# SOCIOLOGY OF SANITATION

# SOCIOLOGY OF SANITATION

*An Edited Volume*

# SOCIOLOGY OF SANITATION
## Environmental Sanitation, Public Health and Social Deprivation

**Bindeshwar Pathak**
*Editor*

KALPAZ

ISBN: 978-93-5128-089-7
Price: ₹ 1050

First Published 2015

*Published by*

**Kalpaz Publications**
C-30, Satyawati Nagar,
Delhi - 110052
E-mail: kalpaz@hotmail.com Ph.: 9212142040

*Laser Typesetting :* Rajender Vashist, Delhi
*Printed at :* G. Print Process, Delhi

**Cataloging in Publication Data--DK**
Courtesy: D.K. Agencies (P) Ltd. <docinfo@dkagencies.com>

**National Conference on "Sociology of Sanitation" (2013 : New Delhi, India)**
Sociology of sanitation : environmental sanitation, public health and social deprivation / Bindeshwar Pathak.
pages cm
Includes bibliographical references and index.
ISBN 9789351280897

1. Sanitation--Social aspects--India--Congresses. 2. Sanitation--Health aspects--India--Congresses. 3. Environmental health--India--Congresses. 4. Sanitation, Rural--India--Congresses. 5. Rural health--India--Congresses. 6. Poverty--India--Congresses. 7. Marginality, Social--India--Congresses. I. Pathak, Bindeshwar, 1943-, editor. II. Title.

DDC 362.10954 23

# Contents

# Preface

The concept of "Sociology of Sanitation" had been on my mind for some time and I often dwell on it. The impetus stemmed from the fact that after working in the sphere of sanitation for more than four decades the strong feeling which emanated was that sanitation and its core problem areas were inextricably linked to sociology as a discipline. Moreover, sociologists and social scientists would be the best protagonists to study sanitation as a sociological subject.

With these thoughts, I had decided to hold the National Conference on "Sociology of Sanitation." Further environmental sanitation, public health and social deprivation were also the primal issues linked to sanitation so much so that one could not delink one from the other.

Despite the short notice, I shall remain ever grateful and beholden for the active cooperation and participation of a galaxy of sociologists and social scientists from all over the country.

We are herein publishing the papers, which we had received which relate to variety of issues and topics covering the various topics embodying Sociology of Sanitation. I am sure these papers will be extremely useful and rewarding for sociologists, social scientists, professionals, experts and policy-makers who are engaged in improving the prevalent conditions of sanitation and the general problems being faced in this sphere.

**Dr. Bindeshwar Pathak**

# List of Contributors

**A. Karuppiah,** Department of Sociology, University of Madras Chepauk, Chennai.

**Amarendra Mahapatra,** Assistant Director, Scientist-D, Epidemiology Division, Regional Medical Research Centre (ICMR), Bhubaneswar, Odisha.

**Anil K.S. Jha,** Asst. Professor of Sociology, F.A.S.C. Mody Institute of Technology and Science, Lakshmangarh, Sikar (Rajasthan).

**Anil Vaghela,** M.K. Bhavnagar University, Bhavnagar.

**Ashish Saxena,** Department of Sociology, Central University of Allahabad.

**B.N. Srivastava,** Vice Chairman, (Admn.) SISSO, New Delhi.

**Bindeshwar Pathak,** Great humanist and Social Reformer of Contemporary India.

**G. Ram,** Professor of Sociology, Assam University, Silchar.

**Hema Gandotra,** Assistant Professor, Department of Sociology, University of Jammu, Jammu.

**Hetukar Jha,** Professor of Sociology (Retd.), Patna University, Patna.

**Jitender Prasad,** Professor and Head, Department of Sociology, M.D.U., Rohtak.

**Madhu Nagla,** Department of Sociology, M.D. University, Rohtak.

**Manish Thakur,** Indian Institute of Management, Calcutta.

**Mohammad Akram,** Associate Professor, Department of Sociology Aligarh Muslim University, Aligarh.

**Om Prakash Yadav,** Probation Officer, Mathura,U.P.

**P.K. Sharma,** Head of Department in Sociology, Pt. RSU Raipur, Chhattisgarh.

**Pankaj Jain,** IAS, Secretary, Ministry of Drinking Water and Sanitation, Government of India.

**Paras Nath Choudhry,** Sanitation Expert, Delhi.

**Prabhleen Kaur,** Associate Professor of Sociology, Udaipur.

**Pranjal Sarma,** Faculty, Department of Sociology, Dibrugarh University, Dibrugarh, Assam.

**Preeti Singh,** HUDCO, New Delhi.

**R. Shankar,** Director, Career Development and Counselling Cell Professor in Sociology, Bharathidasan University, Tiruchirappalli, Tamil Nadu.

**R.S. Tripathi,** Professor of Sociology.

**Ram Updesh Singh,** Retired Senior Bureaucrat, (IAS Retd).

**Richard Pais,** Rtd. Professor of Sociology, Mangalore, Karnataka.

**S.K. Mishra,** Professor of Sociology, Udaipur

**Saroj Ranjan Mania,** Research and Analysis Consultants (RAC), Bhubaneswar.

**Satish Kundu,** Director, R.P. Education Society, Rohtak.

**Shakuntala. C. Shettar,** Professor of Sociology, Karnatak University, Dharwad, Karnataka.

**Sharmila Chhotray,** Assistant Professor, Department of Sociology, Tripura University, Tripura.

**Shaukath Azim,** Professor of Sociology, Karnatak University, Dharwad.

**V. Chandrasekaar,** Department of Sociology, University of Madras Chepauk, Chennai.

**Vishav Raksha,** Associate Professor, Department of Sociology, University of Jammu, Jammu.

**Vishesh Kr. Gupta,** Associate Professor and Head of Sociology Deptt., M.H. (PG) College, Moradabad-244001, U.P.

# 1

# Sociology of Sanitation

*Bindeshwar Pathak*

I am thankful to all of you for participating in the two day National Conference on Sociology of Sanitation which I am proposing as one of the disciplines to be included in the study of sociology. The inclusion of this subject as one of the disciplines will not only enlarge the scope of sociology but will also be helpful in solving the problems of society in relation to sanitation,social deprivation,water,public health, hygiene, poverty, gender equality, welfare of the children and empowering knowledge for sustainable development. As a sociologist, I have been working in these fields for more than four decades and on the basis of my experiences in this sphere coupled with my sociological knowledge, I have an idea that "Sociology of Sanitation" should be included in the discipline of sociology.

I took up sociology in 1961 as one of my subjects in Bachelor of Arts, Part-I in Patna University and later I opted for sociology as a subject in the Honours class. I wanted to be a lecturer in the Department of Sociology in Patna University but that dream remained unfulfilled due to vicissitudes of fortune. However, after passing my secondary school examination I did become a school teacher, did small jobs and finally I wanted to do M.Sc. in Criminology from Sagar University, Madhya Pradesh, but that too did not happen. However, that is a different story.

In the year 1968 by coincidence I joined the Bihar Gandhi Centenary Celebration Committee as a social worker. There I read the autobiography of Mahatma Gandhi as well as other books related to him which had a profound influence and effect on me. The Gandhi Centenary Committee was formed in 1967 to celebrate the birth centenary of Mahatma Gandhi which fell in the year 1969.This Committee had taken up numerous programmes one of which was to restore the human rights and dignity of untouchables who used to clean human excreta manually carrying it as headload for disposal and who were also referred to as human scavengers. Later on I came to know that this subhuman practice stemmed from the genesis of untouchability and had been continuing for the past nearly 5000 years through the Vedic, Buddhist, Mauryan,

**Mughal and British periods**

One day, while I was working in the office, the General Secretary of the Centenary Committee asked me to come and meet him. I went to see him and he asked me to sit down. After that he said "seeing your commitment and performance in this short period that you have worked with the Centenary Committee, I would advise you to engage yourself fully to fulfill the dreams of Mahatma Gandhi – his unfinished agenda to restore the human rights and dignity of untouchable scavengers.This will be the best tribute by the Centenary Committee to Mahatma Gandhi." On this I replied, "how I can work with untouchables because I belong to the Brahmin caste." I then narrated an incident of my childhood days. I told him,"A lady untouchable, at that time referred as "dom", used to come to my house to deliver utensils made from bamboos and when she used to return back my grandmother used to sprinkle water up to the area which belonged to us in order to cleanse it.I was also curious as a child that many other people also used to come to my house but my grandmother did not do like this but why only with that particular lady every time she came to the house. People used to tell me that she was an untouchable and whoever will touch her will be polluted. Being a curious child, when my grandmother was not around, I used to touch her to see whether I became polluted and there was any change of complexion of my body as a result of touching her. One day, by chance when the lady came to deliver the utensils and started returning, my grandmother, started her usual sprinkling of water and cleansing ritual, I touched the lady untouchable which my grandmother saw. She made a hue and cry and asked the neighbouring boys to come, catch hold of me and then she forced me to swallow cow dung and cow urine.Then she gave me Ganges water to drink in order to purify me. It was such a trauma in my childhood which I have never forgotten to this day. So how I can work with these untouchable human scavengers."

Secondly I told him, "Sir, I am a sociologist by background and furthermore I am not an engineer.Unless I give an alternative to bucket or dry toilets which are cleaned by human scavengers how I can ask people not to use these toilets."The General Secretary heard me patiently but said "I do not know your caste or whether you are an engineer or not but by seeing your performance, your dedication as well as commitment in this short period that you have worked with us, I see light in you and strongly feel that you can fulfill the dreams of Mahatma Gandhi to bring the untouchables in the mainstream of the society on a par with others." To this, I had no answer. I became sombre and quietly I left the place.

My knowledge and insight of sociology which has instilled in me a multifaceted approach came to my help here for the first time. In research books of sociology it was taught to us that if somebody wants to work for the cause of a community then first and foremost one has to build a rapport with the community to know in detail their attitudes, their lifestyle, their behaviour and to partake food etc. with them so that one could gather and come up with knowledge and information about the community in depth and in detail. Thus towards this end, to build up rapport with the untouchables I went and lived with them in the colony of untouchable human scavengers in Bettiah,

Champaran, a small town in the State of Bihar for three months, coincidently the same place from where Mahatma Gandhi had started his freedom movement. While I was going to live with these untouchable human scavengers my father was both upset and sad, the Brahmin community turned against me and my father-in-law was very very angry with me. He was absolutely against my living with the untouchables in their habitat as also working in the sphere of sanitation and building toilets. I told him that my entire life has undergone a sea change and these are part of the processes now. I have now started turning over the pages of history of India so far untouchability is concerned. Either I will be successful or I will get lost but I cannot just sit and watch.

While living in the colony many incidents happened. I vividly recall two of them.

One day on a fine morning there was a sudden hue and cry in the neighbourhood. I went and enquired. A newly married girl was weeping bitterly. She was being forced by her in-laws and even her husband himself to go to Bettiah town to clean the bucket toilets. She was crying bitterly and was not at all ready to go. I went and intervened. Her mother-in-law asked one question from me "If she doesn't clean bucket toilets which is our profession, what she will do from tomorrow? If she sells vegetables who will buy from her hands. She has no alternative and is destined to do this job for her whole life."At that time I had no answer.This was certainly a very very tragic situation that a person once born as an untouchable will die as an untouchable. There is no scheme for these untouchables to escape from the social prison where they have to remain imprisoned for their whole life. One can be released from prison one day but not from this social prison created by society.

While I was in the untouchable colony I was in two minds whether to continue or not to continue this work because of the opposition from my family and the Brahmin community and their combined concentrated rage aimed at me and my mission.

After few days I was going to Bettiah town in the afternoon to have a cup of tea with some friends of the colony. We saw that a boy wearing a red shirt was attacked by a bull. People rushed to save him but somebody from the back of the crowd shouted that the boy belonged to the untouchable colony. On hearing this everybody left him in that injured state. With the help of friends I took him to the local hospital but the boy died on the way. That day, there and then I forgot my family, my caste, my community and I took a solemn vow to fulfill the dreams of Mahatma Gandhi to rescue the untouchables from the shackles of slavery which had chained them for the past 5000 years.

Once again the sociological knowledge of tools used for research came to my aid.

Sociology had taught us that for doing any research there should be some tools to test the hypothesis created for the research. Here the tool required was a flush toilet which did not require manual cleaning which could replace the bucket or dry toilets cleaned by human scavengers. In those days hardly any house in rural areas had toilets. No school in such areas also had toilets. I studied in four schools in the villages but none of them had toilets. Women were the worst sufferers because they had to go for defecation in the open either before sunrise or after sunset. Sometimes they were bitten by snakes or scorpions and other times they were subjected to criminal assault and also molestation. Further in those days a large number of children used to die because of diarrhoea, dehydration, cholera and dysentery etc. In fact my own sister died because of diarrhoea while she was being taken to hospital. In urban areas 85 per cent of the houses used to be served by the bucket toilets cleaned by human scavengers and public places had no facilities of there being maintained toilets and baths. So the general picture was totally bleak and dismal. Thus, in this scenario I had to find out a suitable technology which would be appropriate, affordable, indigenous and culturally acceptable in a country like India.

The technology available at that time was the sewerage system which was costly in construction as well as maintenance and it required enormous quantity of water to flush. In the late 60s only 23 cities out of 48 having a population of over one lac have sewerage system. There were 12 other towns which were partially sewercd. About 3 per cent of the total population used to be served by sewerage system in those days. Today out of 7933 towns/cities, 929 towns/cities have sewerage connection of which only 160 towns/cities have Sewerage Treatment Plant (STP). So by this sewer technology it was not possible to stop the defecation in the open or manual cleaning of human excreta by the untouchables.

In those days very little work had been done in this sphere and only rudimentary literature was available on the subject. I went through those literature and here one thing is very important for us to know that application of mind is more important than knowledge. Knowledge can be borrowed but we have to apply our mind in such a way that there is a breakthrough.

To overcome these constraints, I invented, innovated and developed the two-pitpour-flush compost toilet and gave it the name 'Sulabh Shauchalaya'. In this Sulabh Shauchalaya there are two pits, one is used at one time and the other is kept on standby. When the first pit is full, it is switched over to the other one and the first one after two years becomes manure to be used in the fields to raise the productivity of the field and also used in flower plants, or fruit trees etc. It becomes a bio-fertiliser which contains phosphorus, nitrogen and potassium. Moreover, Sulabh Shauchalaya also helps to economise the use of water which is the need of the country. It is said that unfortunately if the world war happens in future that would be for water. Sulabh toilets require only one litre of water for flushing while the conventional toilet requires ten litres.

Most importantly in this toilet, manual scavenging is not required. Anybody can clean the pits because when it is cleaned there is no human excreta as the same has already been converted into ordinary soil and biofertiliser. Thus, Sulabh toilet, has become a tool of social change.

Mahatma Gandhi got freedom for the country through the tool of the spinning wheel and the Industrial Revolution in Europe started from the tool of the spinning jenny. Thus similarly, this Sulabh toilet, has become a tool of social change and has brought vast beneficial effects for the society. In fact this technological innovation was a landmark in the history of sanitation marking a quantum leap and paradigm shift from the centralised system (the sewerage system) of the treatment of human waste to the decentralised system (Sulabh Shauchalaya) which were affordable, accessible, easily constructed and which a country like India could also easily afford. It has been said by a poet,

*"Satsai ke dohre aru naavak ke teer,*

*Dekhan men choten lage ghaav kare gambhir."*

700 couplets of Bihari Lal is called "Satsai"

*"Each couplet of satsai*

*An arrow from the quiver (arrow case) of the archer*

*Both seem to be very small to look at*

*But their impact is very deep, endurable and lasting."*

So on the one hand this Sulabh technology saw a marked behavioural change from open defecation to use of Sulabh Shauchalaya helping people who had bucket toilets to now have flush toilets and are able to use these hygienic toilets with safety and dignity and on the other hand the untouchable scavengers have been relieved from the subhuman occupation of cleaning nightsoil which practice was nearly 5000 years old.This toilet also gives bio-fertiliser to raise the productivity in the field. It has saved enormous quantity of water and the gases produced in the toilet are absorbed in the soil therefore it has also helped to reduce global warming helping to protect climate change.

We now come to the third tool of sociology which is methodology. I used methodology to get the bucket toilets converted to Sulabh Shauchalayas. It was decided that Sulabh International Social Service Organisation which I founded in 1970 will work as the catalytic agency amongst the Government, local bodies and the beneficiaries.Motivators of Sulabh will go from house to house to motivate and educate the beneficiaries and if they agree, get the form filled up for obtaining loan and grant from the local bodies and will build the toilets as per the design and specifications.

To convince the Government, local bodies and beneficiaries a guarantee card would be issued for five years to rectify the defects free of cost if there were any. The job of the Government and local bodies will be to mobilise resources, to do monitoring and supervision, while the work of motivation, education, communication, training, designing, estimation, implementation, maintenance and follow-up would be done by the NGO. Consequently, with close cooperation and collaboration of the Government, local bodies and beneficiaries, the programme became very successful. The role of the NGO is also very important in this field because it requires sustained efforts, social commitment as well as adequate knowledge and expertise. So the methodology as is taught in sociology also worked very well.So far,Sulabh alone has converted 1.3 million bucket toilets into Sulabh flush toilets and lacs of scavengers have been freed from manual cleaning of human faeces and have been freed from shackles of untouchability.

After the human scavengers had been relieved from this subhuman occupation it was then a question of their livelihood.To rehabilitate the scavengers and to bring them in the mainstream of the society which was the dream of Mahatma Gandhi, I took the help of the other tool enunciated by Mahatma Gandhi, the tool of non-violence. Here I took the help of the upper caste people of the society and persuaded them to sit with these human scavengers and to dine with them. For attaining the goal I did not agitate against the social order of the upper caste people. I did not tear or burn the books of Vedas, Puranas and Manusmriti or other scriptures. I did not say a single word against anybody rather I persuaded the upper caste people to have social interaction with the untouchable human scavengers. Here is a great example, where I protested against the

Hindu social order and those who were in favour of the social order right from the Vedic period. I have changed their mind, thoughts, behaviour and attitude towards toilets, sanitation and those who used to work for cleaning the toilets called untouchables.

When I started in 1960 nobody used to talk about toilets. It was a cultural taboo to talk about it specially while partaking food and there was no question of sitting, meeting and eating food with untouchables. So first of all I started giving education to human scavengers for reading, writing and putting their signature wherever required because education is the key of human development. By getting some education they got enlightened, darkness was removed from their minds and they started taking interest in reading, writing and telling their own stories, singing songs and most importantly many of the untouchable scavengers now have become good poets. They compose and recite poems which was earlier totally unbelievable. As Gandhi had given emphasis on basic education so I started giving them vocational education in different trades like making pappadam, noodles, pickles, stitching, tailoring, embroidery, and facial and beauty parlour training etc. so that they could earn their livelihood and be self-reliant.

The products made by them are being sold in the market, hotels and also they sell pappadam and noodles in the same homes where earlier they used to go and clean the toilets. Apart from stitching, tailoring, fashion designing and carpet weaving, they also now do beauty care jobs and they go house to house to do facials to the same women in whose houses they used to clean toilets. Most of their clients are doctors and all the clients provide them with tea and breakfast and exchange pleasantries with them and the scenario is such that as if there was no untouchability in Indian society.

The most important thing is that once again I took the help of sociology and decided to help them to perform rites, rituals and ceremonies of the upper castes people. I took these untouchables to temples where entry of the untouchables was banned. We went to the famous Nathdwara temple, did worship with untouchables and upper caste people and when they came back, the then Hon'ble President of India, Shri R. Venkatraman and the then Hon'ble Prime Minister Bharat Ratna Shri Rajiv Gandhi gave audience to the untouchables. In Alwar there is a temple of Lord Jagannath and the Head Priest, who today will be awarded in this function, opposed the entry of these untouchables, held them up for five hours, not allowing them to enter the temple but finally we became successful after persuading him to allow the untouchables to worship the deity.The minds and attitudes of this Brahmin has changed so dramatically that he invited Smt. Usha Chaumar and others in the wedding of his daughter and his son and provided them food with their family members and accepted the gifts. Now whenever they go from that side this Brahmin always offers them to share a cup of tea. It was good to see that the upper caste people and the untouchables of Alwar dining together on many occasions in the colony of untouchables.

These untouchables were also taken on a trip to Varanasi to see the sacred river Ganges which they had never seen before where they got a chance to worship Lord Shiva and most importantly 200 Brahmins with their family, wives and children had shared food with these untouchables in the holy city of Varanasi which had never happened earlier in history. India is a multi-religious country so I also took them to pay obeisance at the Dargah of Ajmer Sharif,the sacred Church of the Convent of Jesus and Mary at Delhi and the Gurudwara Sahib at Rakabganj so that they may have a feel and experience of other religions as well. They were active participants in the World Toilet Summit held in New Delhi in 2007 where delegates from all over the world had come and for the first time these former scavengers had opportunity to enter the precincts of Vigyan Bhawan. They went to the United States and participated in the proceedings of the United Nations General Assembly where they also walked on the ramp along with top fashion models of India and America who walked side by side with them in a fashion show in the United Nations before a galaxy of diplomats from all corners of the globe. They also went to see the Statue of Liberty, a symbol of equality, liberty and freedom to declare themselves that they are now no longer untouchables. They also went to France to attend the Summit at Le Havre and Marseilles and finally they went to Durban to see the Phoenix Ashram of Mahatma Gandhi where he lived and started the movement and on that visit they proudly proclaimed,"Oh Bapu, because of you we are free from 5000 years of bondage and shackles of untouchability and social discrimination".

Education, as I said earlier, holds the key to any major change and development and is essential to improving the condition of the traditionally oppressed communities specially the untouchables. With the objective of imparting quality education, Sulabh Public School, a premium English Medium School, was set up in Delhi in 1992. The school aims at preparing children from the weaker sections of society for a better life by bringing quality education within the reach of boys and girls from scavenger families. The school is recognised by the Directorate of Education, Government of

Delhi and provides education upto tenth standard. Apart from academic activities,co-curricular activities are regularly organised at school to promote social integration among students. To avoid perpetuation of segregation that characterises the special schools for the scheduled castes, the school is open to the children of families fromnon-scavenging communities also. Children from scavenger families are provided tuition fee waiver apart from free uniforms, books and stationary. In the Sulabh Public School, 60 per cent are the children belonging to the families of erstwhile scavengers while the other 40 per cent are from other castes and communities.

The vocational training centre named "Nai Disha" has also been set up by Sulabh for the women liberated from manual scavenging so that they acquire skills in various trades, engage in gainful employment, start a new life and are easily able to assimilate in the mainstream of society.They are taught food processing, beauty care, cutting and tailoring.

They have now learnt how to prepare pickle, pappad, masala, noodles, jam etc. They are also engaged in stitching frocks, night dress, napkins, bedsheets, saree embroidery etc.

The women who have undergone training at the centre have acquired self- confidence. In fact it has boosted their morale and they now know how to write their names and sign cheques. They have opened savings accounts in the bank and operate it. The vocational training centre at Alwar is a unique case of women empowerment.

Impressed with the success of vocational training centre at Alwar, the Government of Rajasthan entrusted a project to Sulabh International Social Service Organisation for training of manual scavengers in Tonk.The project has been highly successfully and women scavengers who were liberated from manual scavenging have been rehabilitated.

The initiative in imparting training to the liberated scavengers in market-orientedtrades through vocational training centres has yielded laudable results. The liberated scavenges are now settled in dignified employment, trades and occupations. Theirsocio-economic status has gone up. They are now engaged in producing their own products like garments, embroidery, pickles, papads etc. and sending it to the market for sale. Their goods are absorbed locally and are used by the persons belonging to all communities. This attitudinal change among the people towards them is remarkable as at one point of time when they were engaged in manual scavenging the people looked at them with contempt. But now they are using goods, articles, eatables prepared by them gladly and treat them on a par with others. They have been now absorbed in the mainstream of the society.

At this stage I would like to share with you, in a small measure, the views expressed by few eminent personalities.

The first is of the former President of India, Hon'ble Smt. Pratibha Devisingh

Patil at Rashtrapati Bhawan, New Delhi on July 25, 2008. The occasion was when the liberated scavengers women of Alwar called on her apprising her of their visit to the United Nations and United States to participate in Mission Sanitation. Hon'ble

President, Smt. Patil stated as follows:

> "I congratulate you for what you have achieved, which you richly deserve, for which there is no comparison.You have done such a great job and I would like to tell you that Dr. Bindeshwar

Pathak has brought about a revolution, a very big revolution. Financial revolution can come about and can be brought about, but to bring a revolution in the mind-set of people is a very big achievement, a very difficult job which Dr. Pathak has brought about. He increased yourself-respect, your self-confidence and not only your own self-confidence but also showed to society what you are worth and what you can do. What he has shown everyone sees.The whole country looks at it and every village looks at it and tries to do what he has done.

If Mahatma Gandhi was watching today's function from Heaven, his eyes would be brimming with tears of joy. I do not think any other programme in the country would give so much happiness to Mahatma Gandhi as this one."

The second is from the former Ambassador of United States of America in India,

Mr. Timothy J. Roemer, who while addressing the students at the University of Notre

Dame, Graduate School, Indiana, U.S.A. on May 21, 2011 told them a motivational, inspiring story, giving the example of Sulabh and Dr. Pathak. The relevant extract is quoted below:

> "To motivate you, let me tell you a story about ...... toilets!
>
> India is a country with many inspiring people. There is, of course, Mahatma Gandhi, the father of the nation. His teachings of tolerance really are the key to the success of democracy in India and he has influenced civil rights movements around the world including in the United States.
>
> There is Mother Teresa, who lived and worked in India although her legacy now touches the lives of children, women, and the poor all over the world.
>
> There is Rabindranath Tagore, the first non-European to win the Nobel Prize for Literature.
>
> But there are also many inspiring people, lesser known to the world, like Dr. Bindeshwar Pathak.
>
> Dr. Pathak, although from a very high caste, knew at a very young age that there was nothing wrong with touching the untouchables. He has dedicated his life to restoring the human rights and providing dignity to scavengers, which is thebottom-rung caste in India responsible for cleaning up human waste.
>
> To do so, he used technology to develop a safe and environment-

friendly toilet to replace pit latrines, reducing the need for scavenging and improving sanitation and hygiene for both rural and urban poor.

He provided education to the children of scavengers, helping to break thenever-ending family cycle of scavenging.

He provided alternative economic opportunities so that women no longer have to clean toilets for the rest of their lives to provide for their families.

All this has helped tackle a bigger problem – breaking down the caste system in India.

As you leave Notre Dame today, I hope you will remember the story of Dr. Pathak.

He did not start out to change the world. He started out to help some scavengers in a few villages in Bihar, a small state in the north of India on the Nepal border.

As you start out today, you do not have to change the world overnight. But I encourage you to try to make a difference.

As you walk out these doors and leave this campus for your final time as a student, follow the counsel of President John Quincy Adams, who said, "March then with firm, with steady, with undeviating step, to the prize of your high calling. Consecrate above all, the faculties of life to the cause of truth, of freedom, and of humanity."

And lastly, the grandson of the great Mahatma Gandhi, Prof. Raj Mohan Gandhi, when he visited the Sulabh campus in 2010 with students of University of Illinois, U.S.A. He was so overwhelmed that he stated as follows:

> "I am the son of the son of Mahatma Gandhi but Dr. Bindeshwar Pathak is the son of his soul. If we were to go to meet Mohandas Karamchand Gandhi, he would first greet Dr. Pathak for the noble work that he is doing and then meet me. Dr. Pathak has restored human rights and dignity to people engaged in the manual cleaning of human excreta which they carried as head-load".

A word here about the widows of Vrindavan, some of whom you see sitting in the audience today. Vrindavan has become host to widows from all over India shunned from the society when their husbands die, not for religious reasons but because of tradition as well as financial drain in the families.They pass their days in abject poverty and want, begging in the streets and lying on the steps outside temples hopefully waiting for scraps of food and alms. Even when they die there is nobody to take care of their cremation.

The Hon'ble Supreme Court in a recent court order, directed the National Legal Services Authorities (NALSA) to contact Sulabh International Social Service Organisation to find out whether they could come forward to help the 1,780 odd widows living in four government shelters in Vrindavan. On getting this request without giving a second thought, within forty-eight hours I went to Vrindavan and was terribly moved by the plight of these widows and conditions that they live in.There and then I gave them the necessary monetary help and within a month thereafter each of these widows is getting an honorarium of Rs. 1000/- monthly for their needs from Sulabh. Sulabh has also provided five ambulances in each of the five widow shelter homes along with doctors and nurses and regular eye and medical check-ups are also held. Nearly 500 widows have been provided with spectacles as well as other health requirements from Sulabh. Most of all Sulabh has given them what they required most– love, affection, compassion, respect and dignity.

Another area in which Sulabh has played a pioneering role is the development of the concept of community latrines by constructing public toilets on 'pay and use' basis.

Though the concept of public toilet found a place in the Bengal Municipal Act, 1876 as amended in 1878 which provided for operation of community toilets on 'pay and use' basis but it did not take off and it remained at the concept stage itself. I took the initiative in reviving and giving concrete shape to the concept of public toilets on 'pay and use' basis in Bihar for the first time in the year 1974. This was a landmark in the history of sanitation when the system of operating and maintaining community toilets with bathing and urinal facilities (popularly known as Sulabh Shauchalaya

Complex) with attendant's service round the clock was initiated in Patna on 'pay and use' basis with people's participation and without any burden on the public exchequer or local authorities. It received a very encouraging response from the people over the years and the Patna experiment has been replicated throughout the country. Besides toilet, bathing and urinal facilities, some more amenities like public telephone, primary healthcare, drinking water etc. have also been provided at some Sulabh Shauchalaya Complexes.

Sulabh toilet complexes have electricity, 24 hours' water supply and soap powder is supplied free to users for washing hands. The complexes have separate enclosures for men and women. Children, disabled persons and those who cannot afford to pay the user's fee are allowed to use the facility free of charge. These toilet complexes are being constructed at public places like bus stands, markets, railway stations, hospitals etc.

Sulabh has constructed more than 8000 public toilets at important places all over the country which are being used by more than 15 million people everyday. 200 of them are linked with biogas plants. It is further revealing that starting from a small district in Bihar, the organisation is working today in as many as 25 States, 4 Union territories, 506 districts and 1629 towns all over the country. Sulabh International Social Service Organisation has also worked in Afghanistan and Bhutan. Sulabh at the behest of the External Affairs Ministry, Government of India constructed five toilet complexes with biogas plants in Kabul. These projects, have been executed and completed in collaboration with Kabul Municipality.These toilet complexes have been handed over to Kabul Municipality and are in operation. In collaboration with the

Royal Government of Bhutan Sulabh International Social Service Organisation had constructed public toilets there and now Sulabh is planning to do the same in Uganda and fifty other countries.

Recycling and reuse of human excreta for biogas generation is an important way to get rid of health hazards from human excreta. Sulabh is a pioneering organisation in the field of biogas generation from public toilet complexes. During biogas generation, due to anaerobic condition inside digester most of the pathogens are eliminated from the digested effluent making it suitable for using it as manure.Thus, biogas technology from human wastes has multiple benefits – sanitation, bioenergy and manure.

Based on 'Sulabh Model' design, about 200 biogas plants linked with public toilets have been constructed by Sulabh in different states of the country so far. Human excreta based biogas technology remained unnoticed for a long time due to the fact that available technology was not socially acceptable as it required manual handling of human excreta which contains a full spectrum of pathogens. The design developed by Sulabh does not require manual handling of human excreta and there is complete recycling and resource recovery from the wastes. Digester is made underground into which excreta from public toilet flows under gravity.

Biogas is utilised for cooking, lighting through mantle lamps, electricity generation and being converted into energy to be used for lighting street-lights and such other uses. The sludge at the bottom of the digester can be used as fertiliser. Sulabh has also developed a new and convenient technology by which effluent of human excreta based biogas plant turns into a colourless, odourless and pathogen free manure. The technology is based on filtration of effluent through activated charcoal followed by ultraviolet rays.The residue water from the plant too can be used as biofertiliser because it contains phosphorus, nitrogen and potassium for raising productivity in the fields.

Training in Sulabh technologies have been organised for the officers, engineers and architects, etc. from a number of African countries which include Ethiopia, Mozambique, Uganda, Cameroon and Burkina Faso, Kenya, Tanzania, Cote d' Ivorie, Mali, Ghana, Rwanda, Senegal and Zambia. They have also been trained as part of achieving the Millennium Development Goals set for the sustainable development in water, sanitation, health and hygiene sectors. These programmes were sponsored by U.N. Habitat. Sulabh technical team had gone to Ethiopia and Bangladesh for giving training on Sulabh Technologies.

We have also provided training and orientation courses to Government employees specially local bodies. Some, Government departments have been sending their participants from India and abroad to learn this technology. Even at present a 12 member team from Tanzania is under training at Sulabh and this delegation is present in this august audience.

The Sulabh model has also been adopted by a number of countries, including China, Bhutan, Bangladesh, Afghanistan, Burkina Faso, Ghana, Kenya, Mali, Nigeria, Senegal, Tanzania and Zambia for expansion and promotion of sanitation facilities. Here I make a small reference to the Sulabh Museum of Toilets, located in the campus of Sulabh International Social Service Organisation, a rare museum in the world. A large number of visitors, both from within country and abroad have shown keen interest in the toilet museum and they have found it very informative, fascinating and useful.So far about 27,50,000 persons have visited the website and over 5000 people come personally every year to visit the museum. The Sulabh International Museum of toilets has rare collection of artifacts, pictures and objects detailing the historic evolution of toilets since 2,500 BC. It gives a chronology of developments relating to technology, toilets related social customs and etiquettes, the sanitary conditions and legislative efforts of many countries. It has an extensive display of privies, chamber pots, toilets furniture, bidets and water closets in use from 1145 AD to the modern times. The objectives of the museum are to educate students about the historical trends in the development of toilets; provide information to researchers about the design, materials and technologies adopted in the past and those in use in the contemporary world; help policy-makers understand the efforts made earlier in this field throughout the world; help the manufacturers of toilet equipment and accessories in improving their products by functioning as a technology storehouse and to help sanitation experts learn from the past and solve problems in the sanitation sector.

I would also like to inform that Sulabh has also given opportunities to millions of people to be a part of the social reform movement and 50,000 people are regular volunteers and involved with the revolution being brought out by Sulabh. In this way Sulabh is playing an active role in poverty alleviation.

In the end I would like to say that in my journey of sanitation spanning nearly 45 years, I have taken the help of truth, honesty, integrity, ethics and morality to create confidence among different cultures and communities, political parties, the Govt. and the people in general. Gandhiji said "An ounce of practice is worth more than tons of preaching." Very true. I would add further that knowledge and action are both important. Swami Vivekanand said that, "they alone live who live for others." John F. Kennedy stated in his inaugural address – "ask not what your country can do for you; ask what you can do for your country." So I request all the fellow sociologists and academicians to consider these aspects which I have enumerated. It is my firm belief that the time has now come when "Sanitation" should be included as a discipline in sociology because the core problem areas embodying sanitation like social deprivation, hygiene, ecology, water, public health, poverty, gender equality, welfare of children etc. require sociological intervention also being intertwined with spiritual and philosophical knowledge. Hence I have termed it as Sociology of Sanitation. To conclude I have propounded the theory of Sociology of Sanitation which is as follows:-

"Sociology of sanitation is a scientific study to solve the problems of society in relation to sanitation, social deprivation, water, public health, hygiene, ecology, environment, poverty, gender equality, welfare of children and empowering people for sustainable development and attainment of philosophical and spiritual knowledge to lead a happy life and to make a difference in the lives of others."

I am overwhelmed by the response this National Conference has generated and I am both beholden and grateful to the Hon'ble dignitaries, the participants and this august audience who have taken off their valuable time to be amongst us today.

# 2

# Rural Sanitation in India: Obstacles, Challenges and Future Interventions

*Pankaj Jain*

When nineteen year old Anita got married to Shivram Narre and went to live with her husband at his house in Bethul district of Madhya Pradesh, a huge shock awaited her, she had no option but to go and defecate in the open fields as her in-laws house did not have a toilet. After two days as per the custom, Anita returned to her native village but with a firm resolve that she would not go back to her in laws house unless they built a toilet. The shame and repulsion of going out for defecating in the open was too much for her even at the cost of sustaining her own marriage.

When her husband Shivram came to her village to take her back, she conveyed her decision to him in no uncertain terms. A disappointed Shivram went back to his native village without his newly married bride. He approached the Panchayat President who apprised him that he was eligible for incentives for construction of a toilet in his house as he came under the BPL category. Shivram took the initiative and constructed a *leach* pit toilet at his residence premises within a span of three days.

India has made rapid strides in almost every other sphere over the last four decades, but has only attained coverage of just over 50 per cent in sanitation across the country (32.7 per cent in Rural Sanitation and 82 per cent. under Urban Sanitation). Many people would find it hard to fathom that a country which is a nuclear power, has an enviable space programme and is labeled as the next economic superpower, has the largest number of people in the world who defecate in the open. The figure of 626 million as projected by the latest JMP report brought out by UNICEF and WHO is a matter of shame and concern for our nation.

But we need to understand the reason behind this extraordinary phenomenon. Government of India on its part has been providing targeted interventions to its citizens. In fact, India is one of the very few countries in the world which is providing incentive to its citizens to construct individual toilets in their household premises. A sum of Rs 9,100 is provided for people under various categories for this purpose but still it has not led to the desired impact. The above case of Anita Narre makes it clear that there seems to be a lack of will among the people to build a toilet in spite of the various government schemes being made available to them. The underlying message is clear, Toilets have not yet been accepted as a necessity in many parts of our country.

**Hurdles and Obstacles in Achieving Total Sanitation**

There are two facets to this problem in India. The first is a problem of scale. Hundreds of millions of people in India have traditionally practised open defecation, especially in rural areas. In fact, a large number of people living in rural areas believe that having a toilet inside the house is unhygienic and accept the fact that defecating in open spaces is a better option. The second issue is the problem of exclusion. The religious and caste based discrimination that existed in the country led to the problem of exclusion wherein different categories of people were denied access to adequate water which also adversely impacted access to sanitation.

Then there are other groups of excluded that lack access to sanitation. These include the socially and economically marginalised, the aged and the infirm, pregnant women, people with disabilities and populations living in remote areas and in difficult terrains where it is difficult to construct basic toilets, due to high water tables, sandy soils, or hard rock.

**Upward Growth over the Years**

In fact, Government of India has made rapid strides in providing sanitation facilities to its citizens over the years. The rural sanitation coverage in the country was as low as one per cent at the beginning of the 1980s. Government of India launched the Central Rural Sanitation Programme in the year 1986 to address this issue. In the year 1998, the sanitation coverage had reached four per cent and by the year 2001, it rose to a remarkable 22 per cent  to reach the current status of 32.7 per cent.

The urban sanitation scenario has also registered an upward trend. As per the 2011 census, 81.4 per cent urban houses have toilets within their premises, while the remaining six per cent share public toilets while nearly 12.6 per cent of the urban population defecate in the open.

**Table 1: Households by Toilet Facility, Census of India, 2011**

| | *Absolute number* | | | *Percentage* | | |
|---|---|---|---|---|---|---|
| | *Total* | *Rural* | *Urban* | *Total* | *Rural* | *Urban* |
| Total number of households | 24,66,92,667 | 16,78,26,730 | 7,88,65,937 | 100.0 | 100.0 | 100.0 |
| Latrines facility within the premises | 11,57,37,458 | 5,15,75,339 | 6,41,62,119 | 46.9 | 30.7 | 81.4 |
| Without latrines within the premises | 13,09,55,209 | 11,62,51,391 | 1,47,03,818 | 53.1 | 69.3 | 18.6 |
| Public latrines | 79,97,699 | 32,53,892 | 47,43,807 | 3.2 | 1.9 | 6.0 |
| Resorting to Open Defecation | 12,29,57,510 | 11,29,97,499 | 99,60,011 | 49.8 | 67.3 | 12.6 |

*Source*: Census (2011).

As reflected in these figures, the sanitation problem seems to be more of a rural issue than an urban one. But then the challenges in urban sanitation are equally important and need a lot of focus. India is witnessing a huge population growth and is all set to become the most populous country in the world by the year 2030. The country witnessed unprecedented urban growth in the last decade when, for the first time in her history, the net decadal population increase was more urban than rural (90.99 to 90.47 million). The total urban population of India was more than 377 million according to the 2011 Census and is projected to touch 600 million by 2030. By the year 2050, it is expected that 50 per cent of the country's population will be urban. This would prove to be a huge challenge and urban sanitation providers will have to plan for the future to meet these challenges head on.

**Table 2: Sanitation Coverage in India, 1990 – 2011, JMP**

| *Proportion of households* | *Percentage* | | | | | |
|---|---|---|---|---|---|---|
| | *Urban* | | *Rural* | | *Total* | |
| | *1990* | *2011* | *1990* | *2011* | *1990* | *2011* |
| Using improved facilities | 50 | 60 | 7 | 24 | 18 | 35 |
| Using shared facilities | 17 | 20 | 1 | 4 | 5 | 9 |
| Using other unimproved facilities | 5 | 7 | 2 | 6 | 3 | 6 |
| With access to sanitation | 72 | 87 | 10 | 34 | 26 | 50 |
| Resorting to open defecation | 28 | 13 | 90 | 66 | 74 | 50 |

*Source*: WHO/UNICEF (2013).

## Institutional Set Up for Rural Sanitation in India

The responsibility for provision of sanitation facilities for sanitation in the country primarily rests with local government bodies– municipalities or corporations in urban areas and Gram Panchayats in rural areas. The state and central governments act as mere facilitators. As per the envisaged set up, the central government and the Planning Commission, through the Five Year Plans, guides investment in the sector by allocating funds for strategic priorities.

The Ministry of Drinking Water and Sanitation (MDWS) is the nodal agency for the overall policy, planning, funding and coordination of programmes of rural drinking water and sanitation in the country. MDWS provides financial and technical support in sanitation to all the states and UTs, while the respective state governments are vested with the responsibility of implementation of the programme in their respective regions. In most states, the Rural Development department or the Public Health Engineering department is given responsibility for management of the rural sanitation programme-known as "Nirmal Bharat Abhiyan (NBA). The NBA aims to 'transform rural India into 'Nirmal Bharat' by adopting 'community-led', 'people-centred' strategies and a 'community saturation approach' with emphasis on awareness creation and demand generation for sanitary facilities in houses, institutions and schools for a cleaner environment.

## Key Focus Areas under Rural Sanitation

The *Nirmal Bharat Abhiyan* focuses on providing holistic and sustainable sanitation to the rural population. One of the key focus areas is construction of Individual Household Latrines by giving cash incentives to individual households. To promote safe and sustainable sanitation, wider technology options are being provided under the initiative to effectively contain human waste and to completely eliminate the fecal oral transmission routes through water, air, insects and other vectors. To reach out to all populations in the gram panchayats, community-planned and managed toilets known as Community Sanitary Complexes are also provided to target groups of households who have constraints of space and economic difficulties in gaining access to individual facilities.

Another major initiative under NBA is the construction of school and *anganwadi* toilets. The scheme facilitates construction of toilets in all type of Government schools with separate toilet units for boys and girls. In *anganwadis* (pre-school), child friendly toilets are constructed for the use of babies and little children with the intention of inculcating best sanitary practices from a young age.

The NBA programme also places a lot of stress on overall cleanliness and improvement of general quality of life in rural areas. To facilitate this process the Government of India provides focused funding to Gram Panchayats (GPs) to enable them to develop sustainable Solid and Liquid Waste Management (SLWM) projects like construction of compost pits, vermin-composting, common and individual biogas plants, low cost drainage, soakage channels and segregation and disposal of household garbage etc. A lot of focus is also given to ensure proper and timely supply of sanitary materials, services and guidance to the local people for constructing different types of latrines and accessing sanitary materials. As a part of this initiative, provision for setting up of Rural Sanitary Marts and Production Centres has been made under NBA.

**Promoting Sanitation Initiatives to Achieve Key Targets**

The Government of India under Rural Sanitation has set itself a target to achieve universal sanitation coverage in the country by the year 2022. As per the 12th five year plan objectives, 50 per cent of the GPs are to attain Nirmal Gram status by the year 2017.

To attain these objectives the government has planned and is executing some targeted interventions to reach out to excluded communities and all sections of the society. The provision of incentives under NBA have been extended from the existing below poverty line families to certain groups under above poverty line households, all scheduled caste and scheduled tribe families, small and marginal farmers, landless labourers with homestead, physically handicapped and women-headed households. The incentive amount has been increased by Rs 500 to people living in hilly areas and inaccessible terrains.

The government has also given a lot of importance to conjoint approach by providing piped water supply to households as a part of

sustainable sanitation initiatives. To cater to the needs of the community, alternate delivery mechanisms and wider technology options are promoted for providing cost effective and affordable sanitary materials at the local level. In addition to individual incentives, the strategy under NBA makes funds available to Gram Panchayats under Nirmal Gram Puraskar (Clean Village Award) for making the village 100 per cent Open Defecation Free. The Gram Panchayats promote construction and usage of toilets by highlighting the community spirit to make the village open defecation free.

Social marketing approaches are also being adopted to push for attitudinal and behavioural change among the people. Effective mass media based campaigns to change the basic mindsets among people in the villages towards sanitation have been undertaken at national and state levels. An intensive IEC Campaign involving Panchayati Raj Institutions, ASHA and *anganwadi* workers, Women Groups, Self Help Groups, NGOs and other stakeholders have been adopted at the village level, while a generic campaign focusing on key sanitation issues is being run at the all India level by involving Mass Media channels like TV, Radio and Print.

The government recognises the fact that the NBA programme needs to be closely monitored for effective implementation. Keeping this in view, a comprehensive system for monitoring and evaluation of the programme through periodical progress reports, performance review committee meetings, district level monitoring and through the vigilance and monitoring committees at the state and district levels have been adopted. To promote rural sanitation, the programme has incorporated steps to help individual households adopt the sanitation technology based on socio-cultural aspects, hydro-geological conditions and economic status of the incumbents.

For convergence, coordination and better planning with related ministries, a National Drinking Water and Sanitation Council (NDWSC) has been set up with representation from related Ministries (e.g., Human Resource Development, Health, Women and Child Development, Panchayati Raj, Rural Development). This Council will provide national level guidance on the implementation of the sanitation programme.

**Future Plans and Targets**

The Nirmal Bharat Abhiyan visualises a shift in strategy for accelerating the progress of sanitation coverage in the country. The future emphasis would be to attain targets in a planned and constructive manner without compromising on quality and sustainability outcomes. As per 12th Five Year plan objective, 50 per cent of Gram Panchayats (GPs) are to attain Nirmal Gram status by 2017 with the objective of attaining universal sanitation coverage by the year 2022. The total fund allocated for rural sanitation during 2012-2017 (12th plan period) has seen a quantum jump and is Rs 37,159 crores which emphasises the priority the government is placing on achieving sanitation targets.

One of the key focus areas under future interventions would be to attain sustainability of outcomes by adopting a phased approach of implementation wherein fully sanitised (Nirmal) Gram Panchayats shall progressively lead to achievement of *sanitised* blocks leading to *sanitised* districts and eventually leading to *sanitised* states. The pattern of releasing funds is being changed to enable flexibility to the districts to prioritise funding to GPs identified for achievement of *Nirmal* Grams. The basic idea behind this move is to ensure that Gram Panchayats that are declared as *Nirmal* Grams will have full toilet coverage, water availability and systems in place for waste disposal including drainage facilities leading to holistic and sustainable sanitation.

Another key issue under future plan of action is to facilitate convergence between drinking water and sanitation projects. The NBA shall give priority to coverage of areas with functional piped water supply systems (PWSS), followed by areas with ongoing PWSS that are nearest to completion. Similarly, New Piped Water Supply Systems will be taken up in Gram Panchayats of districts where Individual Household Latrine Coverage has reached higher milestones of coverage in a descending order. In all such new and ongoing piped water supply system Gram Panchayats, NBA shall be implemented simultaneously with the planning and execution of PWSS to ensure that behavioural change for usage of toilets are generated. Piped Water Supply Systems shall be planned and executed in such a way as to saturate entire habitations, so that health and other impacts of safe water and sanitation are clearly discernible.

Ensuring running water availability to all habitations would be another priority in future interventions. The stress would be to ensure availability of water to all schools, *anganwadis* and sanitary complexes to facilitate sustainable sanitation practices. Apart from providing toilets in all schools and *anganwadis*, school teachers, ASHA workers and ANMs would be trained to inculcate best sanitary practices. Moreover, sanitation will be made a part of the school curriculum so that safe sanitation practices are ingrained in the minds of children who would be the change agents in the community.

Efforts would also be made to maximise incentive provision to beneficiaries through other rural development programmes like MGNREGA, resulting in increased inflow of funds and incentives for construction of toilets. Apart from up scaling communication interventions, massive training campaign will be launched in convergence with the National Rural Livelihoods Mission (NRLM) which will focus on enhancing skills in masonry work, brick making, toilet pan making, plumbing and related activities.

The whole emphasis would be geared towards bringing sanitation on the national agenda and driving home the importance of safe sanitary practices, thus arousing the consciousness of the country as a whole to achieve total sanitation by the year, 2022.

# 3

# Sanitation, Health and Development Deficit in India: A Sociology of Sanitation Perspective

*Mohammad Akram*

Poor sanitation not only affects the health and quality of life of the people, but also affects the economic development and social empowerment agendas. There are visible sanitation deficits in India which are the accumulated negative consequences of the development deficits, viz., policy deficits, technology deficits and implementation deficits. Even the social and human development strategies have failed to make the necessary corrections. This paper finds that the local surroundings and the macro environments together structure the insanitary practices and social worlds within the deficit cultured development trajectory of India. 'Sociology of sanitation' helps in understanding the larger phenomenon in Indian context.

## Defining Sanitation

By sanitation I mean the principles, practices, provisions, or services related to cleanliness and hygiene in personal and public life meant for the protection and promotion of human health and well being and breaking the cycle of disease or illness. It is also related to the principles and practices relating to the collection, treatment, removal or disposal of human excreta, household waste water and other pollutants. The World Health Organisation (WHO) states that: Sanitation generally refers to the provision of facilities and services for the safe disposal of human urine and feces. Inadequate sanitation is a major cause of disease worldwide and improving sanitation is known to have a significant beneficial impact on health both in households and across communities. The word 'sanitation' also refers to the maintenance of hygienic conditions, through services such as garbage collection and wastewater disposal. According to Mmom and Mmom (2011), environmental sanitation comprises disposal and treatment of human excreta, solid waste and waste water, control of disease vectors, and provision of washing facilities for personal and domestic hygiene. It aims at improving the quality of life of the individuals and contributing to social development. Improved sanitation, according to the WHO/UNICEF joint monitoring programme for water supply and sanitation, refers to the management of human feces at the household level. This terminology is the indicator used to describe the target of the Millennium Development Goal (MDG) on sanitation.

A study conducted by World Bank's 'South Asia Water and Sanitation Unit' estimated that India loses Rs 240 billion annually due to lack of proper sanitation facilities. According to it, premature deaths, treatment for the sick and loss of productivity and revenue from tourism are the main factors behind the significant economic loss. Poor sanitation is something that not only affects the economic development of the country, but also affects the social and human development of the nation. In fact, women are most adversely affected by the hazards of lack of proper sanitation. For instance, in India majority of the girls drop out of school because of lack of toilets. Only 22 per cent of them manage to even complete class ten. On economic grounds, according to the Indian Ministry of Health and Family Welfare, more than Rs 12 billion is spent every year on poor sanitation and its resultant illnesses.

Illnesses caused by germs and worms in feces, wastes and pollutants are constant source of discomfort for millions of people and animals. These illnesses can cause many years of sickness and can lead to other health problems such as dehydration, anaemia and malnutrition. Sanitation related illnesses like cholera can spread rapidly, bringing sudden death to many people. Children have a high risk of illness from poor sanitation. While adults may live with diarrheal diseases and worms, children die from these illnesses. More than 300 million episodes of acute diarrhoea occur every year in India in children below five years of age. Of the 9.2 million cases of TB that occur in the world every year, nearly 1.9 million, are in India accounting for one-fifth of the global TB cases.

More than 1.5 million persons are infected with malaria every year. Diseases like dengue and chikungunya have emerged in different parts of India and a population of over 300 million is at risk of getting acute encephalitis syndrome/Japanese encephalitis. One-third of global cases infected with filaria live in India. Nearly half of leprosy cases detected in the world in 2008 were contributed by India (MOHFW, 2010).

### Holistic Approach towards Sanitation

The 'sanitation phase' of the mid-nineteenth century was an important phase of the 'public health movement' in the industrialised countries. It characterised concentration on issues such as housing, working conditions, the supply of clean water, hygiene and the safe disposal of waste. The motivating force of this public health movement is thought to be a concern with economic efficiency and better social cohesion between the working class and other sectors of society. There has also been a significant investment in many countries in creating infrastructures and services to protect health and to prevent ill health. In most industrialising countries over the last 150 years, public health regulations and health and safety legislation have been enacted to provide safeguards for the industrial workforce, to control pollution levels in rivers, and to ensure proper sewerage and drainage. In nineteenth century England, sanitary reformers and radical politicians argued, on economic grounds, for ill health prevention through public policy interventions. The sanitation phase of the public health movement emphasised environmental change.

The need for effective public health services in the developed countries was also triggered by military concerns, since army casualties from disease were far higher than from battle. Elites also had a stake in disease control because cure was uncertain until antibiotics began to be mass-produced in the mid 20th century. Besides, business interests were at stake, as illustrated by the massive business losses following a cholera epidemic in Hamburg in 1892 (Das Gupta, 2005). This sanitation phase led to a considerable and measurable reduction in infectious diseases-especially diphtheria, tuberculosis and cholera (Sarah Earle, 2007). Sanitation, thus, got engrossed in the notion of public health in the industrialised countries. However, it does not find its origin in western notion of public health only. Sanitation is an integral aspect of several other socio-cultural discourses and institutionalises through many politico-economic, or religious-spatial patterns. The belief systems have promoted different paradigms of sanitation historically. The paradigms include the rituals and practices supported by traditions as well as scientific wisdom.

## Sanitation and Quality of Life

While the term 'quality' implies the degree of excellence of a characteristic, different people may value different areas of life, and therefore, quality of life means different things to different people (Carr, Higginson and Robinson, 2003). Quality of life has been viewed as the extent to which basic human needs have been satisfied; as the degree of satisfaction or dissatisfaction felt with various aspects of life; and as the extent to which pleasure and satisfaction characterise human existence. The basic human needs include food, education, freedom, health, housing, sanitation and several other goods which are necessary for human living and give satisfaction in life. The industrialised societies invented the material and technological supportive bases for satisfying most of the need fulfilling goods. The supportive bases made sanitation a way of life.

The understanding related to quality of life, in less developed traditional societies, did not necessarily find the similar evolution. Industrialisation, in most of the less developed societies, is induced, or adopted. The erstwhile colonies of the western empires witnessed selective inducement of industrialisation mainly meant to promote the material interest of the empires. The uneven development paradigms and the indigenous structural compulsions created a fractured understanding of quality of life. Often, the prevailing ethos and contradictory values created more ruptures than cohesion in the life styles. India, as a less developed society having colonial past, presents a typical meeting point of the caste and varna hierarchy, class differences, ethno-religious plurality and regional diversity.

'Ritual purity', a shared and often contested perception about 'quality' in life, has remained a satisfying value irrespective of the presence, or absence of other need fulfilling goods in the caste system of traditional India. Similarly, 'ritual impurity' condemns 'quality' even in the abundance of material possessions. Ritual impurity, compounded with the absence of other need fulfilling goods, could make life much poorer, distressful and secluded. The 'mythical' rituals created imaginary discourses about the quality of life for the different social categories within the caste system. The availability of the basic need fulfilling goods of life is a precondition for ensuring even the minimum level of satisfaction. But the notions of purity or even sacredness perpetuated unrealistic discourses about quality. Those who were at the bottom of the hierarchy became victim of double disadvantages: there was a lack of need fulfilling goods; and, there was a burden of ritual impurity. Sanitation, an integral component of quality of life, was often a miss under the dearth of material and technological bases of human life.

**Sanitation as Public Good**

The Report of Working Group two of the WHO Commission on Macro-economics and Health on 'Global Public Goods for Health' (WHO, 2002) has explained the notion of 'public goods'. Goods, whether public or private, can be colloquially but accurately described as products, programmes, activities, or services. Public goods differ from private goods in several important respects, but a very central difference is the degree to which they generate spillover effects, or externalities, when consumed. The presence of externalities may lead to government intervention either to encourage the potential for positive spillover effects or to discourage the negative. Public goods have two unique properties: they are non-rivalrous and non-exclusive. A good is non-rivalrous if, for any given level of production, the marginal cost of providing it to an additional consumer is zero. For most private goods, the marginal cost of producing more of a particular item is positive. But for some goods, the costs of production do not increase with each additional consumer. This also means that the ability of any additional individual to enjoy the product or service is not diminished by the use of it by others. A good is non-exclusive if people cannot be prevented from consuming it. A common example of public good is the lighthouse.

Public goods can be local, national, regional, international, or global, depending on the 'reach' of their externalities. Global agencies are coming forward with narratives on 'global public goods', but the actual investment in achieving these is marginal. Civic amenities provided by the nation-states come closer to the notion of public goods. Sanitation is also a public good. The industrialised countries developed the public health facilities including sanitation facilities realising their importance as public goods. India, a developing country, is yet to make sufficient investment in public goods like sanitation, although there is tremendous pressure on governments to treat primary education and primary health care as public goods. The spread of communicable disease in India is a consequence of lesser investment in public goods like sewerage treatment, drainage system, drinking water and public and community toilets.

## Sanitation Infrastructure

India has a population of almost 1.2 billion people. Fiftyfive per cent of this population (nearly 600 million) has no access to toilets. Most of these numbers are made up by people who live in urban slums and rural areas. A large populace in the rural areas still defecates in the open. Slum dwellers in major metropolitan cities, reside along railway tracks and have no access to toilets or a running supply of water. India is still lagging far behind many countries in the field of sanitation. According to Harshal T. Pandve (2008), most cities and towns in India are characterised by over-crowding, congestion, inadequate water supply and inadequate facilities of disposal of human excreta, waste water and solid wastes. No major city in India is known to have a continuous water supply and an estimated 72 per cent of Indians still lack access to improved sanitation facilities. Besides this, the 63 per cent of urban population in India is without proper sanitation. Further, the waste disposal and sewage treatment plants are missing in most of the cities. Most of the wastes are disposed in rivers, canals or outskirts of the cities. The 11th five year plan envisaged 100 per cent coverage of urban water, urban sewerage, and rural sanitation by 2012. Although investment in water supply and sanitation has seen a jump in the 11th plan over the 10th plan, the targets do not take into account both the quality of water being provided, or the sustainability of systems being put in place (Kumar, Kar and Jain, 2011). Thus, the need fulfilling goods of life, in terms of the material and technological bases, are conspicuous because of the rarity of their availability, and sanitation has become more ritualistic than realistic.

## Sanitation and MDGs

The United Nations' Millennium Development Goals (MDGs) are important target set at the turn of the century for the global population. The MDGs include a target to reduce by half the proportion of people without access to basic sanitation by 2015. The United Nations declared

2008 as the 'International Year of Sanitation' in view of the 2.6 billion people in the world, who lack even basic sanitation facilities. It was also in recognition of the slow progress being made towards the MDGs sanitation target. Particular concerns in MDGs for sanitation are:

- Removing the stigma around sanitation, so that the importance of sanitation can be more easily and publicly discussed.
- Highlighting the poverty reduction, health and other benefits that flow from better hygiene, household sanitation arrangements and waste water treatment.

Several research findings suggest that sanitation and hygiene promotion needs to be better 'mainstreamed' in development, if the MDGs on sanitation is to be met. There is a realisation that many institutions should carry out activities to develop better sanitation and hygiene in developing countries. For example, educational institutions can teach on hygiene and sanitation by providing better facilities for them, and health institutions can dedicate resources for promoting preventative works. There is also the need of civil society organisations to provide the necessary infrastructure where national governments cannot do that on their own.

## Sanitation and Health

Health is the basic human right of all the human beings. Health contributes to a person's basic capability to function. Denial of health is not only denial of 'good life-chance', but also denial of fairness and justice (Sen, 2006). *The Universal Declaration of Human Rights* stated in Article 25: 'Everyone has the right to a standard of living adequate for the health and wellbeing of himself and his family....' (United Nations, 1948). The Preamble to the World Health Organisation (WHO) Constitution affirms that it is one of the fundamental rights of every human being to enjoy the highest attainable standards of health. The concepts of health, disease and treatment are related to the social structures of communities (Akram, 2007). The biomedical approach based on the 'germ theory of disease' views health as an 'absence of diseases'. The ecological approach views health as a dynamic equilibrium between man and his environment. The socio-cultural approach considers health as a product of the social and community structure.

The World Health Organisation's Commission on Social Determinants of Health (CSDH) defines the Social Determinants of Health (SDH) as the conditions in which people are born, grow, live, work and age, including the health system. The CSDH considers daily living conditions, inequitable distribution of money, power and resources, as well as inequities in health care as determinants of health. Sanitation, as an integral part of daily living condition, is an important determinant of health. Poor sanitation, then, invariably causes poor health. Inadequate sanitation is a very important cause of causation and spread of communicable diseases, the largest killer in India.

**Sanitation in India**

Sanitation in personal and public life is a joint responsibility of individual, community and the state. Some experts believe health problems caused by poor sanitation can be prevented only if people change their personal habits, or 'behaviours' about staying clean (Conant, 2005). However, experiences in India suggest that there are instances when despite having the necessary infrastructure, people's sanitation behaviour do not change. When behaviours do not change, people are blamed for their own poor health. But this idea does not take into consideration the availability and functioning of the supportive goods related to the material and technological bases and the structural barriers or the development gaps that people face in their daily lives. For example, the modern toilets cannot function when there is no availability of sufficient water, or the community toilets cannot work if there is no long term arrangement for ensuring their cleanliness. Very often, the lack of infrastructure is itself the main problem. Technical solutions are often suggested without taking into consideration the overall social worlds of the people. Sometimes they go unnoticed and often they create more problems than they solve.

**Sanitation in the Colonial Past**

Monica Das Gupta (2005) has reviewed the status of public health facilities in India. Das Gupta has also studied the sanitation regulations in the pre-independence India. In the colonial India, Sanitary Departments started to function at national and provincial levels for civilian public health services (with limited reach), while military hygiene was the responsibility of military medical officers. They were answerable directly to the government, and were administratively separate from the Indian Medical Service (IMS) which provided medical services. Policy making and planning for public health services were done systematically to address all major threats to the public health. The Sanitary Departments issued annual reports with information on disease patterns and associated factors such as seasonal conditions and population movements, and analysed this information to extrapolate the potential for outbreaks for which advance planning might be necessary. Periodic Sanitary Conferences were convened to discuss and refine overall policy thrusts, and coordinate policies and implementation between provinces.

The Sanitary Departments were entasked with ascertaining local sanitary conditions and improving them, vital registration, monitoring disease trends, providing technical advice on disease control and carrying out vaccination programs. They were expected to detect outbreaks early, trace them to their source and extinguish them quickly. Municipal governments hired their own public health staff, consisting of medical doctors, and 'a small army' of supervisors and sanitary inspectors to enforce sanitary regulations. Municipal planning was designed to avert public health threats, for example, an elaborate system of drainage in and around the city of Calcutta reduced the risk of malaria. The Sanitary Commissioners sometimes expressed shame that health conditions in India and Britain had come to diverge so widely since widespread sanitary measures began to be undertaken in Britain in the 1880s.

It is important to note that the sanitary departments were not exclusively meant to take care of the sanitation needs of people during that period. They were responsible for many other public health services. By the end of the colonial era, mortality from diseases such as cholera and the plague had fallen sharply, but diseases such as malaria and gastro-enteric infections continued to take heavy tolls. Independent India's First Five Year Plan notes that only three per cent of households in India had toilets, and that much of the population lacked basic water, drainage and waste disposal services.

**Current Programmes and Approaches**

The first three decades of post-independence India witnessed launch of several vertical diseases control programmes like National Malaria Control Programme (NMCP), National Leprosy Eradication Programme, National Tuberculosis Control Programme, National Cancer Control Programme, etc. The first National Health Policy (NHP) came in 1983 in the aftermath of the Alma Ata declaration of 1978. Public health system as such remained very weak and sanitation could hardly attract the attention of government policy makers till the 1980s. Initiative taken by agencies like Sulabh International to construct public and community toilets and maintain them in many cities brought huge impact but such initiative could hardly get translated into government mission for lack of political will and other handicaps.

### Central Rural Sanitation Programme (CRSP)

The 'Rural Development Department', Government of India had initiated India's first national programme on rural sanitation, the 'Central Rural Sanitation Programme' (CRSP) in 1986. The CRSP interpreted sanitation as construction of household toilets, and focused on the promotion of a single technology model (double pit pour-flush toilets) through hardware subsidies to generate demand. However, the programme could not yield many benefits for several limitations. There are critics related to the scope and design of the programme. An often quoted criticism of the programme is its silence on the key issue of motivating behaviour change to end open defecation and to use toilets. However, the constraint related to 'behaviour change' is a larger issue and has been discussed at length in the later sections of this paper.

### Total Sanitation Campaign (TSC)

The Government of India launched the Total Sanitation Campaign (TSC) in 1999 with the goal of achieving universal rural sanitation coverage by 2012. The responsibility for delivering on programme goals rested with local governments (Panchayati Raj Institutions-PRIs) with significant involvement of communities. The state and central governments had a facilitating role that took the form of framing enabling policies, providing financial and capacity-building support and monitoring progress. The main objectives of the TSC were: bringing about an improvement in the general quality of life in the rural areas; accelerating sanitation coverage in rural areas to provide access to toilets to all by 2012; motivating communities and Panchayati Raj Institutions promoting sustainable sanitation facilities through awareness creation and health education; providing sanitation facilities and promoting hygiene education/ sanitary habits in rural schools and *anganwadis* by March 2013; encouraging cost-effective and appropriate technologies for ecologically safe and sustainable sanitation; and developing community-managed environmental sanitation systems focusing on solid and liquid waste management.

### Nirmal Gram Puraskar (NGP)

To give a fillip to the TSC, the government introduced an innovative incentive programme known as Nirmal Gram Puraskar (NGP) in 2003. The NGP offers a cash prize to motivate Gram Panchayats (GPs) to achieve total sanitation. In addition, the NGP is an attractive incentive as winners are felicitated by the President of India at the national level and by high-ranking dignitaries at the state level. The TSC has recently completed a decade of implementation (1999-2009) and the NGP has completed five years of operation (2005-10). Since its launch, the programme framework of the TSC and NGP has been based on a common national guideline whereas implementation has been decentralised to the state and district levels.

An assessment of the TSC is carried out by the Department of Drinking Water and Sanitation, Ministry of Rural Development, Government of India after completion of one decade of the TSC and a report is published. The report (*A Decade of the Total Sanitation Campaign: Rapid Assessment of Processes and Outcomes*, Vol. 1: Main Report) finds that the TSC has achieved significant success over the last one decade. The sanitation coverage has increased significantly from 21 per cent in 2001 (Census, 2001) to more than 65 per cent. The number of Gram Panchayats which have won the Nirmal Gram Puraskar for achieving total sanitation has also increased to more than 22,000. The report finds that there is an undeniable upward trend in scaling up rural sanitation coverage. But the national performance aggregates conceal significant disparities among states and districts when it comes to the achievement of TSC goals. It also acknowledges that open defecation is a traditional behaviour in India and in most of the states, changing this practice is the biggest challenge.

### National Rural Health Mission (NRHM)

The government of India, Ministry of Health and Family Welfare, launched National Rural Health Mission (NRHM) in 2005. It recognises the importance of health as contributor of social and economic development and adopts the synergistic approach by relating health to the determinants of good health. It brought a strategic shift in the health structure and arrangements in India. It has made provisions of several new initiatives. It has new strategies, goals, plans of actions and institutional arrangements. The goals, core strategies and the plan of action of NRHM promise converging sanitation and hygiene under NRHM. The convergence incorporates IEC activities, rural sanitary marts, individual household toilets, women sanitary complex and School Sanitation Programme. Under NRHM, Village Health and Sanitation Committee needs to be formed in all the 6.38 lac revenue villages of India for promoting sanitation. The District Health Mission guides activities of sanitation at district level, and promotes joint IEC for public health, sanitation and hygiene, through Village Health and Sanitation Committee (VHSC), and promote household toilets and School Sanitation Programme. Accredited Social Health Activists (ASHAs) are incentivised for promoting household toilets by the Mission. The NRHM guidelines specify role of VHSC in ensuring sanitation at local level.

### National Urban Sanitation Policy

The government launched National Urban Sanitation Policy in 2008 and identified 100 per cent sanitation as a goal during the 11th Five Year Plan. According to NUSP, 7.87 per cent of urban households defecate in the open, 8.13 per cent use community latrines, 19.49 per cent share latrines, 18.5 per cent have no access to drainage and 39.8 per cent are connected to open drains. The ultimate objective was that all urban dwellers get access to and be able to use safe and hygienic sanitation facilities and arrangements so that no one defecates in the open. The states were expected to prepare their own strategies and the cities were to prepare model city sanitation plans. The overall goal of this policy is to transform urban India into community-driven, totally sanitised, healthy and liveable cities and towns.

### Sanitation and Development

Sanitation is not only an important indicator of development; it is also an important determinant of development; and it is, above all, an important goal of development. According to Mahbubul Haq, 'the basic purpose of development is to enlarge people's choice' (2011: 32). For Haq, these choices can be infinite and can change over time. According to Amartya Sen, 'the central issue in economic development is to expand the social opportunities open to the people' (2011: 22). Sanitation is one such choice; it is a social opportunity that needs to be open to the people. Sanitation is important not only for the elites; it is important for the masses, and above all, it is important for the social categories that remained absorbed in the occupations which are insanitary. The objective of development is to create an enabling environment for people to enjoy long, healthy and creative lives. Sanitation is an integral component of all the models of development, viz., social, human, sustainable or even economic development.

## Economic Development and Sanitation

Economic progress is an essential component of development. The classical and neo classical theorists of the nineteenth and early twentieth century viewed the process of development as series of successive stages of economic growth through which all countries must pass. Such theorist primarily focused on right quantity and mixture of saving, investment and economic expansion to enable an economic growth path. Development, thus, became synonymous with rapid and aggregate economic growth. Sanitation, under this model of development, was considered as an investment to enhance productivity and combat spread of diseases. The developing countries, in the post-second world war era, came under the direct influence of economic growth model of developed countries, but ignored the investment in widening the civic amenities and public health structures. India, in the first three decades after achieving independence, mainly followed the economic development model. But, it failed to realise the productive utility of sanitation infrastructure. No systematic effort has been made to take care of the sanitation needs of people, especially the rural and urban poor. Sanitation deficit is very visible during these three decades not only at the household or community level, but there is a complete absence of sanitation standards in the industrial developments. Industrial pollutant, urban wastes and sewerage systems never got the attention that they needed in many states of India.

## Social Development and Sanitation

James Midgley (1995) conceives social development as a process of planned social change designed to promote the well-being of the population as a whole in conjunction with a dynamic process of economic development. The goal of social development in the context of modern welfare is to produce a social well-being that makes people capable of acting and making their own decisions in the broadest sense. According to this perspective, equal access to society's goods (such as health, education or civic amenities like sanitation) should be available for all. Equal participation should provide everybody with opportunities for fulfillment. This model of development believes in extension of civic amenities and facilities to all. The need of sanitation facilities can't be ignored in this framework. Further, it believes in social planning for ensuring social justice. Thus, those who lagged behind in the trajectory of development must be guarded to come forward.

This model is very relevant in Indian context because the historically prevailing structural inequality has caused exploitation and seclusion of the several social categories like lower castes, poor, women and workers. Social development gives an inclusive trajectory of development. It not only talks about the fair share in the fruits of development for all social categories, it also assures preferential treatment for those who lagged behind. However, the social development model, which became popular in 1980s and 1990s, could not think beyond the protective discrimination in government services and little specific welfare measure for the specific categories. Availability of public goods, the core of the social development model, could not become the thrust of the social planning. The absence of public goods and especially the public health and sanitation facilities made the social development model a policy deficit model. Social justice could not get translated into social empowerment exhibiting implementation deficits and just remained a political instrument to mobilise voters.

**Human Development and Sanitation**

Human development is about expanding the choices people have to lead lives that they value and improving the human condition, so that people have the chance to lead full lives. Fundamental to enlarging these choices is building human capabilities–the range of things that people can do or be in life. Human development disperses the concentration of the distribution of goods and services that underprivileged people need. Investment in people can enable growth and empower people to pursue many different life paths developing human capabilities. The most basic capabilities for human development are: to lead long and healthy lives; to be educated; to have access to the resources and social service needed for a decent standard of living; and to be able to participate in the life of the community. Without these, many choices are simply not available, and many opportunities in life remain inaccessible. Healthy life needs fulfilment of several choices and removal of all those handicaps which may adversely affect it. Ensuring proper hygiene and sanitation is an integral component of a healthy life.

Human Development Index (HDI) became an important indicator of human development in last two decades reflecting upon the combined achievements in health, education and economic fields of the communities. Quantified and comparative measurement of HDI at the global level exposed India's poor performance in such capacity and capability building measures. The disparity between and among the various states of India also became very visible. The HDI also reflected on the relative positioning of the various indicators of development. Many countries are doing much better in HDI even when their per capita income is not very high because of their better performance in health and education. The government at the union level was forced to make dedicated planning to improve literacy level and health facilities. The macro level changes taking place at economic spheres because of the beginning of the LPG (Liberalisation, Privatisation and Globalisation) era and the changed political equations (because of beginning of the coalition government) at the central and federal levels witness the launch of National Literacy Mission, National Rural Health Mission and National Mission on Skill Development, Right to Education, Employment Guarantee Programmes, etc. Amidst these changed circumstance, there is beginning of programmes like Total Sanitation Campaign and National Urban Sanitation Policy which promise to contribute in enhancing sanitation and combating the premature mortalities caused by large scale prevailing communicable diseases and ever increasing non-communicable diseases.

## Sustainable Development and Sanitation

The last two decades also witness a new development approach in the form of sustainable development because of compulsions related to environmental degradation and sustainability needs. Sustainable development advocates policies that allow for economic growth while at the same time minimising damage to the environment. A holistic view of sustainable development basically opts for the doctrine of inter-generational equity. From this view point, sustainable development is the integration of environmental, economic and social concerns of society so as to arrive at development paths, which meet the needs of present generation without compromising the ability of future generations to meet their own needs. In other words, sustainable development allows a long term utilisation of environmental resources for social and economic development while at the same time, attempts to maintain the quality of the environment. Environmental sanitation is an integral element of sustainable development approach. And further, the sustainable development perspective gives the viable alternatives for the sanitation models in various contexts.

The sustainable development perspective has a long term vision for development planning. It does not believe in excessive exploitation of resources for short term gains. It believes in sustaining utilities. It has redesigned the goals and strategies of economic development. Globally, sustainable development talks about maintaining ecological and environmental equilibrium. It has redefined the technologies also. It believes in minimising pollution and wastages. It believes in recycling of material resources. It talks about protecting natural resources like water. Technologically, it is the most sanitation friendly model of development. However, in India, the model has not been adopted at larger level. Sustainable development strategies, if implemented effectively, will pave the path of achieving sanitation goals naturally.

## Sanitation, Health and Development Deficit

Sanitation, in India, is yet to become an integral part of the development paradigms. Most of the industries in India run without having any standard mechanism of waste disposal. No city in India can claim to have a state of the art sewage treatment plant. No river in India has uncontaminated water. This is a reflection of policy deficit and implementation deficit in India. Indian rail is one of the largest systems of modern transportation. Passengers, travelling in all the classes in Indian rails, unite the rural and urban India by expelling and spreading the feces on the railway tracks through the open floor toilets. The drainage system in most of urban India is inadequate. A good rain in any city and everything that we put under the carpet is coming out! Sanitation, in India, never received the attention that it deserves. No government office in India can claim to have a 24x7 clean premise or even toilets. The local self governments in most of the cities in India are unable to deliver the sanitation rights of citizens of India. This is sanitation deficit in India.

Experience suggests that India's late entry into ensuring total sanitation and a limited sectoral approach for it has not yielded desired results. The disparity among states in outcomes is a cause of great concern. To improve sanitation in a lasting way, the issues related to defecation, waste disposal, water, environment and health must be seen from a comprehensive and sustainable solution perspective. When communities use hygiene and sanitation methods that fit their real needs and expectation, they will adopt sanitation practices and enjoy better health. It is, therefore, very important to understand the structuring of the development trajectory responsible for inadequate and poor sanitation conditions prevailing in India. Sanitation can no longer be seen as a 'segment' or 'isolated' component. Sanitation needs to be seen as an integral component of health structure and development agenda. The problem of inadequate sanitation in India is actually the problem of development deficit. The development deficit is not only visible in the economic or development planning; it is also visible in health planning in terms of the planning deficit.

Health, in India, has not been seen in a holistic perspective and the focus always remained on clinical treatment of 'diseases'. The Primary Health Centres (PHCs) and sub-centres hardly attract the attention that they deserve in many parts of the country, even after the comprehensive recommendations made by the *Alma Ata Declaration* (1978). The declaration states that primary healthcare includes at least: (i) education concerning prevailing health problems and the methods of preventing and controlling them; (ii) promotion of food supply and proper nutrition; (iii) an adequate supply of safe water and basic sanitation; (iv) maternal and child health care, including family planning; (v) immunisation against the major infectious diseases; (vi) prevention and control of locally endemic diseases; (vii) appropriate treatment of common disease and injuries; and (viii) provision of essential drugs. However, India's policy-makers could never include the first three elements, as suggested by the declaration, into India's health policies, plans and programmes. India's health policies are dominated by the bio-medical germ theory and mainly prescribe clinical and treatment oriented curative care. The broad based preventive and promotive health care (except immunisation against select diseases) could hardly find their place in the core health policies and programmes. Food, nutrition, potable water and sanitation could never become component of public health policy in India.

Out of the eight primary elements necessary for primary health care, as suggested by Alma Ata declaration, the author considers unadulterated nutritious food, safe drinking water and sanitation as the 'Basic Health Goods (BHGs)'. BHGs are basic in the sense that they are indispensable for human life and life is impossible without them. 'Health for all' is just an illusion without the comprehensive and sustainable availability of the BHGs to all individuals in any society and more particularly in developing societies like India (Akram, 2012). Most of the states in India have a lackadaisical approach towards making universal availability of primary health care and especially the BHGs. The mechanism and practice of denying primary health care and especially the BHGs to the population or a part of it or even gradual withdrawal from it is denial of health chance and can conveniently be termed as 'dehealthism' or at least 'ahealthism'. Any group, community or state practising dehealthism or ahealthism can't achieve the goal of health for all, no matter how much medicalisation it is promoting.

Thus, health policies and programmes in India don't treat the BHGs and especially sanitation as a component of health or health care. The Total Sanitation Campaign, as discussed earlier, did make some efforts in ensuring sanitation but in the absence of proper budget, infrastructure and strategies, sanitation practices are yet to find their popularisation among the masses in India. A recent policy initiative of government of India in the form of 'Universal Health Coverage' has also missed the importance of sanitation, potable water and nutrition as component of health coverage. It gives the impression that health policies and plans in India are witnessing 'over-medicalisation' and the BHGs are becoming victim of 'medical neglecting'. 'Medicalisation of health', 'privatisation of health care', and 'pharmaceuticisation of health behaviour' are the dominant trends of Indian health scenario.

Universal availability and accessibility of 'public health facility' is the first step towards developing a modern health system in any society. But such facilities are poorly funded in India. And further, such facilities are poorly designed and even more poorly implemented (through bureaucratic targetism). The under achievements of various development plans and programmes and the wastage and pilferage of the resources are 'bureaucratically managed' by blaming the people for their cultural poverty and illiteracy (povertism). On the other hand, the poorly designed public health institutions are further degraded by 'medical absenteeism'. Very often, the absenteeism of the medical professionals from their duties is twisted as people's traditionalism and lack of preference for institutional care. There is an increasing redesigning of the domains of 'health care' and 'health coverage' as 'medical care' and 'medical coverage'. The cumulative and compounding negative consequences of 'medical neglecting', targetism, povertism, absenteeism and 'over' medicalism are manifested in continuous occurrence and prevalence of communicable disease in India. The mechanisms and processes together create a development deficit in the health structure of India.

**Sociology of Sanitation**

'Sociology of sanitation' helps us in understanding the larger phenomenon of lack of sanitation standards and the sanitation deficits in Indian context. It also helps in understanding the structuring discourses which cause inadequate sanitation at personal and public life. It aims at seeing sanitation needs at three different levels: state level; community level; and individual level. A sanitation friendly development trajectory can ensure sanitation at the state level. For this, the state needs to follow the comprehensive social and human development models, as discussed above. The state needs to eliminate the policy and technology deficits in a sustainable way from the existing patterns. The sustainable development perspective has the answer to the most of the problems related to pollution, garbage and waste. The development deficits need to be removed.

The social development perspective has larger implications. It has the potentiality to correct the historical wrongs also. The birth based division of labour, in the form of caste system, has left some social categories absorbed in the occupations of carrying and dealing with human feces. Although the occupation of carrying the human feces on head by human groups is abolished, the stigma associated with it, in the form of ritual impurity, is lingering in several discourses. The need of mitigating such stigma and providing alternative occupations for such human groups is still unrealised. The state needs to work on it in a sustainable way. This is very much possible through the systematic and dedicated human development strategies. There is a larger need of involvement of the communities in achieving these development goals at larger level. Social justice is not only a value that needs to be admired; it is also a solidarity bond that needs to be practised.

Several interventions are required for achieving the goals of social justice and social development at the community level. Development of community life is the core of any development trajectory. The structural inadequacies created and perpetuated at the community level because of incoherent values (historically) and inadequate social planning (politically), need to be mended through conscious community engagement. The community initiative needs to be taken at diverse levels. The elite as well as the masses, the urban as well as the rural, the educated as well as the illiterate, the global as well as the local, the upper caste/class as well as the lower caste/class—all need to come forward in a coherent and integrated way to overcome the challenges posed by the development deficits in general and the sanitation deficits in particular. It needs to be realised that the organs, symbols and vehicles of development and modernity often promote underdevelopment and insanitation in public life because of ignored or neglected deficits. Just as economic growth cannot be achieved through continuous financial deficits or budgetary deficits; development cannot be achieved through continuous or perpetual development deficits. The developed world is developed because it keeps identifying and rectifying such deficits.

The deficits cannot be improved without identifying the acts that cause them. Very often, the development models induced by technology are set in urban spaces by the elites and the rural spaces gradually adopt them. The development discourses are generally set by influential opinion builders. The masses often get trapped in these discourses and simulations. The worldviews often build up surrounding the technology. This is also true about the sanitation practices. Indian rails were designed by the elites. The industries are owned by the elites. The urban spaces are dominated by educated. But all these development tools and designs promote insanitation at public life. India is continuing with the technology deficit trains which spread human feces and urine in the railway tracks (closed door open floor defecation!). The industries pass the pollutants and waste materials in the rivers. The urban spaces dump the garbage and leftovers in the suburbs. The infrastructure deficit is approved by all including the political leadership. Hence, it is very important to identify the deficits and the gaps. A conscious decision to overcome such deficits can only promise to bring a change.

Sanitation practice at individual level is largely affected by the sanitation models and standards followed at the community and the society levels. The sanitation programmes in India (CRSP, TSC, and NGP) consider 'open defecation' of the rural people or urban poor as the main sanitation challenge. They have failed to identify the sanitation deficits grounded at different levels as sanitation challenge. The problem of open defecation is not denied here. The health problem created by it is also undeniable. But what is denied here is that, the problem is caused by only rural or urban poor class. People's behaviour is largely determined by the complex intermixing of the images of the larger environment and his/her local surrounding. People's behaviour is more or less influenced by the social world and the *habitus* (term used by Bourdieu) which are structured by multitude of factors. The contemporary societies are also seen as the administered societies (term used by Foucault); and hence, the behaviour of individual largely gets influenced by the administrative discourses. Behaviour is also seen to get governed by simulations (term used by Baudrillard), which are the signs and the images and never the reality themselves.

The sanitation deficits prevailing in the larger environment composed by polluting industries, sewerage deficient urban spaces, open defecating railways, garbage producing middle class households, dirty public spaces like bus stands, hospitals, offices, toilets, etc. create discourses in which sanitation is not considered as a value or a need satisfying good. When it comes to the personal life of people, there is a lack of faith in having the capacity to maintain the sanitised environment and thus doubts in the sanitation designs proposed by various government programmes. Besides, the local surroundings of the rural people and the urban poor pose serious limitations like non-availability of money and space for construction and maintenance of toilets or absence of other materialistic support bases like water, water storage system, toilet cleaners, in having the affordability of personalised toilets. The complex intermixing of these larger environments and local surroundings create discourses which not necessarily support the government promises. Sanitation needs a conscious decision making.

If rural India can learn to operate ATMs, mobiles, kisan and aadhar cards, they can also learn to sanitise their behaviour. But, for this, they need to volunteer themselves consciously. This conscious decision-making will depend upon removing the local handicaps and structuring the right macro environment. The sanitation deficits prevailing in the macro environment need to be removed first because they structure the images and imaginations of masses. This is perhaps a difficult task for the political leaders and administrative managers, because this needs corrections at multiple levels such as having long term vision, economic investment, bureaucratic efficiency, corporate responsibility, technological and infrastructure upgradation, political will and many more initiatives. Any such initiative by the government will empower people and may further the demand of public goods. The need fulfilling goods needs to be provided to people. The political and managerial elites follow the other short cuts; learn to 'manage' and 'pass the buck'.

The 'difficult to change the traditional behaviour of open defecation' theory is proposed to explain the unmet goals of sanitation programmes in India. The proposition says that the rural people do not want to change their behaviour of open defecation. So, even when they are provided with the toilets, they stick to their traditional behaviour. The remedy suggested, by the supporters of the above theory, is to create awareness and to educate people about the potential benefits. And thus, the rural people and the urban poor are held responsible for not changing their behaviour and having unhygienic taste and preferences. The overall 'sanitation deficit macro structures' is deliberately ignored. The role of the government agencies, industrialists, elites, designers and the powerful, in perpetuation of sanitation deficit environment, is completely ignored.

The state organs in India are yet to become the responsible agencies for designing and implementing holistic change. The enlightened citizens are yet to become the conscious agents in the field of sanitation and health. India needs the active presence of many more conscious agencies like civil society groups, who can help in filling up the various deficits. The social practices both produce and are produced by the social world. Sanitation needs to be a part of the social practice as well as the social world. From a broader perspective, health care needs to become part of the social world. From a holistic perspective, active citizenship needs to be an integral part of the social world. This social world is not confined to rural or urban, elite or masses, rich or poor, or even literate or illiterate. A social world transgresses many boundaries and engrosses the local surroundings as well as the macro environment. A practice is not just traditional or modern; a practice is something that mediates between the individual and the social world.

Sanitation needs engagement not only between a user and a toilet: it needs engagement between responsible citizen and responsible state; it needs engagement between local surroundings and public spaces; it needs reciprocity between needs and need fulfilling goods; it needs to fulfil the gaps between the deficits and the interventions. We need to come above the deficit model we all are habituated in working with. Labelling 'open defecation' as an 'unchangeable traditional behaviour or practice' of rural or poor people is a part of the larger mechanism of blaming people for inadequate institution building, improper policy making, inefficient programme implementing, unprofessional elitism, and diverting all the issues through capitalising povertism. Cleanliness and hygiene is a natural and human choice, universally. Given a coherent and substantial choice and the power to decide, people always prefer sanitation and good environment. The interventions designed by the government should not aim to maintain its comfort zones suggesting half-baked programmes: they should aim to achieve the constitutional commitment of providing right to life to the citizens as given in Article 21 and ensuring all the necessary goods meant for it.

## References

Akram, M. (2007), "Introduction", in Akram, M. (ed.) *Health Dynamics and Marginalised Communities*, Jaipur: Rawat Publications, ix-xx.

Akram, M. (2012), "Looking Beyond the Universal Health Coverage: Health Inequality, Medicalism and Dehealthism in India", *Public Health Research*, Vol. 2 No. 6, 2012, pp. 221-228. doi: 10.5923/j.phr.20120206.08.

Carr, A.J., Higginson, I.J. and Robinson, P.G. (2003), *Quality of Life*, London: BMJ Books.

Conant, J. (2005), *Sanitation and Cleanliness for a Healthy Environment*, USA: Hesperian Foundation.

Das Gupta, M. (2005), Public Health in India: An Overview, Development Research Group, *World Bank Policy Research Working Paper* 3787, The World Bank.

Earle, S. (2007), "Promoting Public Health: Exploring The Issues", in Sarah Earle, Cathy E. Lloyd, Moyra Sidell and Sue Spurr (eds.). *Theory and Research in Promoting Public Health*, London: Sage, pp. 1-36.

Haq, M. (2011), "Human Development Paradigm for South Asia' in *Re-Imagining India and Other Essays* (Collection of D.T. Lakdawala Memorial Lectures, Institute of Social Sciences), New Delhi: Orient Blackswan, pp. 30-43.

Kumar, G.S., Kar, S.S. and Jain, A. (2011), "Health and Environmental Sanitation in India: Issues for Prioritising Control Strategies", *Indian J Occup Environ Med.* Sep-Dec; 15(3): 93-96.doi:10.4103/0019-5278.93196.

Midgley, J. (1995), *Social Development: The Developmental Perspective in Social Welfare*. Thousand Oaks, CA: Sage.

Mmom, P.C. and Mmom, C.F. (2011), "Environmental Sanitation and Public Health Challenges in a Rapidly Growing City of the Third World: The Case of Domestic Waste and Diarrhoea Incidence in Greater Port Harcourt Metropolis, Nigeria", *Asian Journal of Medical Sciences*, 3(3).

MOHFW (2010), Annual Report to the People on Health, Government of India, Ministry of Health and Family welfare, September 2010.

Pandve, H.T. (2008), "Environmental Sanitation: An Ignored Issue in India' http://www.healthizen.com/blog/index.php/general/environmental-sanitation/. Indian Journal of Occupational and Environmental Medicine, April; 12(1): 40, doi:10.4103/0019-5278.40816.

Sen, A. (2006), "Why Health Equity?", in Anand, S., Peter, F., Sen, A. (ed.) *Public Health, Ethics and Equity*, New Delhi: Oxford University Press, pp. 21-33.

Sen, A. (2011), "Beyond Liberalisation: Social Opportunity and Human Capability", in Re-Imagining India and other Essays (Collection of D.T. Lakdawala Memorial Lectures, Institute of Social Sciences) New Delhi: Orient Blackswan, pp. 1-29.

The Declaration of Alma-Ata (1978), [online] available from: http://www.who.int/social_determinants/tools/multimedia/alma_ata/en/index.html (accessed July 15, 2012).

United Nations (1948), Documents. (online) Available from: http://www.un.org/en/documents/udhr/ (accessed July 05, 2012).

WHO (2002) Report of Working Group 2 of the WHO Commission on Macroeconomics and Health on 'Global Public Goods for Health', Geneva: WHO.

# 4

# Scourge of Untouchability and Social Deprivation of Scavengers

***Jitender Prasad*** **and** ***Satish Kundu***

It is somewhat paradoxical to note that certain members of low caste groups labeled as untouchables, provided with a particular service to those belonging to the higher castes are themselves the most deprived section. They belong to the bottom of caste hierarchy and are subjected to the extreme forms of socio-cultural, political and economic deprivation. They are forced to do caste based traditional occupations of manual scavenging. It is considered most polluting work hence it bears the stigma of untouchables on those engaged in manual scavenging. As untouchables the manual scavengers ranked low in *Varna* hierarchy (known as *Shudra*) and they are subjected to the extreme forms of deprivation in social domain.[1] The enactment against untouchability has not changed the mindset of people to whom they extend social service.

In different states, the caste groups involved in scavenging works are termed as *Bhangis, Doms, Balmikis, Mehtars* and *Chudas* etc. They are traditionally associated with polluting work such as sweeping the floor, carrying the night soil on their head, i.e., the most defiling act due to which members of high caste tended to avoid having any bodily contact with them.[2] They are cursed to live in the most unhygienic conditions. In urban areas they occupy spaces adjacent to drains and in rural areas they live in the low lying water logged areas at the corner end of the village in mud houses or huts thatched with dry twigs of plants and trees. Their precarious economic existence in low paid work carries the stigma attached to their social work which make them realise that they are like, 'the worms that crawl in the dirt.'[3]

In the present paper an attempt has been made to highlight the predicament of the scavengers who even after six and half decades of

**Scavengers at work without facemask and gloves.**

our independence and despite 'Article 17 of our constitution declaring that untouchability is abolished' are forced to lead a life that negates the right to a 'life of dignity'. They continue to engage themselves in the most demeaning work that earned them derogatory epithet *untouchables*.

Three illustrations of untouchabilities that cause social deprivation of manual scavengers will be highlighted to address the concerns of one of the subthemes of the workshop.

**(A) Unfinished Legacy of Shaheed Bhagat Singh Addressing the Scourge of Untouchability:** Irfan Habib, a noted historian while paying tribute to Shaheed Bhagat Singh on his 71st birth anniversary, termed him not just a martyr but also a revolutionary thinker, a visionary and an intellectual who had a secular vision of India.[4] He alluded to two articles of him which were published in June 1928 issue of *Kirti-Firstly, Achhoot ka Sawaal* (The Question of Untouchability) and Second, *Sampradayik Dange aur Unka Ilaz* (Communal Riots and their Solutions). Irfan Habib (who now holds Maulana Azad Chair at National University of Educational Planning and Administration, New Delhi) praises Bhagat Singh who was a voracious reader and some of his journalistic writings on, "Poverty, Religion and Society: The Global Struggle against Imperialism and on issue of caste, communalism and conditions of the working class and peasantry" still continues to be quite relevant.

Bhagat Singh talked about Leo Tolstoy's division of religion into three parts: First, that concerns with essentials of religion; second, philosophy of religion and third, with rituals of religion. In his concluding part Bhagat Singh stated that if religion means blind faith by mixing rituals and philosophy then it should be blown away, but if we can combine essentials with philosophy then religion may be a meaningless idea. He felt that ritualism of religion has divided us into touchables and untouchables and these narrow divisive religions cannot bring about actual unity among people. For us freedom should not mean a mere end to British colonialism, our freedom implies living together happily without caste and religious barriers.

**A thinker and a Doer: Bhagat Singh (left) with DSP Gopal Singh Pannu, Lahore Central Jail, 1928.**

"Bhagat Singh's idea", writes Irfan Habib, "needs to be invoked even today to bring about the changes he yearned for". While writing the questions of untouchability he observed, "Our country is unique where six crore citizens are called untouchables and their touch defiles the upper caste. Gods get enraged if they enter the temples. It is shameful that such things are being practised in the 20th century. We claim to be a spiritual country but hesitate to accept equality of all human beings while materialist Europe is talking of revolution since centuries. They had proclaimed equality during American and French Revolutions. However, we are still debating whether the untouchable is entitled for the sacred thread, or can he read the Vedas or not. We are chagrined about discrimination against Indians in foreign lands and whine that English do not give us equal rights in India." Given our conducts Bhagat Singh wondered, "Do we really have any right to complain about such matters?"

He also engaged with a solution to this malaise. "The first decision for all of us should be, that we start believing that we all are born equal and our vocation as well need not divide us. If someone is born in a sweeper's family that does not mean that he/she has to continue in the family profession cleaning shit all his life with no right to participate in any developmental work."

He attributed discrimination as contributory factor responsible for conversions, a burning issue of 1920s.[5] Despite his anticolonialist fervour he did not condemn the missionaries, nor did he instigate Hindus to kill and burn all those who had accepted new faith. He wrote self critically, "If you treat them worse than animals, then they will surely join other religions where they will get more rights and will be treated like human beings. In this situation it will be futile to accuse Christianity and Islam of harming Hinduism." Singh was convinced, "That no one would be forced or tempted to change faith if the age old inequalities are removed and we sincerely start believing that we are all equal and non is different either due to birth or vocation." Finally commenting on ideas of Bhagat Singh, Irfan Habib observed that he has left behind an easy legacy and has "bequeathed us an unfinished task of nation building where no caste, class or religious barrier will ever exists.

### (B) Burying Democracy in Human Waste—The Strange Alchemy of Law and Practice of Manual Scavenging

Parbha Sridevan, a former judge of Madras High Court and Chairperson, Intellectual Property Appellate Board, in one of the most ponderous reflections pointed out that the Supreme Court had recently admonished a District Magistrate for filing a wrong affidavit stating that there was no manual scavenging in districts of Madras.[6] In fact, it was also pointed out by the former judge that earlier Union Minister of Rural Development Jairam Ramesh had publically apologised for the continuance of the practice of manual scavenging. The judge pointed out the woeful tale of a poor *bhangi's* child. When enquired about her going to school, she informed the judge that she had earlier used to go to school but now she has stopped. Reason for dropping out of the school was the continuation of painful practice of untouchability. She stated that in the school she used to sit in the front row but her classmates objected to her sitting in front row and the teacher asked her to sit in the last row. She continued to sit on the back row for some time and later she got so disheartened with the discriminatory practice that she stopped going to that Government school.

The story narrated by the small girl named Neerottam is not the only one as the eight year old girl had the dream to become a nurse or

a teacher. There may be several cases of such discriminatory practices which still continue but go unreported. It is the dignity of the individual and the unity and integrity of the nation that denies the fraternity and affection towards *dalits* engaged in manual scavenging work. No wonder Ambedkar, who was involved in the framing of constitution, treated caste as an antinational institution. When the constitution was being framed Ambedkar observed, "Fraternity means a sense of common brotherhood of all Indians... It is the principal which gives unity and solidarity to social life... Castes are antinational, in the first place because they bring about separation in social life. They are antinational also because they generate jealousy and antipathy between caste and caste... we must overcome all these difficulties if we wish to become a nation in reality. For fraternity can be a fact only when there is a nation. Without fraternity, equality and liberty will be no deeper than coats of paints". That means in the absence of substantive equality there will always be groups whose dignity is not acknowledged resulting in a negation of fraternity

Sridevan writes, "Of the five senses touch is the least understood... it is the only sense that establishes fraternity that also establishes kinship. A bridge is built when you touch another in kinship in a way that it is not when you look at, talk to or listen to the other... we have not understood the principal of fraternity, that there is no 'they' and 'us', there is no us.

The broken dreams of young girl Neerottam is not the only one. She represents a group to which the right to fraternity is consistently and brazenly denied and is the most marginalised of the marginalised groups. It is acknowledged in public meetings that manual scavenging is a human rights issue and not about the sanitation. In the newspapers it is reported that this practice would soon be banned and that we would become Nirmal Bharat.[7] The state has committed itself for eradicating this inhuman practice by a deadline that was March 31, 2010. Such deadlines have come and gone but manual scavengers continue their work anaesthetising themselves with drinks and drugs from these assaults on their dignity. The former judge observed, "Their lives are a daily negation of the right to a life with dignity though they have court orders affirming that right."

The judge further narrated an excruciatingly painful experience shared by Bezwada Wilson who campaigns against manual scavenging. One day he saw some manual scavengers digging in a pile of excreta. When enquired about their digging work he was told that their pale had got buried in the filth and they were trying to retrieve it with their bare hands. When Wilson asked them why were they doing they said, "If we do not get it back we cannot do our job tomorrow and will not get paid." It shook the heart and soul of Wilson who states, "I stood there and cried to the moon. I cried to the wind. I cried to the water. I cried and asked why?"

Justice Albie Sachs of South Africa observed in his book *The Strange Alchemy of Law and Life*, "There are some things human beings cannot do to other human beings." He said so in the context of torture and it is just the same in the context of abomination. In *State of M.P. vs Ramakrishna Balothiya* [1995 SCC (3) 221] the Justice rejected the attack on the provisions of the *SCs* and *STs (Prevention of atrocities) Act, 1989*, saying that a special legislation to check and deter crimes against them committed by non-scheduled castes and non-scheduled tribes is necessary in view of their continued violation of their rights, S.3(1)(ii) states, "Whoever-(1)…(ii) acts with intent to cause injury, insult, or annoyance to any member of SC or ST by dumping excreta…in his premises or neighbourhood is punishable."

Needless to add, the work of manually lifting and the removal of human excreta is inextricably linked with caste and is another form of dumping democracy in human waste. B. Wilson in his foreword to Gita

Thamaswamy's book *India Stinking* (2005) writes that, "(A)n estimated 1300000 people from Dalit communities continue to be employed as manual scavengers across the length and breadth of this country—in private homes, in community dry latrines managed by the municipality, in the public sector such as Railways and by the Army."

**(C) *Mehtars' Slog* to Keep the *Kumbh Mela* Ground Clean-A Paradox of Development**

Few days back, about 7-8 thousands members of *Mehtar* community (known as *bhangi*) arrived from neighbouring districts of UP to Allahabad in the *Mahakumbh* that began on January 14, this year.[8] The *Mahakumbh* is held at *Allahabad Sangam* every twelve years. Omar Rashid reported that the *Bhangis* who will be living in the tents will have to slog hard to keep the vast area of *Sangam* clean. The *Bhangis* who are called with different caste names, at different places are all involved in scavenging work, are mostly concentrated in Uttar Pradesh, Bihar, Delhi, Haryana, Punjab and Gujarat. They are still identified as untouchables in various districts of these states and are marginalised and forced to do manual scavenging. The *Mehtars* who have visited the *Sangam* this year will sweep the vast stretch of *Kumbh Mela* ground clean and live in deplorable conditions. For eight hours of daily work they will earn daily wage of Rs 156, the nominal wage fixed for all the sweepers.

**Cleaning up the *Sangam* Ground in Uniform.**

The 7000-8000 members of the *Mehtar* community belonging to the *Bhangi* caste have indeed shifted to less *ostracised* jobs, the stigma attached to their traditional occupation still remains. In the late 19th century, the members of the scheduled caste resorted to extensive conversions to *Islam* and Christianity to escape the discrimination and inhuman conditions in which they were forced to live. Now in the second decade of 21st century, majority of them are devout *Hindus* and the religiosity along with the guarantee of work is a good reason why they travel all the way to Allahabad to attend the *Magh Mela*. For them, it serves the twin objectives of (a) earning wages that they would get compared to their hometowns and (b) the second objective of getting an opportunity to have holy dip in the sacred *Gangaji* on occasion of a *Kumbh Mela*. Needless to add it is the second objective which is a far more compelling reason for them to travel all the way to attend *Magh Mela*. When enquired about what they earned in their home towns, in their local language they said, *"Kaam bhi hota hai aur Gangaji ke darshan bhi."*

**Living in trying conditions in makeshift homes.**

The local sweepers forced the migrant *Mehtars* to pay circle tax for the work they get in *kumbh mela*. At times, they have to part with grease money of Rs 700 for the period of their stay at *Sangam,* otherwise they will be harassed by the local sweepers. Omar Rashid interviewed some of local *Mehtars* to record their experience about the sweeping work that they do. "What else can we say, we are like the worms that crawl in the dirt", says Ashok, a *Mehtar*. The dirt, pools of stagnant water and excreta, he is referring to, besides being un-aesthetic, are also perfect breeding grounds for illness.

## Economic Reforms and Social Deprivation

In the early decades of 90s, when three issues, namely, *Mandal*,

*Kamndal* and economic reforms portrayed the grim social, economic and political prospects of our country's development, the British magazines *The Economist* adorned the cover page with 'a tiger in a cage'. The informative survey diagnosed a state of India's economy pointing out the role of ever proliferating bureaucracy, the *license raj* and expressed the dialectic hope that with the election due, the new government might immediately face a fiscal crisis. Subsequently, reforms introduced in 1991and the succeeding years thereafter followed liberalisation programme giving India a dubious distinction of best emerging market at the global level. Amartya Sen lamented that "the potential benefits of accelerated economic growth appear to have been diluted by severe imbalances in growth patterns, growing inequalities and continued state inertia in crucial social fields–eliminating deprivation is as much a matter of public action as one merely of economic growth."

In the eleventh plan approach paper themes titled *Disparities and Divides* and *Bridging the Divides: including the excluded* provided some concerns about the social deprivation that particular sections of society face. While a salutary commitment to abolition of the inhuman practice of manual scavenging by the middle of eleventh plan is made, no reference to women and girls who traditionally dominated this activity is made. C.P. Sujaya observes, "Untouchability, caste biases, illiterate backgrounds of parents and families, poverty, learning disabilities, etc., are examples, which, compounded with vulnerabilities of being females…" the real and complex face of discrimination against women and girls still continue. For them there is neither the escape from the social evil of untouchability, nor the freedom from the manual scavenging. The problem of manual scavenging is considered the most despised and defiling activity that still continues to be part of their vocations.

The irony of the situation with regard to manual scavenging is that it stands statutorily prohibited in 1993. The convention on the elimination of all forms of discrimination against women suggests women expressing their concerns over it. The Governments also pointed out the adverse health implications of manual scavenging. While no government data on the women's involvement in manual scavenging seems to be available the Action Aid in its press release referring to government statistics point out that 98 per cent of those engaged in scavenging work consists of women and girls out of the estimated one million total scavengers in the country.

Padma Velaskar (2001) refers to vast and complex literature on caste, i.e., silent on women and gender issue. She pointed out that though Ambedkar and Phule seriously engaged themselves on the question of women, theories of caste have paid scant attention to women's specific role and position when analysing the system. Phule-Ambedkar critique on caste patriarchy did not highlight the problem until *dalit* women themselves decided to deal with the scourge of untouchability issue in the context of their daily experience of caste, class and gender oppression.

It is pertinent to mention here that forty-three years after its prohibition in the Constitution, in 1993, a law was passed which outlawed the practice. Later, it turned out to be a feeble and toothless law and hence a new bill promising to correct the historical injustice and indignity suffered by the manual scavengers and to rehabilitate them to a life of dignity was passed. While the 1993 law defined a manual scavenger as 'a person engaged in or employed for manually carrying human excreta,' the 2012 bill defined a manual scavenger as 'a person engaged or employed... for manually cleaning, carrying, disposing of, or otherwise handling in any manner, human excreta in an unsanitary latrine, or in an open drain or pit into which the human excreta from the insanitary latrine is disposed of, or on a railway track...' The irony of the change in definition provided a new escape route which meant the employers may issue gloves and protective clothing and that would be sufficient to allow the demeaning practice to persist.

**Hazardous cleaning of sewer and chemical waste in a pool of water**

**carrying filth**

The bill, however, brought in to force certain innovative ideas, namely, (a) prohibition of dry latrines to be constructed and prohibitingthe employment of manual scavengers in the hazardous cleaning of sewer and a septic tank. It was strange enough to find that the bill did not prohibit cleaning railway tracks as hazardous cleaning. Thus, it is clear that human dignity was not considered important. In view of these

loopholes mentioned above, Harsh Mander rightly pointed out the schemes of Rehabilitation of the Manual Scavengers, when he observed that women should have the option of receiving a monthly pension of Rs 2000, or an enterprise grant of up to Rs 1 lakh, supported by training and counselling facilities. Highly subsidised housing should be ensured in mixed colonies. In yet another write up by Rane, it was pointed out that manual scavengers… are out there on a routine job, "without any form of protective shield. Employers of sewage divers don't even provide proper clothing, face mask or gloves as a scavenger who enters a sewer is exposed to many forms of toxic chemicals and disease causing bacteria." What was all the more alarming that the manual scavengers "are provided with a bottle of booze to dull their senses while they are on their jobs." This shows callus neglect and insensitivity about the problems of manual scavengers.

In view of government's apathy and lack of concern for the problems of manual scavenging, the role of Sulabh International, Centre for Action Sociology over last four decades is indeed quite commendable. The man behind the movement Bindeshwar Pathak's efforts in providing a platform to cross section of people of different backgrounds is decidedly a paradigm shift in the field of sociology. The scavenging people are found inhabiting the urban areas retaining their caste identity wherever they live. The concern shown by the Sulabh International in raising the problem of Manual Scavenging would go a long way in heralding a new initiative in two fields in particular, first, social upliftment of *dalits* and second, empowerment of *dalit* women and girls. It is in this backdrop that in this paper three illustrations of manual scavenger's plight were presented here to suggest that despite the total sanitation campaign launched as one of the flagship programme of the government why the campaign has not yet succeeded in removing the scourge of untouchability.[9]

## Notes

1. Four main divisions of Hindu society under *Varna* scheme-in descending order are *Brahmin*, *Kshtriya*, *Vaishya* and *Shudra*.
2. S.C. Dubey observes, 'India still has 41,000 open latrines; the excrements from them have to be carried as headloads in closed containers or even in open baskets by one particular *jati*' (1990:63).
3. Omar Rashid uses the expression to portray the *Mehtars* engaged in scavenging work.
4. A noted historian Irfan Habib observed that Bhagat Singh was not just a martyr but also a revolutionary thinker and intellectual who had a secular vision of India.
5. Change of Religious belief pattern.
6. Prabha Sridevan has pointed out the predicament of manual scavengers who do not get a descent treatment in our democracy.

7. The Total Sanitation Campaign (TSC) was one of the flagship programmes of the government. The annual budgeting support has gradually increased from 202 crores in 2003-04 to 1500 crores in 2011-12. The TSC follows a community led and people centric approach laying emphasis on information, education and communication (IEC) for demand generation for sanitation facilities. To motivate the community towards creating sustainable sanitation facilities and their usage, the incentives for individual household's latrines (IHHL) for BPL households have been increased from Rs. 600 to Rs. 3200 w.e.f. 1st June, 2011. TSC has been turned into an exclusive programme ...inclusive growth for all sections of society. The *Nirmal Gram Purskar* incentive scheme has been launched to encourage PRIs to take up sanitation promotion to realise the dream of *Nirmal Bharat.*
8. The *Mahakumbh* is held at *Allahabad Sangam* every 12 years. This year it started at Allahabad on January 14, 2013 in which about one crore people were reported to have taken a holy dip in the *sangam.*
9. TSC campaign was launched enthusiastically in three districts of Haryana namely Hisar, Fatehabad and Sirsa. In all these three districts the enthusiastic implementation of the programme was carried out but Sirsa was declared the first ever district of northern India which won *Nirmal Puraskar*. The credit goes to the then Deputy Commissioner Dr Yudhbir Singh Khyalia and his team.

## References

Crook Clive, *A Survey of India*, The Economist, May 4, 1991.

Dreze Jean and Sen Amartya, *India Development and Participation* Oxford University Press, New Delhi, 2002.

Habib Irfan, *An Unfinished Legacy*, Hindustan Times, March 23, 2012.

Mander Harsh, *India's Great Shame*, The Hindu, Nov. 17, 2012.

Pathak Bindeshwar, *Evil that Refuses to Go*, The Times of India, Nov., 31, 1998.

Planning Commission, 2006, *Bridging divides: Including the excluded.*

Prasad, Jitender, *Myth and Reality of Women's Status; The Case of Working Women,* Samaja Shodhana; Journal of the Manglore Sociology Association, Vol. 13, No. 1-2, 2004.

Rane, *Diving in Sewers to Make a Living*, Punjabi Portal, August 24, 2012.

Rashid Omar, *Worms that Crawl in the Dirt*, The Hindu, January 11, 2013.

Sridevan Prabha, *Burying Democracy in Human Waste*, The Hindu, January 8, 2012.

Sujoya C.P., *Women, Disparities and Development India Social Development* Report 2010, Oxford University Press, New Delhi, 2011.

Velaskar Padma, *Theorising Dalit Women's Oppressions* (paper presented at the workshop on Dalit Feminism, Tata Institute of Social Science, August 1-2).

# 5

# Sanitation in Mangalore: A Case Study

*Richard Pais*

## Introduction

India is urbanising very fast. India's urban population which was 10 per cent in 1900, rose to 17 per cent in the next fifty years. By 2001, it went up to 28 per cent and in 2011 the urban population stood at 31 per cent which indicates that India is facing rapid urbanisation. The problem of sanitation is a serious problem confronting not only rural society but more so urban population. With increasing population and rising income, the lifestyle of urban residents is also changing. There exists a direct link between affluence and municipal waste. Urban India is adopting a 'throw-away culture'. The residents generate various kinds of wastes of bio-degradable and non-biodegradable categories. If proper disposal and management of the waste is not taken up, it could lead to disastrous effects. On the other hand, the waste could become a resource and the society can benefit from these wastes, with proper collection and disposal technologies. Majority of wastes can be recycled and the recycling technology has a promising employment and energy generating options.

This paper examines the methods of waste disposal undertaken in Mangalore city. It also examines both the causes and effects of inefficient method of waste disposal. In 2008, I had a visitor from New Delhi, visiting Mangalore for the first time. So, I decided take him around Mangalore. First, I took him to Kadri Park and he commented that the place is very clean. After showing him two-three places, I took him to Gokarnatheshwara Temple and he again commented that the place is really clean. I really felt proud of my Mangalore and started observing the places in terms of cleanliness and I found that Mangalore was much cleaner compared to the many towns and cities of India, I had visited. It is partly because the city can boast of being the headquarters of *Buddivantara Jelle* (the district of wise people), as it is known in Karnataka. The district is also cent per cent literate. In fact, Mangalore City Corporation was presented with an excellence award for the first position, in the category of tier II cities, in solid waste management in the second international conference on "Solid Waste Management and Exhibition on Municipal Services, Urban Development, Public Works, and Clean Technology" held from November 9 to 11, 2011 in Kolkata, organised by Jadavpur University, Kolkata.

In spite of the first impression a visitor gets and the award it has won in solid waste management, the city is experiencing the rising social costs of development in the form of negative externalities. Increasing levels of pollution, congestion, environmental degradation and depletion of natural resources, displacement of people from their local habitats and also the menace of urban wastes and associated health hazards. The city woefully lacks the most modern and forward looking infrastructure – and is not well managed in terms of environment in general and waste disposal in particular. Mosquitoes and malaria have been the perennial threats to our health, here. Growing garbage has been an eye sore, a challenge to aesthetic sense and health consciousness. In spite of the negative externalities, there is a call and a drive for a clean and green city.

**Mangalore**

Mangalore (now known as *Mangaluru*) is the coastal city situated in the West coast of India in the state of Karnataka. It is a small city having a population of nearly 5 lakhs. Because of the large sea port it is considered as the 'Gateway of Karnataka'. Since Mangalore is close to Western Ghats, the terrain is hilly. For the last 2000 years, Mangalore had connection with the outside world, specially the Arab world. In the 16th century, Mangalore came under the Portuguese rule and with the fall of Tippu Sultan in 1799, it came under the British. In 1860, the district of Canara was divided into South Canara and North Canara and Mangalore became the headquarters of South Canara district. In 1866, Mangalore municipality was established under Madras Town Municipal Act. After independence, with the establishment of Karnataka Regional Engineering College, Kasturba Medical College, Mangalore Hassan Railway link, establishment of National Highways, Konkan Railway, Mangalore University and many industries, Mangalore further developed.

Following the re-organisation of States, the Mysore Municipalities Act, 1964 came into force as a uniform act throughout the state on 1 April, 1965, replacing the Madras District Municipalities Act of 1920. The provisions of this act gave a new phase to the municipality and it became a city municipality. Mangalore City Corporation came into existence on 3 July, 1980, which was formerly a municipality and was expanded during 1996–97 by including Surathkal Town Municipality, Katipalla Notified area, Panamboor, Baikampady, Kulai, Hosabettu villages.

The headquarters of MCC is at Lalbagh. Its sub-offices are at Surathkal and Bikarnakatta. As of 2001, the Mangalore municipality covered an area of 73.71 km$^2$ (28.46 sq.m.). The city of Mangalore, as corporation unit, is having an area of about 132.45 sq.kms. and as per 2011 census, a population of 4,84,785 of which 2,40,651 are males and 2,44,134 are females. Mangalore has a sex ratio of 1014 and literacy rate of 94 per cent. The city is divided into 60 corporation wards. The Mangalore urban area had 32 recognised slums, and nearly 22,000 migrant labourers live in slums within the city limits. Further during April 2002, it was further extended to include Bajal, Kannuru, Kudupu and Thiruvail panchayat limits into Mangalore City Corporation. There is a proposal to increase the area of MCC to 304 km$^2$ by including Mulky in the north and Ullal in the south. Mangalore is now famous for banking, education and health facilities.

One of the serious problems faced by the city– its people and its management is waste management, particularly the solid waste management. The city seems to be generating more waste than it can collect and dispose off.

## Sanitation in Historical Perspective

Till the beginning of 20th century, Mangalore was a small place having a trading community living around the old port. The mode of transport was bullock cart. People used to live in traditional tile roofed houses and each house had a big compound. In the end of the compound there were dry latrines. These latrines were cleaned by *thotis* (lowest among Scheduled Castes) and they used to take the waste in buckets and *wheelbarrows*. Around 1940s, wet latrines became common where the human waste was directed to a *leech* pit dug near the latrines. Kitchen waste and other waste was dumped in the drains nearby which was washed away during the monsoon. At this time elephantiasis and malaria were common. It was very common to see in each house one or two person, suffering from elephantiasis. In this last 2-3 decades due to constant spying by the Corporation health authorities both elephantiasis and malaria have reduced considerably.

**Waste Management**

From 1960s, Mangalore municipality started the work of drainage and the latrines and the waste water were connected to the drains and the waste was recycled at Mullakad. However, because of the topography of Mangalore which consists of hills and valleys latrines at the lower levels could not be connected to the drains. Still latrines at the low levels are connected to the leech pits. As a result, water from the surrounding wells could not be used for drinking and the people have to wait for water connection from the City Corporation.

**Solid Waste Management**

Solid waste management and its disposal is better in Mangalore compared to that in Bangalore and in other places. In fact, last year Mangalore stood second, after Mysore in Karnataka, in cleanliness. It is attributed to the good literacy rate of the city and the district.

For the sake of waste management 47 wards are out-sourced and 13 are being maintained by the MCC. In 2003, under the Karnataka Urban Development and Coastal Environment Management Project, a plan was drawn up to upgrade the city's solid waste management capability to 120 tonnes a day by 2020. However, the city is already producing 200 tonnes waste per day. In 2009, the MCC spent Rs 9.88 crores for garbage management (or Rs 1,350 a tonne) with more than one-third of it going to staff salary, according to the draft estimates originated by the Administrative Staff College of India, Hyderabad. The college, which has prepared a draft sanitation plan for Mangalore, found the following: staff requires proper training on solid waste handling and collection, waste is not being segregated at source, vehicles collecting waste do not have segregated compartments, sanitary workers are not provided with any protective equipment posing health hazards, bio-medical waste from smaller hospitals finds its way into municipal waste, and that there is illegal disposal of waste into the sea which will cause 'serious public health and environmental issues'.

Solid waste management is one the most important service which is handled by the health department. The most pressing problem faced is rapid urbanisation and changing lifestyles have led to the generation of huge amount of garbage and wastes in the urban areas, so much so, over the past few years; just handling this municipal solid waste has assumed the proportion of major organisational, financial and environmental challenge. Despite municipal solid waste management, being major task of the local government, typical accounting for a sizeable portion of the municipal budget, yet the urban local body is unable to provide effective services. Previously the waste was disposed in an unscientific manner, with crude open dumping in low lying areas being the prevalent practice followed by most urban local bodies. The results of these are foul smell, breeding of flies and other pests and generation of liquid runoffs (*Leacheate*), which pose a serious threat to the under-ground water reserves. The area coming under the jurisdiction of Mangalore City Corporation produces an average of 220 tonnes per day of wastes, with a daily collection frequency of 200 tonnes per day. The waste collected has a composition of 60 per cent of organic, 25 per cent of inorganic, five per cent of combustible and 10 per cent of recyclable wastes.

As per Municipal Solid Waste Management and Handling rules 2000, including all administrative, financial, legal planning and engineering functions involved in the whole spectrum of solutions to problems of solid wastes thrust upon the community by its inhabitants. The major components of solid waste management are: Segregation at source, Primary (door to door) collection, Secondary storage, transportation, treatment or processing and disposal.

## Source Segregation

This involves separation of wastes into wet, dry/recyclables and household hazardous waste, familiarising people about the solid waste management, system adopted; training programme for retrievers regarding importance of segregation, proper handling of waste and its hazards due to improper handling, and littering of waste to be banned. So far Mangalore has no method of source segregation.

## Primary Collection

In December 2012, the MCC launched door-to-door collection of solid waste in some wards by entrusting the job to eight contractors in eight packages. As per the terms of the contract, it was mandatory on their part to collect waste from doorsteps. The contractor could collect a monthly user fee of Rs 30 for collecting waste from residential houses. The monthly user fee for commercial establishments ranged between Rs 100 and Rs 1,000. For hotels and marriage halls, it was between Rs 300 and Rs 1,000, and for traders in vegetable markets it ranged from Rs 100 to Rs 500. But, the odd collection time in some wards has made the efforts go waste. For instance, workers reach some places at around noon to pick waste when none of the inmates are at home. Now the MCC has decided to collect the waste either before 10 a.m. or late in the evenings. MCC has given a mobile number where the residents can SMS their complaints to this number if solid waste is not picked from their doorsteps. Since two months MCC has banned the use of plastic bags and awareness is created in people's involvement in maintaining the city clean. Similarly, efforts are afoot in the segregation of dry and wet waste. Pushcarts and tri-cycles are being used by the contractors for the same. Household wastes bulk generator wastes and street wastes are deposited into secondary collection points.

### Secondary Storage

Closed metal secondary storage containers are provided. Closed bins systems for secondary storage are provided. Manual handling of waste is minimised by reducing the secondary storage location by transferring garbage directly from door to door collection system to the transportation vehicle. There are approximately 600 RCC bins of 0.8 CC, 24 bricks masonry dustbins, 30 fibre containers and more than 130 other containers.

### Secondary Transportation

Covered transportation vehicles are provided. The authorities want avoiding multiple handling of waste. Regular day wise clearance frequency is maintained. Twin container dumper placers, compactors (back loaders) and side loaders are being used for transportation of waste to the processing site. Rs 214 lakh was the capital investments made on the procurement of the transportation vehicles and containers for MSW transportation and reduce manual handling under Karnataka Urban Development and Coastal Environmental Management Projects (KUDCEMP). Presently, there are two trucks, two tippers, one mini lorry, three single container dumper placers and eight twin container dumper placers owned by MCC and one compactor and two side packers and 19 contract trucks operating. These are used to carry wastes to the landfill site at Vamanjur which is 15 kms. away from the heart of the city.

**Disposal Site**

Mangalore City Corporation processing and disposal site is having an extent of 37.32 acres of land for the disposal of solid waste located on top of a hill. The site is divided into two portions by a road passing through with 26.69 acres on the north side and 10.63 acres on the south side. To the south side of the existing landfill 25.4 acres of land have been acquired for the construction of new sanitary landfill site. The landfill area is adequate for about 25 years of life. The landfill is constructed in phases to enable progressive development. The development of the landfill over the life would be done in four phases: phase I, for six years time frame, phase II, III and IV respectively for three years, six years and for 10 years time frame. To the north side, compost yard for a capacity of 120 tonnes per day of waste is being treated and 68 vermin-composting pits for a capacity of 25 tonnes per day are constructed. The construction of the municipal solid waste processing and sanitary landfill site was done under KUDCEMP funded through Asian Development Bank loans at a cost of Rs 6.48 crores and Rs 9.39 crores respectively. The compost plant is partially operational with the outsourced 12 personnel, I JCB and one tipper. It generates an average of six tonnes of compost/day taking a feed of 55 tonnes per day.

**Landfilling**

Sanitary landfill site is provided in a six acre land as phase I. Rejects from the compost plant will be land filled. Daily soil top cover of 10 cm. will be provided. Presently, the sanitary landfill site constructed is not being used. Previous dumped landform will be covered with soil and will be provided with green cover.

**Treatment**

Aerobic composting and Vermin-composting is provided. There is provision of 120 tonnes per day of waste is aerobically composted and 25 tonnes per day of waste is vermin-composted. Rejects from Compost plant will be transported to sanitary landfill site. Presently, MCC is handling the operation and maintenance of aerobic compost plant. Compost plant is generating four to five tonnes of compost/manure through windrow method of aerobic composting. Operation of Vermin-composting is not yet started. Provision is made for running the aerobic compost plant in two shifts. Arrangements have been made for outsourcing the entire treatment and processing unit.

## Bio-medical Waste Management

The Bio-medical Waste (Management and Handling) Rules notified in July 1998, under the Environment (Protection) Act, 1986, make mandatory for all healthcare facilities irrespective of their size to treat Bio-Medical Waste (BMW) generated by them. In order to comply with the provisions of the rules, some of the healthcare facilities have installed their own treatment facilities and others are availing services of Common Bio-medical Waste Treatment Facilities (CBWTF). CBWTF has been set by M/s. Medicare Incin Private Limited, No.47-B, Karnad Industrial Area, Mulky, Dakshina Kannada. MCC has issued notices to all the hospitals/ clinics/nursing homes to treat the BMW as per the BMW rules 1998 and keep informing regularly to hospitals/clinics/nursing homes not to mix the BMW with regular waste. M/s. Medicare Incin private Limited has installed 7500 kg/day capacity incineration plant but Karnataka State Pollution Control Board has given authorisation for a capacity of 2500 Kg/day. M/s. Medicare Incin Private Limited has provided their own vehicles for collection of bio-medical waste from the hospitals/ clinics/nursing homes/laboratories of total 6200 beds throughout Dakshina Kannad. Father Muller's Hospital and Yenepoya Medical College have installed their own treatment facilities.

## Information, Education and Communication

There is door to door campaigning for educating the public on segregation and door to door garbage collection. Educating school and college students through various activities on solid waste management is being done. School and college level competitions are conducted for students with cash prizes. Also, ward level meetings are held to educate the public on municipal solid waste rules, 2000. Street *jathas* are also organised to create awareness among public. Children and students have become messengers of solid waste management. Some of the colleges in association with MCC have started creating awareness on solid waste management, among the school children and public. St. Agnes College of Mangalore has constituted a 'green army' to create awareness in various parts of the city limits on waste management through *skits* and *mime* shows. Another NGO called Round Table has expressed its desire to create awareness on solid waste management, segregation of waste from the source in schools. Taking cue from vermi-technology unit at the Department of Zoology in St. Aloysius College, the MCC has also started vermi-compost units in two wards, namely, Court and Padav–in the city on a pilot project basis.

For any study on waste management, the study of people involved is essential. This study also takes the people into account involved specially the sanitary workers.

## Caste Structure

MCC employs around 400 people to clean the streets and transport the waste to the dumping yard. These sanitary workers are known as *Paura Karmikas*. During the times of dry latrines, *thotis* used to collect the night-soil and carry it to the dumping yard. After the starting of wet latrines, these *thotis* have been absorbed into MCC. Due to their occupation of carrying night-soil, the *thotis* have the lowest status among the untouchables or the Scheduled Castes (SCs). *Adi-dravida* is the new name acquired by some Scheduled Caste groups to obliterate the stigma of untouchability (Pais, 2004: 60). According to Kakade, the idea that change of name would obliterate the stigma of centuries perhaps led the depressed classes to give up their old names and adopt new inoffensive and generic names like *Panchamas, Adi-Dravida, Adi-Karnataka, Harijan* etc. (1949:5). Probably the process of sanskritisation in caste name is complete because in the socio-economic survey of 1993 conducted by MCC not a single Scheduled Caste householder has given his caste name as *thoti*.

These *paura karmikas* together with other SCs live in colonies. Valencia (Souterpete), Kodikal, Urwa Market (Welspete), Bejai (Kapikad), Kodialbail (Ballalbagh), Kankanady (Narigudde) and Attavara (Babugudde) are the colonies of SCs in Mangalore. At the turn of the last century these areas were outside Mangalore but due to urbanisation, the city has grown around these colonies. The important groups working as paura karmikas are: *adi-dravida, adi-karnataka* and *koragas*. While *adi-dravida* and *adi-karnataka* are SCs, *koragas* are Scheduled Tribes (STs). *Koragas* is a unique group. While they have all the tribal features such as separate dialect, occupation, etc., untouchability is also found among them. In fact, they rank lower than SCs. A deeper study how the *koragas* entered this profession is required.

## Conditions of Paura Karmikas

Unemployment, inadequate housing and poor health may be considered as the major problems faced by the SCs in Mangalore. In spite of the efforts of the government, there is large-scale unemployment among them. Their housing condition is poor in many colonies where they live. It is a common place to find three-four household living under one roof, with separate kitchens. Often these households are forced to depend upon a single ration card to avail the facilities of public distribution system. Abject poverty, unhealthy living conditions, lack of nutritious food, lack of entertainment and the nature of work give rise to various diseases and early death. The worst affected are the *paura karmikas*. As most of them are engaged in cleaning the drains, roads and disposing of the waste, they are exposed to a variety of infectious diseases. Besides, they also have the habit of heavy drinking and smoking. As a result they succumb to various diseases and die early. The survey of MCC has traced 282 widows and 29 widowers out of 3693 married persons. An officer in Wenlock Hospital in Mangalore told the researcher that he has seen three generations of workers in the hospital during his 30 years of service.

## Problems and Challenges

The main problems of Mangalore's waste management are as follows:

1. Increasing quantity of solid waste generation and improper management,
2. Inadequate availability of public/community storage bins and their haphazard use,
3. Objectionable open-space throwing of solid waste,
4. Unsatisfactory and unhealthy practice of municipal solid waste collection and transportation,
5. Irregular sweeping of streets and public places,
6. Crude methods of (open) dumping–health hazards and deterioration of environment,
7. Unscientific burning of wastes in some places,
8. Not a high level of civic consciousness,
9. Inadequate machinery and equipment,
10. Lack of sufficient and efficient manpower – In MCC today there are 18 A Group employees allotted posts but only 11 are filled, B Group 12 out of 20 filled, C Group 229 out of 352 and D Group 643 out of 788 are filled, and
11. The poor socio-economic condition of sanitary workers.

## Needs and Plans for the Future

With increasing funding becoming available and keen interest shown by educational institutions and NGOs, MCC has been drawing good plans for the future. Some highlights of these plans:

- A new System would be in place: Waste will be collected from the household and business establishments during fixed time every day. The waste is likely to be collected twice every day. For this purpose Mangalore city would be divided into two zones – North and South, sanitation in 47 wards would be carried out by contractors and in 13 wards by the MCC, for a period of seven years. Compost plant operation would be outsourced for six years. Private security checks for littering with wide use of media and educational institutions. Hydraulically operated vehicles would be used for collection. Sweeping machines would be used to sweep concrete roads.
- Waste being dumped on the roadside between Balmatta and Hampankatta in Mangalore will soon become a thing of the past. Mangalore City Corporation is planning to declare Balmatta-Hampankatta as litter free zone. 'Dustbin-free' garbage collection will be introduced from Balmatta-Hampankatta and garbage collected at the doorstep of residents. This will be a pilot project.
- Dustbin-free garbage collection is a part of three package scheme on the solid waste management proposal which is pending before the government for approval. This will be a good step in segregation. Three contract agencies will handle the solid waste management in the jurisdiction of Mangalore City Corporation in three packages.

## Some Recommendations

Under present circumstances, solid waste management is a challenge as people have started opposing areas being earmarked for waste management for they cause damage to the environment. A community-centred scheme involving all would help to tackle the problem. We understand that health and prosperity in our city can be threatened by ignorance, indifference and unhygienic conditions, too. The present study would offer the following suggestions regarding solid waste management to the city authorities as well as waste generators and the general public:

1. Beware of the worsening problem of solid wastes in the city: sustained involving of citizens, NGOs etc.,
2. Make compulsory the rules of waste management by households and establishments,

3. Increase and handle community storage bins healthily,
4. Give recyclable waste if possible to trained ragpickers,
5. Debris to be disposed at specific areas in a utilitarian way e.g., landscaping,
6. Treat organic waste via vermiculture at the community level itself,
7. Medical waste to be autoclaved and disposed in a particular way,
8. Implement source segregation at the earliest,
9. Improve means of carrying the wastes,
10. Increase staff involved and improve safety with required devices and health care,
11. Enhance professionalism in waste management,
12. Decentralise waste management, and
13. Improving the socio-economic condition of sanitary workers.

**Conclusion**

MCC is making sincere efforts in the direction of better waste management. In April 2011, MCC has embarked on a mission to dispose of the electronic waste systematically. The then Corporation Commissioner K.N. Vijayaprakash said that the Sarvodaya Jagruti Trust, a non-governmental organisation, would collect e-waste from people. Initially e-waste would be collected on a trial basis on a seven km stretch from Infosys in Kottara to Mphasis in Morgan's Gate. The trust would send the waste to *e-parisara*, a government authorised e-waste recycler in Bangalore. On March 16, 2013, MCC launched a new project for solid waste management in the city. The endeavour which has two schemes under it was flagged off. Deputy Commissioner N. Prakash inaugurated the Street sweeping machine and symbolically distributed the waste bins to the residents of the pilot wards, Mannagudda and Court ward in front of the City Corporation.

Waste management should be viewed in the larger context of environmental management. China is facing enormous challenge in this regard. But they see it as an opportunity to improve environmental quality and are introducing new strategies to improve solid waste management in China. Mangalore needs 'growth with a future'. We need to restore the ecological balance. Curtail consumerism. Revert to good old practices of gardening, composting etc. We need to go from waste creation to waste utilisation with strong economic, environmental, resource conservation, employment generation, quality of life reasons. We need a whole city, not a city with holes: potholes and loopholes. We the people of Mangalore city must have positive environmental ethos. Fiscal and financial incentives/disincentives along with environment-friendly technologies would be the plus points.

**Acknowledgment**

I am grateful to Dr Basil Hans, Associate Professor and Head, Department of Economics, St. Aloysius Evening College, Mangalore, Karnataka for making available his paper, *Solid Waste Management in an Urban Agglomeration: A Case Study of Mangalore City* presented at the Seminar on Mangalore: Yesterday, Today and Tomorrow, organised by St. Aloysius (Autonomous) College, Mangalore and Mangalore Sociology Association held from February 24 to 26, 2011 at St Aloysius (Autonomous) College, Mangalore.

## References

Kakade, R.G. 1949. *Depressed Classes of South Kanara.* Poona: Servants of India Society.

Mangalore City Corporation. 1993. *A Survey of Scheduled Castes and Tribes of Mangalore City* (Unpublished).

Pais, Richard. 2004. *Scheduled Castes: A Study in Employment and Social Mobility.* Mangalore: Mangala Publications.

# 6

# Right to Sanitation and Dignity of Women

*Anil K.S. Jha*

*"Injustice anywhere is a threat to justice everywhere."*

**Martin Luther King**

The history of women has been a history of silence. Indian women have hitherto functioned under rigid hierarchies, learned to curb their freedom, condition themselves to suppress their needs, silence their senses and sublimate their selves in a philosophy of self-denial, self-effacement and services. Girls are tamed to become housewives and domesticated to undergo their reproductive roles only; whereas boys are trained to earn and generate income and take up responsibilities. The social, cultural and religious fibre of India is pre-dominantly patriarchal contributing extensively to the secondary status to women. This spectre, reflected in the Indian society, has raised several questions on the status and dignity of women.

India has been the great champion and votary of the concept 'dignity' from times immemorial. Various texts of earlier Indian civilisation bring forth the testimony of India's serious concern over this valuable issue. As the frontrunner of human values and human norms, India has made abundant contributions in this field and has acted as the torchbearer for others in this venture. Hence, the concept of dignity is not new for Indian society and culture. The term *garima* is the Hindi counterpart of the term 'dignity'.

In this backdrop, the makers of the Constitution have given due place to dignity in the Constitution. After independence, theoretically India has impressive record of rights given to its citizens. The Constitution of India contains fundamental rights violation of which is neither possible by the executive nor the legislature. However, in practice, India's record in the field of human rights and dignities related to women is not satisfactory.

The concept of human rights is related to the concept of human dignity. Human rights mean to provide all the rights and dignities to human being as human. Liberalism believes in the unity of mankind, therefore, the rights of men and women are the same but because of certain situational factors it is imperative to discuss the women's human rights and dignities separately. There are several reasons behind this: first, women are representing almost half of the population; secondly, women are discriminated throughout the world in different spheres and at different stages; thirdly, women are supposed to carry out some special functions, therefore they needed human rights separately. The women's human rights can be categorised in many ways, i.e., right to equality, right to education, right to life with dignity, right to liberty, political rights, right to property, right to equal opportunity for employment, right to free choice of profession, right to livelihood, right to work in equitable condition, right to get equal wages for equal work, right to protection from gender discrimination, right to social protection in the eventuality of retirement, old age and sickness, right to protection from inhuman treatment, right to protection of health, right to privacy in terms of personal life, family, residence, correspondence, etc., and right to protection from society, state and family system.

Societal values and norms operating within the framework of patriarchy impact on women's rights at various levels—of family, community and state. The forces of globalisation, industrialisation and urbanisation have been an addition in exacerbating women's ordeal and denying them of their rights and dignities. In India, women's lives are governed by multifaceted and nuanced realities where class, caste and religion intersect with each other in complex ways to intensify women's subordination. These vexed realities make it an imperative to analyse the issues of right to sanitation and the issues of women within a broader socio-economic and cultural context. Every individual has certain rights bestowed by nature which are preserved, protected and promoted in this era of globalisation in the name of human rights and human dignity. These rights are sacrosanct, inalienable and inviolable by nature and are the prerogative of every human being without any discrimination.

The concept of sanitation was earlier limited to disposal of human excreta by cess pools, open ditches, pit latrines, bucket system, etc. Today it connotes a comprehensive concept, which includes liquid and solid waste disposal, food hygiene, personal, domestic as well as environmental hygiene. Proper sanitation is important not only from the general health point of view, but it has a vital role to play in our individual and social life, too. Sanitation is one of the basic determinants of quality of life and human development index. Good sanitary practices prevent contamination of water and soil and thereby prevent diseases.

The concept of sanitation was, therefore, expanded to include personal hygiene, home sanitation, safe water, garbage disposal, excreta disposal and waste water disposal.

Individual health and hygiene is largely dependent on adequate availability of drinking water and proper sanitation. There is, therefore, a direct relationship between water, sanitation and health. Consumption of unsafe drinking water, improper disposal of human excreta, improper environmental sanitation and lack of personal and food hygiene have been major causes of many diseases in India and millions of lives are still claimed every year, and human development is held back on a massive scale. Women are responsible for health, hygiene, sanitation and other productive activities at the household level. Lack of access to water and sanitation directly affects women's health, education, employment, income and empowerment. The gendered dynamics of water and sanitation underscore the close inter-linkages between poverty, gender and sustainable development. Access to water and sanitation – as human rights – has, therefore, gained growing attention over the last few years at a global level.

In 2008, the UN Human Rights Council appointed an independent expert, Catarina de Albuquerque, with a mandate to further clarify and define the obligations of states related to the right, both to water and to sanitation. Furthermore, a new milestone was reached as the UN General Assembly adopted a resolution recognising access to clean water and sanitation as a human right essential for the full enjoyment of life and all human rights. A recent trend has evolved towards recognition of sanitation as a distinct right. Safe water is not possible without functioning and sustainable solutions for sanitation. In this sense, water and sanitation are inextricably linked.

On 28 July, 2010, the UN General Assembly and UN Human Rights Council recognised a human right to water and sanitation, which means that everyone, without discrimination, should have access to adequate amounts of safe, accessible, affordable, acceptable water and sanitation. On September 30, 2010, the Human Rights Council in Geneva adopted a resolution on 'The human right to safe drinking water and sanitation'. In Resolution, it affirmed that the human rights to water and sanitation derived from the right to an adequate standard of living and was inextricably related to the right to the highest attainable standard of physical and mental health, as well as the right to life and human dignity. The United Nations General Assembly explicitly recognised the human right to water and sanitation and acknowledged that clean drinking water and sanitation are essential to the realisation of all human rights. The Resolution calls upon states and international organisations to provide financial resources help capacity-building and technology transfer to help countries, in particular developing countries, to provide safe, clean, accessible and affordable drinking water and sanitation for all.

The right to water and sanitation is a human right, equal to all other human rights, which implies that it is justifiable and enforceable; hence society has greater responsibility to concentrate all its efforts in the implementation and full realisation of this essential right. The Millennium Development Goals (MDGs) have been valuable in galvanising international support around a certain number of poverty reduction targets, including with respect to water and sanitation. They have generated broad and high level political commitment to water and sanitation, by putting them on the international agenda. Integrating the rights to water and sanitation within MDG monitoring and policy-making can help to make progress towards the MDGs more inclusive and sustainable, while promoting equity, accountability and policy coherence. The MDG target on access to water and sanitation aims for a 50 per cent reduction in the lack of access to improved water sources and improved sanitation facilities by 2015.

India cannot achieve real development if majority of its people, particularly women, live in an unhealthy and unclean surroundings due to lack of access to safe water and sanitation. Poor water and sanitation facilities have many other serious repercussions. A direct link exists between water, sanitation, health, nutrition and human well being. Consumption of contaminated drinking water, improper disposal of human excreta, lack of personal and food hygiene and improper disposal of solid and liquid waste have been major causes of many diseases in India.

It is distressing to note here that as per the census of India, 2011, a majority of households (53 per cent) in India has no toilet facility, the proportion of households without any toilet facility is much greater in rural areas (74 per cent) than in urban areas (17 per cent). Table-1 presents the per cent distribution of households without toilet facilities. Within India, there are significant geographical differentials; most of the households (78 per cent) in Jharkhand and Odhisa have no toilet facility, the situation in these two states is worst, closely followed by Bihar (77 per cent), Chhattisgarh (75 per cent) and Madhya Pradesh (71 per cent). The proportion of households without any toilet in the state of Lakshadweep (two per cent) is better, followed by Kerala (five per cent), Mizoram (eight per cent), NCT of Delhi and Manipur (11 per cent each). The figures of the Table-2 indicate the per cent distribution of urban, rural, and total households by type of toilet/ latrine facilities, which reveal the deteriorating and alarming conditions, especially in rural India.

## Table 1: Availability of Latrine Facility: 2001-2011

| *Percentage of Households Having No Latrine* | | |
|---|---|---|
| 2011 | 2001 | State/UT |
| 53 | 64 | India |
| 49 | 47 | Jammu & Kashmir |
| 31 | 67 | Himachal Pradesh |
| 21 | 43 | Punjab |
| 12 | 21 | Chandigarh |
| 34 | 55 | Uttarakhand |
| 31 | 56 | Haryana |
| 11 | 22 | NCT of Delhi |
| 65 | 71 | Rajasthan |
| 64 | 69 | Uttar Pradesh |
| 77 | 81 | Bihar |
| 13 | 37 | Sikkim |
| 38 | 44 | Arunachal Pradesh |
| 24 | 29 | Nagaland |
| 11 | 18 | Manipur |
| 8 | 11 | Mizoram |
| 14 | 19 | Tripura |
| 37 | 49 | Meghalaya |
| 35 | 35 | Assam |
| 41 | 56 | West Bengal |
| 78 | 80 | Jharkhand |
| 78 | 85 | Odisha |
| 75 | 86 | Chhattisgarh |
| 71 | 76 | Madhya Pradesh |
| 43 | 55 | Gujarat |
| 22 | 56 | Daman & Diu |
| 45 | 67 | D & N Haveli |
| 47 | 65 | Maharashtra |
| 50 | 67 | Andhra Pradesh |
| 49 | 63 | Karnataka |
| 20 | 41 | Goa |
| 2 | 11 | Lakshadweep |
| 5 | 16 | Kerala |
| 52 | 65 | Tamil Nadu |
| 32 | 50 | Puducherry |
| 30 | 47 | A & N Islands |

**Table 2: Toilet/Latrine (Types)**

| *Type of Toilet/latrine Facility* | *Urban* | *Rural* | *Total* |
|---|---|---|---|
| *Improved, not shared* | 52.8 | 17.6 | 29.1 |
| Flush/pour flush to piped sewer system | 18.8 | 0.6 | 6.6 |
| Flush/pour flush to septic tank | 27.6 | 10.6 | 16.1 |
| Flush/pour flush to pit latrine | 4.7 | 4.1 | 4.3 |
| Ventilated improved pit (VIP) latrine/biogas latrine | 0.2 | 0.1 | 0.2 |
| Pit latrine with slab | 1.4 | 2.2 | 1.9 |
| Twin pit, composting toilet | 0 | 0 | 0 |
| *Not improved* | 46.7 | 82.2 | 70.6 |
| Any facility shared with other households | 24.2 | 5.3 | 11.5 |
| Flush/pour flush not to sewer/septic tank/pit latrine | 4.4 | 0.2 | 1.6 |
| Pit latrine without slab/open pit | 0.7 | 2.2 | 1.7 |
| Dry toilet | 0.5 | 0.6 | 0.5 |
| No facility/open space/field | 16.8 | 74.0 | 55.3 |
| Other | 0.4 | 0.1 | 0.2 |
| Missing | 0.2 | 0.1 | 0.1 |
| Total | 100.0 | 100.0 | 100.0 |

*Source:* IIPS and Macro International. 2007. National Family Health Survey (NFHS-3), 2005–06: India: Volume I. Mumbai: IIPS.

The data provided by NFHS-3 decipher that most people in rural areas obtain their drinking water from a tube well or borehole (53 per cent); however, one in eight rural households gets its drinking water from unprotected wells or springs. Women and girls are most often the primary users, providers and managers of water in their households and are the guardians of household hygiene. If a water system falls into disrepair, women are the ones forced to travel long distances over many hours to meet their families' water needs. In rural areas, for one in seven households, each round trip to collect water takes at least half an hour (NFHS-3). In 81 per cent of households that do not have a source of drinking water on the premises, it is an adult female who usually collects the water. Female children under age 15 are more than four times as likely as male children of the same age to go to fetch drinking water (NFHS-3). The figures of the NFHS-3 reveal that 81 per cent Indian women (aged 15+) collect drinking water compared to just 13 per cent Indian men (aged 15+), which is clear indication of gender inequality existing in every sphere of life and claimant to women's detrimental status in the field of sanitation also. Lack of sanitation is a serious health risk and an affront to the dignity of women.

No issue touches the lives of women as intimately as that of access to sanitation. A disproportionate share of the labour and health burden of inadequate sanitation falls on women. In rural areas and low income settlements of urban areas, where there are no individual toilets, women have to queue for long periods to gain access to public toilets; some have to bear the indignity of having to defecate in the open, which exposes them to the possibility of sexual harassment or assault. Although men also suffer from the burden of poor sanitation, they are more likely to resort to other means to relieve themselves. For women living in slums, a long wait at the public toilet can mean that children are left unattended, or that a household chore is delayed. Unhygienic public toilets and latrines threaten the health of women, who are prone to reproductive tract infections caused by poor sanitation. For women who are menstruating, the need for adequate sanitation becomes even more acute. Moreover, because it is generally women who are responsible for the disposal of human waste when provision of sanitation is inadequate, they are more susceptible to diseases associated with contact with human excreta.

Despite all this, the sanitation crisis affecting women has not been given a high priority on the agendas of human rights and women's organisations. United Nations and other international bodies tend to confine women's issues to reproductive health and education. This could also be partially explained by the fact that improving access to sanitation was only recently recognised as a pressing issue. India's progress towards fulfilling Gandhian dream of villages with total sanitation has been steady. With exponential growth in population, unplanned urbanisation and industrialisation, there is an imperative need for the provision of good sanitation to the poor and the marginalised sections of the society.

Rural sanitation came into focus in the Government of India in the World Water Decade of 1980s. The Central Rural Sanitation Programme (CRSP) was started in 1986 to provide sanitation facilities in rural areas. It was a supply driven, highly subsidy and infrastructure oriented programme. As a result of these deficiencies and low financial allocations, the CRSP had little impact on the *gargantuan* problem.

The experience of community-driven, awareness generating campaign based programmes in some states and the results of evaluation of CRSP, led to the formulation of the Total Sanitation Campaign approach in 1999. Total Sanitation Campaign (TSC) was launched by the Government of India in 1999, which advocates a shift from high subsidy to a low subsidy regime, greater household involvement, demand responsiveness, and providing for the promotion of a range of toilet options to promote increased affordability.

India has shown high country commitment to sanitation with increased support to India's rural sanitation flagship programme, Total Sanitation Campaign (TCS). In order to promote urban sanitation and recognise excellence in performance in this area, Government of India has instituted the *Nirmal Shahar Puraskar,* a bi-annual exercise that recognises sanitation initiatives of cities.

Equitable access to water for productive use can empower women and address the root causes of poverty and gender inequality. Successful pro-poor sanitation programmes must be scaled up. Assistance is still not reaching large numbers of the poorest of the poor. Successful models must be replicated and scaled up to serve those who cannot provide for their own needs under existing community-based solutions. An approach known as Community-Led Total Sanitation (CLTS) has been found to be effective in promoting change at the community level. Efforts must address socio-cultural attitudes towards sanitation and involve women as agents of change. Another innovation is the socialised community-fund raising, which has met great success among the rural poor. Access to adequate sanitation literally signifies crossing the most critical barrier to a life of dignity and fulfillment of basic needs. Providing adequate sanitation will have profound implications for human health and poverty alleviation. Lack of sanitation obstructs the right to life and health and it also hampers the right to education as girls are often forced to miss school or even drop out of education due to lack of sanitation facilities in their schools, education of children, especially the girl child, is also significantly impacted by poor sanitation. Sandwiched between the problem of sanitation and traditional patriarchal mindset of people, girl children suffer a lot. The social response and attitude towards the girl child shows a grim picture of the status of women (Jha, 2009). The neglect of girl child and discriminatory behaviour against her leading to excess female mortality has been widely documented in several studies (Visaria, 1971, Miller, 1989, Das Gupta, 1987, Kishor, 1995).

Indian women are socially humiliated, politically bonded and economically exploited. To the extent that societies allocate resources on the basis of one's gender, as opposed to one's skills and abilities, their approach comes at a cost. The economic costs of gender inequalities, due to the persistence of traditional norms and to overt discrimination, can be considerable. Many women find that their right to participate freely in economic interchange has been shaped, and often circumscribed, by societal values and norms that deny them access to and control over crucial productive resources for development. To ameliorate the existing inequality, society must institute what Kabeer and Subrahmanian (1996) refer to as 'gender redistributive policies' that are intended to transform existing patterns of resource allocation in a more egalitarian direction. These relate to the full range of productive assets (e.g., land, labour, and financial capital) required by active participation in economic processes. Nobel prize-winning economist Amartya Sen transformed the discourse on development when he argued that development is not only about raising people's incomes or reducing poverty, but rather, it involves a process of expanding freedoms equally for *all* people (Sen, 1999). Amartya Sen feels that the empowerment of women is one of the main issues in the process of development and more importantly, that "the factors involved include women's education, their ownership pattern, their employment opportunities and the working of the labour market" (Sen, 1999). Thus, economic empowerment of women is required not only for the improved sanitation, but for their dignity also.

It is only by a combination of monitoring, education campaigns and effective legal implementation that the deep-seated attitudes and practices against women and girls can be eroded and women can really enjoy human right to sanitation with dignity. Deepening and consistently implementing human rights instruments can be a powerful mechanism to motivate and mobilise governments, people, and especially women themselves. With a view to converting the equality of women from *de jure* to *de facto,* female literacy in general and human rights education in particular is necessary, which is well recognised as a *sine qua non* for gender equality (Jha, 2013). Empowering women can save them from psychological issues such as low self-esteem and a general sense of worthlessness. Bridging the gap between an ideology of individual freedom and equality, and a reality in which women are discriminated is the need of the hour, which demands an immediate intervention to arrest this growing unhealthy situation of sanitation and a greater advocacy for improving the lot of the fairer sex.

## References

Das Gupta, M. (1987). '*Selective Discrimination against Female Children in Rural Punjab, India*'. Population and Development Review, 13(1), pp. 77-100.

IIPS and Macro International, *National Family Health Survey (NFHS-3), 2005–06: India,* IIPS, Mumbai, 2007.

Jha, A.K.S., (2009), *Demography and Development: Challenges of Change*, Gautam Book Company, Jaipur.

Jha, A.K.S., (2013), *Unheard Voices: Human Rights of Women* in ed. Alok Kumar Meena, "Human Rights: Evolution, Implementation and Evaluation", New Delhi: Palm Leaf Publications, pp. 83-93.

Kabeer, N. and R. Subrahmanian (1996), *Institutions, Relations and Outcomes: Framework and Tools for Gender-Aware Planning*, Institute of Development Studies, Sussex.

Kishor, S. (1995), *Gender Differentials in Child Mortality: A Review of Evidence*, in Monica Das Gupta, Lincoln C. Chen and T. N. Krishnan (eds.), *Women's Health in India: Risk and Vulnerability*, Bombay: Oxford University Press.

Registrar General and Census Commissioner of India, Census of India, 2011, Government of India, New Delhi.

Sen, Amartya, (1999), *Development as Freedom*, Alfred A. Knopf, New York.

Visaria, P. (1971). *The Sex Ratio of the Population of India*, Census of India, 1961, Monograph No. 10, New Delhi: Office of the Registrar General, India.

# 7

# Sociology of Sanitation: Incorporating Gender Issues in Sanitation

*Shakuntala. C. Shettar*

Sanitation and gender are closely related. Most of the sanitation issues are gender issues and *vice versa*. Hence the present paper is an attempt to understand the gender issues in sanitation sector with special reference to India. Women are not only responsible for water in the house and hygiene at home, they are not only responsible for health of the family especially of children but also for the sick and elderly. Women menstruate, get pregnant and give birth. All these issues involve sanitation and health of women. Hence proper sanitation facilities help to achieve social status of women, thereby improving gender equality. It also helps in improving women's health and education, livelihood and life chances, and in total the health of the family. Hence gender balanced approaches and inmates should be encouraged in plans and structures to enhance the dignity of women.

## Sociology of Sanitation: Background

Sociology of Sanitation is a sub-branch of medical sociology that emerged in the United States during 1940's. The discipline that investigates the social causes and consequences of health and illness was inspired by the health and sanitary reforms that took place in western society. It was well recognised that the relations between sociology and sanitation are extremely intimate. The individual is the essential element of the society, his social values depends largely upon his health. Good health is a pre-requisite for the adequate functioning of an individual or society. If our health is sound, we can engage in numerous types of activities. But if we are ill, distressed, or injured, we may face the curtailment of our usual round of daily life and we may also become so pre-occupied with our state of health that other pursuits are secondary ,or quite meaningless. Therefore, as Rene Du Bos (1981) explains "health can be defined as the ability to function". While in turn his health is partly determined by the conditions which society imposes. Social factors play a critically important role in health. Social conditions and situations not only promote the possibility of illness and disability, but they also enhance prospects for disease prevention and health maintenance. The disheartening status of mankind today is undoubtedly the result of the sanitary and social conditions of past ages and former generations. Clean food, adequate clean supply of water, sanitary schools, public baths, adequate housing are sanitary measures which are most effective in both sanitary and social results. Hence sanitation and sociology must go hand in hand in their effort to improve the race and now their relations are consciously and openly recognised. Dr Bindeshwar Pathak, Sociologist and social reformer, working in the sphere of sanitation, has aptly defined, Sociology of Sanitation is a scientific study to solve the problems of society in relation to sanitation, social deprivation, water, public health, hygiene, ecology, environment, poverty, gender equality, welfare of children and empowering people for sustainable development and attainment of philosophical and spiritual knowledge to lead a happy life and to make a difference in the lives of others.

The present study has adopted this definition for incorporating gender issues in the sociology of sanitation.

### 1. Gender and Sanitation

Gender is a concept that refers to socially constructed roles, behaviour, activities and attributes that a particular society considers appropriate and ascribes to men and women. A useful definition of the concept of gender mainstreaming is provided by the United Nations Economic and Social Council (1997), suggests that mainstreaming a gender perspective is the process of assessing the implications for women and men of any planned action, including legislation, policies or programmes, in all areas and at all levels. It is a strategy for making the concerns and experiences of women as well as men, an integral dimension of the design, implementation, monitoring and evaluation of policies and programmes in all political, economic and societal spheres, so that women and men benefit equally and inequality is not perpetuated. The ultimate goal is to achieve gender equality. Sanitation refers to the principles and practices relating to the collection, removal or disposal of human excreta, household waste water and refuse as they impact upon people and the environment. Good sanitation includes, appropriate health and hygiene awareness and behaviour, and acceptable, affordable and sustainable sanitation services. A lack of adequate sanitation or inadequately maintained or inappropriately designed systems can, therefore, constitute a range of pollution risks to the environment, especially the contamination of surface and ground water resources.

Considering 'gender' in water and sanitation is not only about considering women, it is about considering women and men of all socio-economic backgrounds and their interactions with water and sanitation resources; it is also important to consider the different needs and preferences of both men and women.

There are many gender issues in sanitation which need to be taken into account to improve development efforts. Many scholars deal with the different tasks men and women have, in fact, all tasks related to sanitation are women's duties. And sanitation issues also relate with gender ideology as a major obstacle, blocking change.

The following are the gender issues related to sanitation:

1. *Women are responsible for water in the house:* Women and men usually have very different roles in water and sanitation activities, these differences are particularly pronounced in rural areas. Women are most often the users, providers, and managers of water in rural households and are the guardians of household hygiene. If a water system breaks down, women, not men, will most likely be the ones most affected, for they may have to travel further for water or use other means to meet the household's water and sanitation needs. In case of drought or flood, women remain responsible for water, and have to go even further to find it, or compromise by using less and less clean water, which influences the hygienic situation of the household.

2. *Women are responsible for hygiene at home:* Even though the responsibility for cleanliness and hygiene should be with all, in reality it is the women of households and also of villages who are seen as the cleaners of the yard, the house, the kitchen, the bathroom and the toilet facilities. In those situations women are usually also responsible for getting water to the house, from far away, from less far, or from close by. Both the cleaning and the fetching of water take a lot of time. Women are responsible for the hygiene of themselves, their children and men folk; women have to do the work for all of them; and women suffer when they themselves have negative influence of bad hygiene, by getting ailments and diseases, but also if their children are ill, which

means extra work for them. When their men folk and parents are ill that also gives them extra work, and more water to carry. So women are at the centre of hygiene for all. Either way, with or without diseases, it means a lot of daily work provided for them. Not all women are in the same position; the younger women in the household have more duties than the senior ones.

3. *Women are responsible for health of family, especially of children:* Women, who are aware of the connection between the dirtiness and illness of family members, will do extra effort to keep the house, the kitchen, the food and the sanitary facilities clean. This is extra daily work, but when somebody is ill, women usually have the responsibility to care for him or her and that may be even more work.

4. *Women are responsible for the sick and elderly:* Both men and women can get ill, but women are the caretakers *perse*. Hygiene becomes doubtly important when there are sick family members who could infect the others. Extra water is needed, and a lot of extra work needs to be done. Gender ideology prescribes that women do all this, there is no other real reason. The same is true for the elderly, with the difference that sick people in the house should be an exceptional situation, whilst to get old will happen to all who are healthy and lucky.

5. *Women menstruate, get pregnant and give birth:* Women in their menstruating period are generally seen as unclean. They should clean their blood themselves, and that is one of the reasons that women always have to clean everything. Not according to reason, but according to the prevailing gender ideology. During the time of being pregnant, giving birth and breast feeding, the risk of getting infections is high. All women try to avoid that by giving lots of attention and spending extra energy in hygiene. The direct relation with the quality and quantity of water available during that time, and the fact that she will not always be able to get it, makes her very vulnerable. Maternal mortality is directly related to hygiene, and hygiene to sanitary facilities and their cleanliness.

6. *Gender issues of toilets:* In both rural and urban areas, women without toilets only go out to relieve themselves in the dark, because their gender ideology tells them that they cannot take the risk to be seen. They often face risks, by snakes, scorpions, or other creatures, but also by men. There are endless stories of women getting harassed and even raped when going out in dark. For men and children this is no problem, they can go anywhere and anytime. For them urinate or

to defecate has no relation to sex at all, but women who go out even in the daylight, ask for trouble.

This is again gender ideology, and even discrimination. Furthermore, to wait till the dismal results of constipation and adapted diet and drinking habits, which give serious health problems. In densely populated urban areas, public toilets, if available, are to be cleaned by women only. They often cannot be locked, and here again women suffer from violence.

## 2. Why are Gender Issues Important in Sanitation Sector?

Gender issues are important in Sanitation Sector for the following four important reasons:

1. *For improving gender equality:* Proper sanitation facilities with toilets help to achieve the social status of women. It is known that parents do not marry their daughter to a household without toilet. The economic value of clean sanitation facilities ensure women fewer days of illness and therefore more days to work and more income: less unpaid work in caring for the sick, daughters with higher education so with more income.

2. *Improving women's health and livelihood:* Proper sanitation facilities are essential for fewer infections for women, for less sexual harassment, for security, and physical dignity; sanitation will empower poor women. Time savings also have a considerable impact on women's livelihood. There is an economic benefit of having water close to home so that the saved time can be used to generate some income.

3. *Improving education and life chances of girl children:* In rural areas fetching water takes more time which keeps girls out of school and limits the economic productivity of women. Globally, more than one in five girls of primary school age are not in school, in most cases this is due to lack of clean water and sanitation facilities available at the community and schools. Girls like their mothers must often walk miles to fetch the daily water supply. Girls who have reached menstrual age may also be deterred from school by inadequate sanitation in public places. Simple measures such as providing schools with water and latrines, and promoting hygiene education in the classroom can enable girls to get education.

4. *The health of families:* Improved sanitation facilities with regular and safe water supply, good latrine facilities enhance not only the health of women, but also the health of entire family. The time saved from

fetching water far from places can be best used to maintain the health of the family members.

In this connection gender differences is of particular importance with regard to hygiene and sanitation. Initiatives and gender balanced approaches should be encouraged in plans and structures for implementation. Access to adequate sanitary latrines is a matter of security, privacy and human dignity, particularly for women. Access to adequate and clean, near water is a matter of women's health, their access to education, employment, livelihood and their empowerment.

Keeping this in mind, the following initiatives should be taken to improve sanitation programmes:

1. At the national government level, line ministries, such as the ministries of health, water resources and social services are key actors and have important roles to play in ensuring that sanitation, hygiene, promotion, education and gender are incorporated into water resources and health policies. The line ministries should be motivated and willing to address gender in sanitation policies and legal frameworks.

2. At the community level, hygiene and sanitation are considered a women's issue, but they impact on both genders. Yet societal barriers continually restrict women's involvement in decisions regarding sanitation improvement programmes. Thus, it is important that sanitation and hygiene promotion and education are perceived as a concern of women, men and children and not only of women. Separate communication channels, materials and approaches have to be developed to reach out to men and boys. It is also important to target community leaders for gender sensitisation; this would facilitate mainstreaming gender in sanitation and hygiene promotional activities.

3. Attention and funds should be focused on sanitation and hygiene in schools, in order to reduce transmission of water-related diseases and implement hygiene and health education. School children are key change agents because they can influence their parents and will be tomorrow's adults. When they learn sanitation-related behaviours, such as hand washing, they can bring about change in their families and communities, leading to health improvements and higher school attendance of girls. It is critical that school sanitation and hygiene programmes address both boys and girls.

One problem that has been observed is that the latrine designs, especially for primary and secondary schools, are mainly prepared by male masons. The tendency, therefore, has been to construct latrines which are not sensitive to the special needs of girls. This has resulted in girls staying away from schools when they are menstruating, even when their schools have latrines. In the case of small boys, too, the urinals are often too high. Moreover, it is important that separate sanitary latrines are constructed for boys, in order to prevent boys from taking over the latrines that are meant for the girls. And toilet blocks for girls and boys should not be constructed next to each other. Sanitation design needs to be sensitive to physically challenged girls and boys too. In India, a survey carried out among school children revealed that about half the ailments found were related to unsanitary conditions and lack of personal hygiene (UNICEF and IRC, 1998).

### 4. Water-Sector Professionals

Water-sector professionals may adopt a more gender-sensitive approach for water and sanitation projects. Gender mainstreaming is incorporating gender-awareness into all aspects of intra-organisation and institutional process such as planning, mainstreaming approach requires collection of sex-disaggregated data for planning, involvement of women and marginalised communities for planning and management, and engagement in policy dialogue on gender, water and sanitation.

## References

1. A gender approach to sanitation, for empowerment of women, men and children www.GenderandWaterAlliance.JokeMuylwijk2006.for SACOSAN
2. Gender aspects of water and sanitation www.wateriad.org/documents/plugin_documents/microsoft_word_gender_aspects.pdf
3. Gender, Sanitation and Hygiene www.genderandwater.org/content/..../chapter3.4_july per cent2006doc
4. Gender and Sanitation www.tilz.tearfund.org/Publications/Footsteps+7180/Footsteps+73/Gender+and+sanitation.htm
5. Gender in Water and Sanitation www.unhabitat.org/content.asp?typeid=19andcatid=303andcid=6847
6. Gender, Water, and Sanitation www.waterfortheages.org/gender-water-sanitation-faq/#2.
7. Sanitation and Sociology www.jstor.org/stable/27617.4?seq=8.
8. Sanitation: A woman's issue www.unhabitat.org/documents/mediacentre/APMC/sanitation-Awoman'sissue.pdf

which are not sensitive to the special needs of girls. This has resulted in girls staying away from schools when they are menstruating, even when their schools have latrines. In the case of small boys, too, the urinals are often too high. Moreover, it is important that separate sanitary latrines are constructed for boys, in order to prevent boys from [illegible] the latrines that are meant for the girls, and toilet blocks for girls and boys should not be constructed next to each other. Sanitation [illegible]

[illegible] Development

[illegible] sanitation projects. Gender mainstreaming [illegible] all aspects [illegible]

# 8

# Environmental Sanitation and Social Deprivation in Dibrugarh, Assam: A Case of Dibrugarh Public Health Department, Dibrugarh Municipality—Their Manual Workers and Deprived Scavengers

*Pranjal Sharma*

## I

This chapter tries to highlight the scenario of environmental sanitation and social deprivation in Dibrugarh District of Assam. To depict the overall picture of the district in case of both rural and urban areas, we have taken the case of public health department which deals with rural areas and the municipality of Dibrugarh town which deals with the urban scenario. The manual workers of Dibrugarh municipality are also taken into account in order to reflect upon their deplorable social statuses who are engaged as cleaners and sweepers. There is also a considerable amount of scavengers (around 500) living in and around Dibrugarh slum pockets under municipality area. Their deprived social status as a downtrodden community in the field of public health, environmental sanitation, their liberation and rehabilitation really deserve attention for their social upliftment.

The master plan area of Dibrugarh City is divided into two zones: Urban zone and Rural zone. Urban zone comprises of: Dibrugarh Municipal area, Barbari (Assam Medical College Area), Dibrugarh University Area, Japaragaon and Rajabheta Tea Estate; and the Urbanised Villages. The Rural zone comprises of Eastern, Central and Western Rural areas. The population of Dibrugarh has increased from 11,227 in

1901 to 1, 86,214 in 2001. A rapid growth has been noticed since then, specially in the municipal board area and a projection of 0.275 million is envisaged for 2021 in municipality area which is due to natural increase as well as increase due to emigration and immigration flows. Besides that, in Dibrugarh town there are ten slum pockets notified by the Government of Assam, which are Gangapara, Paltanbazar, Grahambazar, Pathanpatty, Tulsigaon, Santipara, Loharpatty, Mirzabagh, Tinkunia and Dibrujan. A total of 21,652 populations live in ten pockets as in 2001, which means 17.6 per cent of the total population of municipal area, have been living in the slum pockets with 1.163 sq. km. in area under the notified slum pockets. During rainy season most of the slum areas of Dibrugarh town becomes water-logged due to which the existing *kuccha* roads as well as gravel roads has become badly damaged. Other problems of the slum areas are sanitary, water supply, street light, refuse disposal and so on. Moreover, there are seven blocks in entire Dibrugarh district which are namely, Barbarua, Lahoal, Panitola, Tengakhat, Joypur, Khowang and Tingkhong.

## II

The sanitation (rural and certain parts of urban slums) coverage in Assam is very less. It is still a common practice for open defecation and using *kuccha* pit latrines which are the sources of infection. It encourages foul gases and odour and fly breeding that spread the excreta related diseases. In view of the suspected health hazards and environmental degradation, open defecation and the use of *kuccha* pit latrines is being discouraged to ensure safe disposal of excreta. Environmental sanitation has become important to safeguard the society from the spread of diseases and to keep the surrounding clean and odourless. Toilets are a sign of civilised society.

In India, many diseases are caused by lack of proper sanitation affecting the population as whole. These include, intestinal, parasitic, infectious diarrhoea, dysentery, typhoid and cholera. Further, women have to go for defecation before dawn or after dusk, which implies suffering in the daytime. The school dropout of female child is also very high, as toilet facility is rarely available in rural areas.

India's caste system is a unique method in the world which divides the society into different strata. Lower caste people occupy a very low position in the society and are socially, economically, educationally and culturally backward. Changes are coming in the caste system but Pathak (2009: xxii) has mentioned that, "... there still remains a class of persons belonging to the scavenging caste, who were traditionally ordained in the Indian society to clean and carry human waste. Their appalling hardship, humiliation and savage exploitation have no parallel in human history. Living in the filthiest of surroundings under most trying circumstances, scavengers are hated even by those whose excreta they carry on heads. Reduced to the depth of degradation as untouchables and forced to live a sub-human existence, they are the worst victims of a cruel caste based social order. Their story is the sordid story of utmost violation of human rights. Their heartrending plight stressing over centuries is a blot on India's civilisation…" Making toilet as a tool of social change by *Sulabh* in terms of low cost sanitation technology and suitable methods of relieving the scavengers from the oppressive stranglehold of the country's caste system is a positive step towards their liberation from the clutches of the societal deprivation.

In the entire north-eastern region of India, there is no proper system of the disposal of the human waste. Excessive flood and rain creates major problem in sanitation programmes. Even in some areas, especially in Dibrugarh, there is dispute in demarcation of land. Sometimes the land is claimed by municipality and sometimes by *panchayats*. There is a politics in it. In this indecisive exercise, the construction work for sanitation never gets underway as the question of jurisdiction comes.

Usually we have septic tanks but no proper system of cleaning the tanks are there in any of the municipalities in entire north-east India. The rural areas do not figure in this as there are areas where even the septic tank systems are not yet implemented. That is why the system of scavengers still exists even after sixty-six years of India's independence. Even after the ban imposed by the Indian parliament in 1993 regarding human scavenging [Adoption of the employment of manual scvangers and construction of dry latrines (Prohibition) Act, 1993]; the scavenging class of people are still cleaning the septic tanks manually and disposing the human waste in open yards and drains. In Dibrugarh town, the main *harijan* colonies are located in Graham Bazar, Santipara, Loharpatty slum pockets as well as in Chiring Chapori harijan colony. There are more than five hundred scavengers including small children, men and women living mostly in slum pockets, who are engaged in unclean manual works. They often collect plastics, other scrap metals and even food from the garbage bins, dumping grounds, etc., and lead a very miserable life and most of them are migrants.

Pathak (2006: 5-6) mentions that, "It would, thus, be evident that sewerage system is beyond the means of the common people to adopt. Although the sewerage system has been introduced in the small cities and the town also, this does not cover the entire urban areas." He further remarks that "As of septic tanks, it has hardly been adopted even by 10 per cent of the urban population. This system, too, has its obvious limitations and problems. On the one hand, the septic tank system requires more space to set up the tank and on the other, it is a costly affair to get it constructed. In this system, it requires at least 10 liters of water per person, every time to flush the night-soil, from the pan to the tank. For the proper functioning of the system, therefore, it will require a huge quantity of water which is not available in the country. Therefore, it cannot be adopted by the common man. The gas pipe attached to the septic tank discharges the gas formed in the septic tank which pollutes the environment. For cleaning the tank, the traditional class or caste of scavengers is needed because the deposit in the tank remains in the forms of digested and raw night soil and nobody else can do this job."

Kalbermatten (1980:3) writes that "Among the fundamental problems of increasing sanitation services are the high cost of the conventional solutions and the large number of people presently being without such service. Today, around 114 billion people in developing countries lack sewage facility and an almost equal number do not have any access to safe water. If to this number the predicted growth in population up to 1990 is added, over two billion will have to be provided with water and sewerage (or other excretes disposal facilities) during 1980s. A general estimate based on the existing per capita cost indicates that up to $ 500 billion would be needed for conventional (western style) water supply and sewerage. The per capita investment cost for sewerage alone ranges from $ 150-250, which is totally beyond the capacity of the beneficiaries in developing countries to pay.

Total Sanitation Campaign December 2012 by Public Health Department gives a picture of the present scenario in the rural area which is given in Table below:

**Report on Total Sanitation Campaign (Dec. 2012)**

Govt. of India vide letter no.W11044/1/2003-CRSP DTD 24/02/04 sanctioned the okriginal TSC project for Dibrugarh district amounting to Rs. 383.45 lakh, Government of Assam accorded administrative approval vide letter no., PHED-374/2004/5 dated Hengrabari, the 18/07/05 and implementation started since 2006-07.

GOI sanctioned revised project proposal with project outlay is Rs. 2770.10 lakh, in which central share, state share and beneficiary share are Rs. 1884.52 lakh, Rs. 651.16 lakh and Rs. 234.42 lakh respectively.

**A. Break up of target and achievements in the district are shwqn in the following tables:**

| Year | Target as per (Revised sanctioned) | Target as per (as per available BPLID) | Target 2012-13* | Achievement Dec., 2012 (with ID) | Achievement 2012-13 (upto Dec. 2012 (With ID) | Cumulative Achievement | | | % Achieved against target of 2012-13 | % achieved (Cumulative) |
|---|---|---|---|---|---|---|---|---|---|---|
| | | | | | | with ID | Without ID | Total | | |
| IHHL (BPL) | 77606 | *58262 **(52515) | 1095 +465 | 34 +875 (IAY) | 1542 +3518 (IAY) | 51815 | 18099 | 69914 | 141% | 90.09% |

*The target fixed against actual BPL ID available in the field. **The target as per available BPL ID in P&RD website list.**The target is shown after segregation of Anomalies/constraints in field situation, etc.

| Year | Target as per (Revised sanctioned) | Target 2012-13 | Achievement Dec. 2012 | Achievement 2012-13 (Upto Dec. 2012) | Cumulative Achievement | % achieved against target of 2012-13 | % achieved (Cumulative) |
|---|---|---|---|---|---|---|---|
| IHHL (APL) | 45384 | 10213 | 160 | 1962 | 36781 | 19.2% | 81.04% |
| SSB toilet (no. of units | 517 (969) | 0 | 0 | 0 | 518 (972) | 0% | 100% |
| AWC toilet (no. of units) | 559** | 0 | 0 | 0 | 559 | 0% | 100% |

**No. of AWC having Government Bld. As per SWD record: 641 out of which 82 AWC constructed after 2005-06, which has been surrendered and district target fixed at 559.

| Sl No. | Financial Share | Revised Approved | Released | Cumulative Expenditure | Available Fund |
|---|---|---|---|---|---|
| 1 | Government of India | 1884.52 | 1775.00 | 1543.26 | 231.74 |
| 2 | Government of Assam | 651.16 | 350.57 | 499.35 | –148.78*** |
| 3. | Beneficiary contribution | 232.82 | 209.742 | 209.742 | 0.00 |
| 4. | Bank Interest | | 52.722 | 28.94 | 23.78 |
| | Total | 2768.5 | 2388.03 | 2281.29 | 106.74 |

***Due to non receipt of GOA share the expenditure has been incurred from the GOI share.

In the seven blocks of the Dibrugarh district, several NGO's like NESPYM, Jan-Kalyan Consumer Co-operative Society Ltd., Jyoti Krishak Sangha, UNDFA, Prerana SHG, Sammaniye Krishak, Natures Care and Friends, Jagaran SHG, Dristirekha, Udioman SHG, Alok, Tipomia Mahila SHG, Jagriti SHG, Janak SHG, Kiran, Dinabandhu SHG, Akota SHG, Hemkosh SHG, SPOT NGO are working with public health Engineering department in different sanitation programmes. Besides these, a Delhi based NGO, Feedback Foundation, is working for triggering community led total sanitation (CLTS) in villages under the blocks.

## III

In case of Dibrugarh municipality, there are 165 number of manual workers, out of which 65 were permanent workers who get a salary of about 5500 per month and 100 of temporary workers, which were further divided into skilled and unskilled workers. Skilled workers get Rs 150 per day whereas unskilled workers get Rs 135 everyday. There are 15 *sardars* and three supervisors and one sanitary inspector. These workers are divided into road sweepers, garbage carriers/cleaners and drain cleaners. Sixty-two were road sweepers, all of them were female. About 60 were given quarters in Kalibari and Graham Bazar area. There are nine tractors, two dumpers, three excavators and two robots with 16 of drivers.

As of now, there is no solid waste management plant and garbages are dumped in a place in Maijan, near the *Brahmaputra* river bank which has contributed to pollution in and around the surrounding. A project was proposed five years back in Lahoal, but due to objection of Airport authority, it was abandoned as it fell within 22 kilometres radius of the airport. Recently, more than 21 *bighas* of land was allotted by district administration, Dibrugarh for the proposed solid waste management project in Mankotta Ghoramara.

Dibrugarh municipality is constructing low cost latrines costing 10 thousand rupees and they are 70 in numbers for schedule caste people under SC Annual Plan 2009-10 and about six for scheduled tribes under ST Annual Plan 2009-10 for those whose family income does not exceed 3300 rupees per month. Besides, municipality has constructed community latrines costing one lakh to two lakh rupees in Santipara Harijan Colony, Suwani gaon, Grahambazar under 13th Finance Commission. Moreover, four numbers of pay and use toilets are constructed in Naliapool, Grahambazar, Phul Bagan and in front of the District Court under Assam Bikash Yojana.

In case of dustbins, municipality of Dibrugarh have constructed four different types of dustbins, which are given below:

1. Hume Pipe type removable dustbin costing rupees 1200 to 1500, 200 in numbers;
2. Permanent small dustbin, costing 60 to 80 thousand, 10 in numbers;
3. Mini permanent dustbin costing 10,000 rupees, 30 in numbers; and
4. Platform type dustbin costing rupees one lakh, five in numbers.

To conclude one can say that status of urban and rural sanitation coverage in Assam is very less. Issues of open defecation are a common problem, especially in tea gardens. There is no permanent dumping ground and solid waste management project in Dibrugarh town. The status of scavengers and manual workers are deplorable. Sanitation, drainage and maintenance of these services are important functions of municipal bodies in urban areas but their work is not sufficient. In villages and tea gardens, where people defecate in fields, the natural biological degradation processes take place. Unless all the people are aware of the ill effects of improper sanitation habits, the situation will never improve.

## References

Kalbermatten, J. M., 1980. *Sanitation- Convenience for a Few or Health for many; the report on the International Seminar on low-cost Techniques for Disposal of Human Wastes in Urban Communities,* Calcutta, Annexure II.

Kalbermatten, J. M., 1980. *Appropriate Technology for Water Supply and Sanitation—A Sanitation Field Manual,* Washington, World Bank.

Pathak, Bindeshwar, 2006. *Road to Freedom—A Sociological Study on the Abolition of Scavenging in India.* Xtreme Office Aids Pvt. Ltd., Delhi.

Pathak, Bindeshwar., 2009. *New Princesses of Alwar: Shame to Pride.* Sulabh International Social Service Organisation, New Delhi.

# 9

# Social Construction of Hygiene and Sanitation in Haryana

*Madhu Nagla*

Idea about dirt and hygiene vary from culture to culture and has changed from century to century. What is dirty in one place is clean in another. What was seen as clean by our forebears is unacceptably dirty in the late twentieth century. The explanation offered by anthropology for dirt is that it is matter out of its proper place. As each society has rules that create order, violations of that order constitute a threat to society. As physical objects which are in the wrong place, or hard to classify are labelled as 'dirty', so the label 'dirty' is given to marginal behaviours and social categories which provide a threat to the social order (Douglas: 1966). Hence the lipstick has to stay in its proper place on the lips, and the dirty old man has to keep his behaviour within society's boundaries.

To combat the dangers of dirt there is hygiene, which serves to preserve order, to chase away dirt and to preserve health. As dirt is multiple in natures and ubiquitous, so is corollary to hygiene. Rules about hygiene are to be found throughout every society. Hygiene is not only the private practice of individuals, but it is requirement of each society. Hygiene provides not only a barrier to the transmission of disease, but it also provides a barrier to disorder, chaos and social collapse.

Simply providing public services, whether in water supply, sanitation, curative services or health education does not in itself guarantee improvement in health status. Just because a service is there does not guarantee that it will be used, or that it will be used to the best possible health advantage. Some households contrive to preserve health even without these services. A framework that goes beyond the provision of services, beyond the standard public health perspective, is needed, if we are to find more effective way of working.

Berman *et al.* (1994) offer a solution and suggest that at household level external conditions and internal processes come together to produce health. They propose that households combine their own knowledge, resources and beahvioural patterns with available technologies, services, information and support from outside the home, to produce desired outcomes, one of which is good health. Similarly, in a paper on the public and domestic domains of disease transmission, Cairncross (1996) points out that the endemic disease that is responsible for the vast majority of the toll of death and illness in developing countries is largely transmitted within households.

**What is Hygiene?**

What image comes to mind when one thinks of hygiene? A European might think of a spotless bathroom, or of a child learning to put her hand in front of her mouth when she coughs. An African might think first of a well-swept courtyard and a child learning not to eat with her left hand, whilst someone from Asia might first imagine a *verandah* carefully smeared with dung and a child learning to brush her hair. Hygiene means different things to different people. Hygiene is a social phenomenon in the context of the social reality.

Boot and Cairncross (1993) provide a useful definition of hygiene: "the practice of keeping oneself and one's surrounding clean, especially in order to prevent illness, or the spread of infection'. The idea of hygiene thus comprises of two concerns; the avoidance of dirt, and the prevention of disease. The ideas about hygiene are not absolute. They vary from culture to culture and have through history. If we are to understand hygiene, it is necessary to explain both dirt and concept of disease causation. According to MacLaughlin (1971), "dirt is the evidence of the imperfection in life". He suggests that there is no such thing as absolute dirt: soup on a plate before we eat is food, the leftovers on the plate are dirt; lipstick on a girl's lips may make the boy friend want to kiss them, lipstick on a cup will ensure that he does not drink from it. Secretions; pus, vomitus, urine and faeces are inescapably dirty. The anthropologist, Mary Douglas was one of the first to realise that dirt was the reflection of the culture which defined it. Dirt is a by-product of a systematic ordering and classification of matter. That which does not fit within the system is rejected and labeled as dirt. Douglas shows that hygiene is not a matter of mere health, but is a construct that can only be understood in relation to other fundamental social values; cleanliness, order, purity, sacredness, veneration and their corollaries: dirt, disorder, pollution, profanity and defilement.

Everywhere, people have their hygiene rules in terms of a search for health and the avoidance of disease, whether they believe in microbes or not. Arguments about the natural consequences of unhygienic aces are roped in to uphold existing belief about disease, whether they spring from pre-scientific, quasi-scientific, or scientific understanding of disease causation. To elicit the emic (inside) view of hygiene in any society we have to scratch beneath this rationalist surface, to find out the cultural and psychological foundation of hygiene.

## Social Significance and Functions of Hygiene

Hygiene springs from a need for individual and social order; good order creates harmony and health. Religion, natural philosophy and science have contrived to offer satisfactory post-rationalisation for what is a fundamental need for order. If we want to promote safer hygiene therefore, we do not need to confine ourselves to arguments about disease avoidance. For example, in India one could build on the existing idea that water possesses the power of purifying, reviving and regenerating to encourage hand washing.

Hygiene and pollution rules are found in each society and are to be understood in the social framework of ideologies, underpinning forces and rationality behind them. In India, the religious conception of the pure/impure dichotomy subtends the whole hierarchical order of society. In his classic work, *Homo Hierarchicus* (1966), Dumont states that the fundamental institution in India is caste. Caste is based upon a hierarchical opposition of the pure and the impure, the superior and inferior. If the ritual and purity of the *brahmins* helped to set them apart from society, this would have also contributed to the legitimisation of the *brahmins*' position at the top of the hierarchy. Eventually *brahmin* religion became dominant throughout India among Hindus as did a rigid hierarchical ordering of society based on degrees of purity. Nowhere is it clearer that social rule which are founded on, and justified by, scriptural prescriptions about pollution and purity help to keep each group in their allotted rank in the social hierarchy. The relationship of one group to another is defined by their ritual purity with *brahmins* at the top of the purity scale and 'untouchables', who traditionally have the polluting professions (leather work, garbage and night-soil collection) at the bottom of the scale (Dumont: 1980). Social sanctions, which work all the way up the edifice of caste, keep the system in place (Curtis, 1998). In other countries, secular morality often plays a similar role (Curtis, 1998), for example, elaborate cleanliness, fresh clothes and perfume are not only more available to the rich, but serve to reinforce the distinction between rich and poor and thus perpetuate the inequality. If poverty and oppression can be justified on the grounds of a lack of hygiene, then we are dealing with a potentially explosive concept. Efforts to promote hygiene that are founded on the notion of the ignorance of the peasant, or the shanty down dweller, are still the rule rather than the exception in India, Africa and Latin America. If hygiene is intimately related with power, rank and caste, then no effort to promote hygiene can afford to be dealing with a purely scientific issue.

Hygiene keeps society in order because of the threat of diseases. But for this order society has to believe in it. Society provides two categories of explanation of natural phenomena such as birth, growth, the changing of the seasons, or disease, calamity and death. The first is the agency of some external forces deriving its power from religion, magic or symbolism. The second is the agency of properties that are intrinsic to the natural world and designated as naturalistic or scientific. While it is commonly thought that societies have evolved away from mystical explanation and towards the scientific, the two categories cannot be separated so easily. The ancient Hindu science of health, *Ayurveda* does not separate the divine from the earthly. It gives a central role to the balance of the humors. Disease is but one consequence of offences against the natural order. Burkert (1992) suggests that to try to separate the divine from the earthly in early societies is wasted efforts: "In archaic societies the social and physical ills were not clearly differentiated… the administration of justice and healing can be seen to fuse…An offence is the source of illness, illness is the result of an offence, be it in the personal, the social, or the religious sphere. Even the Greek word, *Nosos* embraces both the physical and the social ailments and disturbances."

Thus, we conclude that societies require coherent explanations of natural phenomena, especially disease, to create order and to explain and control calamity and disease, thus keeping threat at bay. Religious and naturalistic explanations have always overlapped and that one of the key concerns is with the policing of social and body boundaries. Any substance which transgresses these boundaries, which makes the transition from without to within or from within to without are potentially dangerous and need to be hedged with ritual. Religious, symbolic and scientific ideologies are the way in which society makes sense of and controls disease. Of course, contemporary explanation of germ theory cannot be ignored.

Throughout history people have been advised, exhorted and ordered to conform to certain rules of hygiene behaviour. The explanations offered have included factors such as public and private morality, religious purity and the preservation of health. As the scientific understanding of disease transmission has advanced, so the case for hygiene for health reasons has come to dominate in our supposedly scientific societies. However, motivations for domestic hygiene lie not in the avoidance of specific diseases, but in subtle social forces. On the other hand, health scientists ignore the social forces in the path of disease transmission.

## Meaning of Sanitation

Sanitation is the hygienic means of promoting health through prevention of human contact with the hazards of wastes as well as the treatment and proper disposal of sewage wastewater. Hazards can be physical, microbiological, biological or chemical agents of diseases. Wastes that can cause health problems include human and animal faeces, solid wastes, domestic wastewater (sewage, sullage, greywater)), industrial wastes and agricultural wastes. Hygienic means of prevention can be by using engineering solutions (e.g. sewerage and waste water treatment), simple technologies (e.g. latrines, septic tanks), or even by personal hygiene practices (e.g. simple handwashing with soap).

World Health Organisation (2000) states that: "Sanitation generally refers to the provision of facilities and services for the safe disposal of human urine and faeces. Inadequate sanitation is a major cause of disease world-wide and improving sanitation is known to have a significant beneficial impact on health both in households and across communities. The word 'sanitation' also refers to the maintenance of hygienic conditions, through services such as garbage collection and wastewater disposal.

## Sanitation and Public Health

The importance of the isolation of waste lies in an effort to prevent disease which can be transmitted through human waste, which afflict both developed countries as well as developing countries to differing degrees. It is estimated that up to five million people die each year from preventable water-borne diseases (Gleick: 2002). Sanitation is necessity for a healthy life.

There are two schools of thought: the 'miasmatists' who regarded *miasmas* as being responsible for disease; and the contagionists who regarded that disease came from bodily contact, sharing of substances such as food and water, or proximity. Edwin Chadwick (1800-1890), the great sanitary reformer, explained that epidemic fevers sue to *miasmas* arising from decaying animals and vegetable matter. In the wake of industrialisation and urbanisation came the concern that urban population concentrations were the breeding ground for filth, epidemic and vice; all of which threatened the social order. In pre-revolutionary Paris Joseph Guillotin proposed the setting up a health committee in 1790 to look into health conditions of the urban masses. Social unrest in England led to the Edwin Chadwick's sanitarian movement and the Public Health Act of 1848. Boards of Health were set up in Philadelphia, Boston and New York and Public Health legislation was enacted throughout Europe. DeSwaan suggests that a collective effort to pacify the urban poor was required to maintain the social order in the interest of elites (1988). But the stated concern of sanitarians was that "epidemic disease was the product of dirt and decomposing matter". Pickstone points out that the 'expert' explanation of disease did not coincide with what the masses perceived; their emic vies was that fevers and other diseases were due to privation and the high price of corn (1992). The elite used new theories about disease to explain their fear of the threat of the poor; the poor saw their disease as a consequence of their property.

## Objective of the Study

There has recently been considerable concern in scientific discourse regarding the social determinants of hygiene and sanitation. The concern is further expressed in the need to influence the hygiene and sanitation related behaviour through various policies and programmes interventions for the practising of safe hygiene and sanitation in the day to day life. Sulabh International from last several years has been doing a commendable job in improving the sanitation facilities and also removing the burden of carrying night-soil on the head by the untouchables. They not only rehabilitate them, but also provided them the alternative livelihood. They have also introduced various technologies for latrines which are available according to different climatic conditions of the country. They have also introduced the technique which is successful in saving the use of water.

This paper will delineate on the individual/communities in terms of understanding of hygiene and sanitation. Further, it also tries to understand their unhygienic behaviour and what efforts are made to bring the proper scientific hygienic sanitation behaviour. It results in a concern for understanding certain questions at two levels, viz., individual and community and in two ways, i.e., not merely 'what' but the 'why' people do. For example, why people do not follow the scientifically guided hygiene and sanitation behavior? Why people do not want to change, or what obstructs them to change?

The research questions might not necessarily be explanatory alone, but exploratory as well to understand community's perception about the hygiene and sanitation and their behaviour pattern. Such concern for research questions, which are beyond numbers, has resulted in an acknowledgment (among medical scientists) of the contributions of qualitative research through the work of social scientists. Thus, recently there have been studies that advocate for triangulation of research tools and methods (quantitative method typical, or epidemiological surveys and qualitatively characteristics of social science more particularly sociology/anthropology). The study of hygiene and sanitation thus provides a platform for greater academic exchanges between these two streams, a fact increasingly acknowledged both by anthropologists and medical scientists, including public health specialists. This has resulted in a growing interests of studies exploring possibilities of combining research methods (qualitative and quantitative) and perspectives from these different streams in the larger interest of public health (Baum, 1995; Carey, 1998; Roberts et al., 2002; Goering and Streoner, 1996; Nakaash et al., 2002; Nichter et al., 2002).

## Methodology

We conducted a study to explore community members' understanding of hygiene and sanitation and their practices, perceived risk factors and their views on possible improvement. This study is a part of another study on health and its various dimensions during period of 2006-2007. We conducted Focus Group Discussion (FGD) with people from different caste, class and gender category between April to June 2006. People for group discussion were drawn on the basis of housing structure, occupation, education, income and gender. Profiling of people was done on the basis of consultation with *sarpanch* and our own observation. In all five FGD were conducted in Dhandhlan village, in Jhajjar district in Haryana with a total of 30 respondents (13 males and 17 females). The age group ranged between 25 to 62. Data were analysed concurrently with data collection. This helped us to identify issues emerging in one FGD to bring back for discussion in subsequent ones, thus each FGD enriched the process of data collection. The following section discusses the results.

## Interpretation of Data

### Idea and Practice of Sanitation

Sanitation is an important index of socio-economic development. Low sanitation levels lead to a host of diseases, making sanitation a key public health issue ad concomitant of a clean water supply. Reddy and Snehlatha (2011) did field work in two urban slums of Hyderabad, Andhra Pradesh and concludes that sanitation implies much more than defecation issues and it converges on several important aspects of life, such as shame and dignity and personal hygiene. Women themselves defined what appropriate sanitation is. Cleaning tasks are primarily performed by women who receive little support from men. Reddy and Snehlatha (2011) argued for the need to give women a central role in decision-making, designing, planning and implementation of sanitation programmes. Women's definitions of the minimum standards of hygienic practices are clearly brought out by study. Idea and practice of sanitation revolves around women. In our study, the women are disposing the stool of children outside their houses. Majority of the houses are having flush latrines, therefore, they need not go outside except very poor people.

### Hygiene and Sanitation in Community Understanding

There are many hygiene behaviours, however, according to WHO they include: hand-washing, having and using latrines, safe disposal of excreta and storing drinking water supply. Community members across socio-economic group highlighted the hygiene and sanitation behaviour. The *vignettes* given below are only a few from the large numbers recalled during the FGDs.

### Hand Washing

Having clean hands is important to prevent disease. For example, one common way to get a cold, or serious disease such as *hepatitis A* or diarrhea is by rubbing your nose, mouth or eyes after your hands have been contaminated with germs. Hand washing is a complex behaviour, for which several things are needed such as knowledge, skills and an enabling environment. Knowledge of hand washing times is important for health reasons. These critical hand washing times are usually considered to be: before eating, after defecation, after handling excreta of infants. Rubbing both hands with soap, or ash and using enough water is important. Dongre et al. (2007) found that need based, focused, skill based child to child education is effective for behaviour change. Mukhopadhyay et al. (2012) found in their study that many food handlers disregard their illnesses like diarrhea, sore throat and skin infections and continued to do work under such conditions. Disregarding these illnesses can contribute to the occurrence of frequent food-borne diseases to their consumers in eateries.

Knowledge and practice of hand washing with soap is common in the study population. However, fifty per cent respondents wash their hands using soap and water and rubbing both hands together. The entire households had soap for washing hands, however, washing of hands with soap was only observed after defecation not after urinating. Washing hands before eating is also not found common, however, after eating food it is found among 80 per cent of the respondents.

**Disposal of Excreta and Habit of Defecation**

The condition of the disposal of the house dirt and waste need to be seen against the background of the local traditions, customs and practices which reflect the lack of understanding of the rule of sanitation and hygiene and in turn knowledge about the disease. People are used to the conditions as they are today in the nature of things, a characteristics feature of village life. They will hardly think about it, or talk about it. This has created indifference in these people regarding the disposal of house filth, or waste and general sanitary conditions of the village. It may be out of place to quote Karve's explanation of the indifference of the people to environmental sanitation. Karve says, "When people cannot afford to spend adequately even on food and clothing, they do not just bother about environmental sanitation…experience strengthens the view that sanitation is inextricably woven with the economic and social life of people, and to the extent to which the latter improves, the sanitary consciousness of the people also correspondingly improves…" (Report on Environmental Sanitation in Rural India: 1957). Curtis and Cairncross (2003) found that inadequate hand washing after defecation and the cleaning was important source of transmission of enteric diseases in the countries like Bangladesh and India. On the other hand, Curtis, Cairncorss and Yonli (2000) evidenced that hand washing after defecation; especially by the children was significant factor in diarrhea transmission.

Generally in the cities houses are usually swept daily and the refuse is thrown out near some empty plot, or some vacant place. Alternatively sweepers of the municipal corporation come and load in their carts and throw them outside the city. In the planned colonies the refuse is not thrown outside the house but house maids collect them in some poly bags and dispose it off in the big bins collected in the corner of the colonies.

One of the respondents replied that "he also wants to live like the other rich people live, but in the rich locality the municipality people regularly come and clean it. On the other hand, they hardly bother to clean it and they do not come regularly".

Another respondent said that "it is not the house waste, or filth which bothers but it is the disposal part which worries us. There is no proper place to dispose them, moreover, the refuse of polythene bags create many problems. When the wind blows, therefore, it turns into heaps and ultimately it stinks and invites breeding of mosquitoes and flies."

Another respondent said, "that heaps of the house refuse may be seen decaying and emitting foul smell. Here house flies and mosquitoes are found on large scale and thus it results in the malaria and other diseases."

**Habits of Defecation**

The proper disposal of human faecal material is important for the environmental sanitation of a community. Report on Environmental Sanitation in Rural India (1957:75) reports that a complete drainage systems laid out has been unearthed in Mohanjodaro and in all these places, there are latrines and bathrooms in each house, with drains. All their men and women among Hindus go to the fields for defecation with the exception of one family. Among the Muslim families, latrine was there, but only females were using that as they are supposed to observe *purdah* (Hasan: 1979). Furthermore, nearly 90 per cent did not want to have latrines in their houses as they it is unhygienic and uncomfortable. The foul smell inside the latrine makes them feel bad. Hasan also observed that inside the house they failed to excrete and resulting in to constipation or their bowels did not move. Going outside in the morning has an additional advantage as one enjoys morning walk and breeze.

In the present situation of the village, people have latrines, except very few houses. However, the houses in which latrines were there, we asked them that where the children defecate? Except those houses where mothers and fathers were educated, their children defecate in the latrine and in the toddler stage they defecate on the floor of the house, or in plastic pot and then stool are thrown in the latrine and pot is washed. Children aged between three-four years to six-seven years defecate outside the house where drainages are there. They reported that it is convenient for children as well as for parents to send them outside the home for defecation as for this age group of children, as they have only one latrine and in the morning time all the members go for defecation, for there is rush for it. Therefore, for this age-group of children it is better to send them outside. Generally, latrines do not have tap water, only one container filled with water along with the mug is there to wash the latrine and flush it out with mug of water. They have given the argument that by fixing tap in the latrine for water, water will be spent in the liberal manner. There is already a shortage of water and it has to be collected either from the supply of municipality water or from private sources. Private source of water is very popular in Haryana. Generally each household has private connection of water by paying Rs 100-150 per month. The private water supply owners bring tanks and whosoever pays them they fill their tanks and charge the money. Thus, the role of parents' education, economic condition and role of water supply is the determining variables in the hygienic behaviour.

There are certain uncomfortable situations which we observed at the level of sanitation facilities at home and in turn they brings nightmare for disabled and old age people. We are citing them below:

**Case Study-1**

Sarita and her husband Ramphool both are disabled and struggle to make ends meet to support their three young children. They are disabled, therefore, they are unable to do any type of work and moreover, they are not so efficient also. They are daily wage labourers. The physical effort required to get water from different water points is an exhausting and time consuming chore, limiting time available for other productive work and causing considerable hardship for the family. Local support is also not available particularly for the daily routine things like collecting water etc.

**Case Study-2**

Twenty-five year old Farzana suffers from severe mental and physical disabilities. She is unable to walk to move without the capacity to walk. Farzana cannot independently visit the nearby fields to practise open defecation as other community members do. She is forced to defecate where she lives in bed. Consequently, her mother spends hours each day giving her bath and cleaning her bed. This is a source of distress for Farzana and her family.

**Case Study-3**

Ompati an elder women living in outskirts of the village, lost her eyesight by both eyes 20 years ago. Life is difficult for Ompati because water is not easily available in her community and she does not have a toilet at home. When she needs to collect water, she uses tube well with the support of others. If she goes alone, she is often injured.

**Case Study-4**

Krishna, middle aged women, suffering from knee pain. She lost her husband and does not have her son. She has three daughters and all are married and living in distant villages. When the winter approaches, she severely suffers from the severe pain in her knees and even unable to walk properly. All the more, it is difficult for her to sit in the ordinary toilet and defecate. She wants something like chair system on which she can sit and defecate. Till now, every winter she suffers from severe pain and wants some alternative. Like her there are many people in the village who are suffering from this type of problem.

**Storing Drinking Water**

Safe storage of drinking water means at least keeping it covered. There should be no visible particles in the water and there should be no contamination in the water. Although the study found reduced contamination at village water sources, household water quality did not improve. Except countable households, people in village do not likely to purchase and use household water purifier, filter, indicating that price is the barrier. Most of the household in the village strain water through a cloth.

**Implication for Public Health**

Modern health promotion programmes counsel hygiene, ostensibly for reasons of disease avoidance. But the multiple and confusing messages that are issues contain other values. Why do some programmes advise disinfecting vegetables and boiling drinking water, others concentrate on food storage and handling, and still others issue certificates of food vendors, advice cutting fingernails, disinfecting latrine labs, or cleaning nipples before breastfeeding? Perhaps concern with order, morality, or purification ritual to render safe that which crosses the body boundary can be discerned behind such counsel. Take, for example, hygiene education programmes that encourage the boiling of drinking water. However, this may be misleading and costly advice for mothers, whose children could be getting much higher doses of intestinal pathogens from their domestic environment, than for water they drink. But the fear of polluted substances crossing the body boundary, epitomised as microbes, is such a potent threat that it is easy to see why hygiene educators tend to keep prescribing purification rituals such as boiling, or filtering. It may also explain how marketers contrive to sell vast quantities of bottled water (which may even be less bacteriologically pure than tap water) on images of purity.

**Intervention**

Non-Governmental Organisations should be invited to promote community led sanitation models that trigger demand for improved health and hygiene behaviour. Hygiene awareness campaigns and inter-personal communication for behaviour change by involving in communities, schools and *anganwadi* centres are appreciated. NGOs should work with communities that have already sanitation facilities and water points to make sure these are better used and maintained.

**Conclusion**

Rules about hygiene are to be found throughout every society. Hygiene is not only the private practice of individuals, but it is requirement of each society. Hygiene provides not only a barrier to the transmission of disease, but it also provides a barrier to disorder, chaos and social collapse. Sanitation is the hygienic means of promoting health through prevention of human contact with the hazards of wastes as well as the treatment and proper disposal of sewage wastewater.

Majority of the houses are having flush latrines, therefore, they need not go outside except very poor people. The entire households had soap for washing hands however; washing of hands with soap was only observed after defecation, not after urinating. Generally, in the cities, houses are usually swept daily and the refuse is thrown out near some empty plot, or some vacant place. Alternatively sweepers of the municipal corporation come and load in their carts and throw them outside the city. In the planned colonies, the refuse is not thrown outside the house but house maids collect them in some polybags and dispose it off in the big bins collected in the corner of the colonies. The study found reduced contamination at village water sources, household water quality did not improve. Except countable households, people in village do not likely to purchase and use household water purifier, filter, indicating that price is the barrier. Most of the households, in the village strain water through a cloth. Outside defecation and collecting water from distant place is a difficult task and it becomes more difficult in the case of physical, mental disabilities and in old age.

## References

Baum, F. (1995), *Researching Public Health: Behind the Qualitative Quantitative Methodological Debate*, Social Science and Medicine, 40(4), pp. 459-62.

Berman, P et al. (1994), *The Household Production of Health: Integrating Social Science Perspectives on Micro-level Health Determinants*, Social Science and Medicine, 38 (2), pp. 205-215.

Burkert, W. (1992), *The Orientalising Revolution: Near Eastern Influence on Greek Culture in the Early Archaic Age*, USA: Harvard University Press.

Cairncross, C. et al. (1996), *The Public and Domestic Domains in the Transmission of Disease*, Tropical Medicine and International Health, 1, pp. 27-34.

Carey, J.W. (1998), *Linking Qualitative and Quantitative Methods: Integrating Cultural Factors into Public Health*, Qualitative Health Research, 3(3), pp. 298-318.

Curtis, Valerie (1998), *The Dangers of Dirt: Household Hygiene and Health*, Wageningen: Grafish Service Centrum.

Curtis, Valerie, S. Cairncross and R. Yonli (2000), *Domestic Hygiene and Diarrhea, Pinpointing the Problem*, Tropical Medicine and International Health, 5: pp. 22-32.

Curtis, Valerie and S. Cairncross (2003), *Effect of Washing Hands with Soap on Diarrhea Risk in the Community: A Systematic Review*, The Lancet Infectious Diseases, 3: pp. 275-281.

DeSwaan A. (1988), *In care of the State: Health Care, education and Welfare in Europe and the USA in Europe and USA in Modern Era*, Oxford: OUP.

Dongre, A.R. et al., (2007), *An Approach to Hygiene Education Among Rural Indian School Going Children*, Online Journal of Health and Allied Sciences, Vol. 6, 4, Oct-Dec.

Douglas, M. (1966), *Purity and Danger: An Analysis of Concepts of Pollution and Taboo*, London: Ark.

Dumont, L. (1980), *Homo Heirachicus: The Caste System and Its Implications*, Complete revised English edition, Chicago: University of Chicago Press (First published in 1966).

Gleick, Peter H. (2002), *Estimated Deaths from Water-related Diseases 2000-2020*. Pacific Institute Research Report, Pacific Institute for Studies in Development, Environment and Society.

Goering, P. and D.L. Streiner, *Reconcilable Differences: The Marriage Between Qualitative and Quantitative Methods*, Canadian Journal of Psychiatry, 41, pp. 491-497.

Hasan, K.A. (1979), *Medical Sociology in Rural India*, Ajmer: Sachin Publications.

MacLaughlin, T. (1971), *A Social History as Seen Through the Uses and Abuses of Dirt*, Dorset Press.

Mukhopadhyay, Prianka et al., (2012), *Indentifying Key Risk Behaivours Regarding Personal Hygiene and Food Supply Practices of Food Handlers Working in Eating Establishments Located within a Hospital campus in Kolkata*, Al Ameen Journal of Medical Science, 5(1), pp. 21:28.

Nakkash, R. et al., (2002), *The Development of a Feasible Community-Specific Cardiovascular Disease Prevention Programme: Triangulation of Methods and Sources*, Health Education and Behaviour, 10, pp. 405-421.

Nichter, M. et al., (2002), *Using Qualitative Research to Inform Survey Development on Nicotine Dependence Among Adolescents*, Drug and Alcohol Dependence, 68, pp. S41-S56.

Pickstone, J.V. (1992), *Dirt, Dearth and Fever Epidemics: Rewriting the History of British Public Health, 1780-1850*, in T. Ranger and P. Slack (eds.), Epidemics and Ideas: Essays on the Historical Perception of Pestilence, Cambridge: Cambridge University Press.

Reddy, B. Suireh and M. Snehlata (2011), "*Sanitation and Personal Hygiene: What does it mean to Poor and Vulnerable Women?*" Indian Journal of Gender Studies, Vol. 18, No. 3, pp. 381-404.

Report on *Environmental Sanitation in Rural India* (1957), Government of India, Ministry of Health.

Roberts, et al., (2002), *Factors Effecting uptake of Childhood Immunisation: A Babyesian Synthesis of Qualitative and Quantitative Evidence*, The Lancet, 360 (9345), 1596-1599.

World Health Organisation (2000), *Global Water Supply and Sanitation Assessment, 2000, Report*, Geneva.

# 10

# Social Deprivation in Present Scenario: Motivating and Liberating Scheduled Castes from an Inhuman Profession

*R.S. Tripathi*

The way people live should be seen with an eye of a sociologist, rather than a hygiene scientist. The system of discrimination among castes, is still prevalant in our society. This discrimination in Indian Society is far bigger than financial discrimination and is resulting in social strain. On lower level. The broader and practical results of untouchability as a regular phenomenon are linked to the system of discrimination. Although there are so many options for career building now that the children of people belonging to the castes who carried human excreta still harbor a feeling of negativity for them in society. This means the lives of scheduled castes people are full of deprivation, discrimination and lower standards of living.

The youth belonging to scheduled castes do not regret for being born as such. Schedule castes people living in cities have gone through some social change rather than people living in the villages.

In India the deprived sections of society live in isolation. Their main work is to clean the roads, carrying human excreta, cleaning toilets and dumping the city garbage. In cities the above mentioned works are mainly done through municipal corporations. But now a days in metro cities the cleaning work is undertaken on contract basis. Change can be clearly seen as the people belonging to lower casts are now working in school, hospitals etc. This is the result of change in professional situation during the last three decades.

Education, health, business, banking facilities are taking the society towards broad mindedness. Due to migration of this class into cities the youth of this class are able to secure better jobs. One could even say that these migrants are more enterprising than the local people. The third generation of the lower castes people living in the cities are now mixed up with the mainstream. It has been found in the sociology studies that people's mindset has reached a point where they think that these people, working in any organisation are there just because of their caste and reservation. This means casteism is still prevailing. There are still instances of caste discrimination. There are provisions in law against it, but the caste of an individual does keep an important indentity in an organisation. Employees belonging to lower caste are easy prey to social deprivation and this is also true when it comes to some agitation against reservation, a person belonging to lower caste is the first victim. Although these lower castes people have made their unions and they are registered and are not speechless. Person in any job of this class is always worried about the ill-treatment. There are very rare chances when a person from lower caste can sit and chat with a general category worker. In this way, the feeling of casteism remains ahead of the harmony. It is very unfortunate that a person belonging to lower cast gets a job due to his cast but he does not get the same respect as a person from the general category.

The deprived classes are a category that is out of the bounds of mainstream of society. It is very painful to be illiterate today. When the pain of untouchability is mixed up with the pain of being illiterate there is a situation of social exclusion in society. The condition of social discrimination can be very rightly understood by study of Mure (1990). He clearly describes the social conditions of black in Britian and under class theory. Anthony Giddens has described three stages of detachment:

1. Labour market Exclusion,
2. Service Exclusion, and
3. Exclusion from social Relations.

The detachment from the labour market is focused on increasing number of the unemployed. Unemployed house wives and students are left outside the labour market. An area or a group of people can be deprived of certain services like Electricity, Water, Light, Roads, Bank, Post Office, School, Doctor, Park, Bus Stand and places of amusements. A person who is totally detached from his friends, family friends and others is never called on certain occasions. The mental harassment on this stage is such that one lacks social support or advice.

Sixty per cent of illiteracy in any society is a matter of concern. And when it is in the schedule castes society, one could easily understand the condition of women. The fact is that person belonging to the last surf of society is left out of the societal benefits. In India, a lower cast, or backward class person is ill treated. The difference between education level of man and women of lower castes and general castes people is an important data for the analysis of 'underclass theory' and social deprivation. Under section 46 of Indian constitution it is the responsibility of the administration to develop the activities regarding the education of the lower and backward classes.

The makers of economic policy in India have been accepting the system of reservation on the basis of castes and classes. In Indian society castes and classes are almost synonomus to each other.

In the framework of globalisation, privatisation and liberalisation, the revaluation of new economic policies is being done. In India, weaker sections are mostly feeling the heat of poverty. 100 per cent of poor people are from lower castes. These include scheduled castes, backward muslims and other backward classes. Other than these some scheduled tribal classes are also included. Eight per cent scheduled castes and 27 per cent backward classes 15 per cent. The area wise regional sectoral population is divided into such a way that people living in Bihar, Odisha, Uttar Pradesh are poorer than the people living in Gujarat, Punjab, Haryana. When we look into the index of regional development we reach the conclusion that backward states are hardly moving forward. The situation of the weaker sections in backward states is very critical. The per capita GDP of developing states during 1992-2005 is rising in an impressive way while the per capita GDP of the poor states has not shown any development.

The GDP of 1992-1993 and 2004-2005 growth have many differences, on one side in 1992 Madhya Pradesh and Bihar were far behind and contrary to this they achieved six per cent and five per cent GDP in 2004-2005. The weaker sections are given priority in the development policies, but on ground reality is not so that could prove to be suitable for sustainable development.

If we see the new economic policy in regard to the economic index of scheduled castes we can easily understand the eco-political system. The aims of development are regularised by the states, center and the ruling parties. Scheduled castes-tribes are constitutionally listed and they are known to everyone without mentioning the name of one's caste.

'Dalit' in our society is a person who belongs to one of the lowest classes that are exploited and whose life is full of misery. He is a victim of economic backwardness for generations. He is very poor. He has to fight for his children to get to schools due to lack of work, lack of land and social deprivation, all these are results of poverty. For the development of this class some policy at the national level should be made that is based on reality, although we have seen a great change in education and professional movements, on account of the reservation policy. Dalits take this as their right that they got after a strong movement.

## Ratio of Poverty

The poverty level is 26.5 per cent in general category in comparison to 35.44 in scheduled castes. This means scheduled castes are feeling the heat of poverty in rural as well as urban areas.

Another table shows the comparison of domestic in SC's and general classes. The table shows that the schedule castes living in urban areas are getting the facilities of drinking water, toilet and electricity much more than their counterparts in rural areas. The toilet facility that is enjoyed by only 5.15 per cent of scheduled castes living in villages, 21.8 per cent of SCs in villages and 56.3 per cent in urban areas is the percentage of scheduled castes getting electricity.

**Ratio of Poverty**

**(A)**

| *Caste* | *Rural* | | | | *Urban* | |
|---|---|---|---|---|---|---|
| | *1983* | *1987* | *1993`* | *1997-2000* | *1987* | *2000* |
| ST | 63.89 | 56.31 | 47.5 | 44.35 | 52.26 | 37.42 |
| SC | 58.96 | 50.79 | 48.27 | 35.44 | 54.42 | 39.13 |
| Others | 40.40 | 33.80 | 31.20 | 21.14 | 36.87 | 20.78 |
| Total | 46.51 | 36.36 | 37.28 | 26.50 | 39.16 | 23.98 |

*Source:* NSSO, 58th round.

**(B)**

| *Source* | *Year* | *Scheduled Caste* | | | *Non-Scheduled Caste* | | |
|---|---|---|---|---|---|---|---|
| | | *Total* | *Rural* | *Urban* | *Total* | *Rural* | *Urban* |
| Safe Drinking Water | 1991 | 63.6 | 59.8 | 30.6 | 64.1 | 56.4 | 82.0 |
| | 2001 | 81.1 | 78.5 | 94.0 | 79.2 | 74.1 | 90.0 |
| Toilet | 1991 | 11.6 | 5.15 | 38.25 | 28.63 | 11.52 | 68.38 |
| | 2001 | 23.7 | 15.1 | 54.5 | 42.3 | 25.8 | 78.0 |
| Electricity | 1991 | 28.1 | 21.8 | 56.3 | 48.1 | 34.6 | 79.3 |
| | 2001 | 44.3 | 35.1 | 77.4 | 61.4 | 48.2 | 89.9 |

*Source:* Bharat Mei Dalit: Samanya Lakshya Ki Khoj, Sukhdev Thorat, 2011, p. 116.

As per population census, 16 per cent of the total population are scheduled tribes and are mostly settled in northern India. Almost 80 per cent of them are in villages. The *dalit* colonies are known by different names and are still at a distance from the general colonies. The positive results and symptoms can be seen in the fields of education and professional life due to positive steps taken by the government.

The system of casteism prevailing since thousands of years is the basic of reservation system. Economic, educational and social backwardness are also companion to the caste system. Although in 1955 untouchability became illegal but still the administration is feeling the pulse of it.

The slums in urban areas are the places where a big number of scheduled castes live. The sweepers (earlier called *bhagis*) also live here. Their work and social life is full of social deprivation. The system of scavenging is still prevailing in India. In western Uttar Pradesh touching the capital of India, one could see scavengers cleaning human excreta. Government has formed several committees to end the problems of these scavengers (Barre committee: 1949, Bose committees: 1990). Malkani scheme in 1981 was formed to rehabilitate them. The aim of the government was to raise the standard of living of the poorer in scheduled caste people. The idea was to raise the level of their income, their social standard would automatically rise.

In 1993, a new Act was passed for the welfare of scavengers. Scavenging was banned and construction of flush toilets was provided.

A national commission was formed for the welfare of scavengers (12 August, 1994). The aim of the commission was to provide facilities to this class so that they could come into the mainstream of society. The comparable table of wages in urban and rural areas is as follows:

| *Employment Area* | *Rural* | | *Urban* | |
|---|---|---|---|---|
| | *SC* | *Non-SC* | *SC* | *Non-SC* |
| Engaged in Non-Agriculture Employment | 12.0 | 14.4 | 27.3 | 36.6 |
| Labour | 10.2 | 7.1 | 26.5 | 12.4 |

*Source:* NSSO 55th round.

Social deprivation is still prevailing because of low wage work. Scheduled castes are not able to get two-third of the non-agricultural jobs. As per available data, 65 per cent of SC's are without any land and without resources. By looking at current daily status one can say that there is big economical inequality in the society. NSSO 55th round data show that the situation in urban unemployment was not better. There was a downfall of 5.2 per cent during 1982-2000. The fall in the percentage of unemployment in the cities shows that there is a positive result of the reservation policy. Due to reservation policy, about 16.6 per cent of scheduled castes (in 2003) were working in central government. In 2005, nearly 5.46 lakh people were working in the central government in comparison to 2.28 lakh in 1960. This is also a positive sign.

There is a view that through education the fact of social deprivation can be eliminated but still the goal is far away. In 2001, the literacy rate in scheduled castes was 54 per cent while all round literacy was 68 per cent. This means SCX are 14 per cent behind that is a little less than that of 10.27 per cent (SC) in comparison to 27.9 per cent. We have to be concerned with all the classes specially those who are engaged in manual scavenging as the Sulabh International and few other organisations are doing. An Act to ban manual scavenging and use of bucket toilet was passed on 5th June, 1993. When we compare different states some important data come our way. In India, around 42 per cent of general people were enjoying the facility of toilets. In cities, it was 80 per cent and 25 per cent in villages (2001). But when it comes to scheduled castes, it was 15 per cent in villages and 54.5 per cent in cities. Overall it was 23 per cent. These figures give us the impression of inequality.

Scheduled castes were using toilet facilities in rural areas in following states as under: Bihar 5.5 per cent, Karnataka 10.5 per cent, Madhya Pradesh 5.5 per cent, Orissa 4.4 per cent, Rajasthan 13 per cent, Tamil Nadu 10 per cent, Uttar Pradesh 13.7 per cent, Kerela 66 per cent, Delhi 42.6 per cent, and Assam 57.7 per cent. In urban areas the condition was much better than that of rural areas (13 per cent-78 per cent).

The situation of *mahadalit* is economically deprived. A scheme ' Pratishtha' was introduced in Madhya Pradesh. Under this scheme a research was done in Indore (about 200 families); about 57.5 per cent of people in these families were doing scavenging. 84 youths among these families were given vocational training.

In the research it was found that 55 women started doing same old work even after getting training. Former Central Minister Hon'ble Sh. Jairam Ramesh has said, "Construct toilets before temples". A UN reports says that about 60 per cent of Indians still go for open defecation. In urban areas five local people go for open defecation. About 70 per cent houses in 15 main cities are equipped with a separate bathroom and toilet that is connected to sewer line. 80 per cent of slums do not have toilet (*Kehnan Samayantar* – August 2012-13, Toilets vs Weapons).

The problem that is harming human dignity cannot be solved through capitalist policies and that, too, overnight. It has been seen that these sweepers and cleaners are affected adversely by the septic tank gas. Sometimes the gas even kills them. The involvement of women is no less in this. The scheduled castes live in different conditions in different states.

As per Namisharay, scheduled castes have no choice to do other works other than pig farming, excreta cleaning, road cleaning etc. All these professions are unhealthy. *Safai karamchari* union has been established on the rational level, but they, too, are not able to raise their voice at higher level. The standard of social deprivation that is focusing on the critical condition of scheduled castes is challenging for the functioning of sociologists. Although 60 years have passed since freedom and we have more than 300 sub-castes in scheduled castes those are still not getting the power of social justice. We still cannot imagine India as a country that is free from casteism, although to get the benefits of reservation polices, several castes are pressurising media and the government.

## References

Sukhdeve Thorat, 2011. *Bharart Mein Dalit: Samanya Lakshya Ki Khoj,* Hindi translation of Rawat, Vijay Kumar Pant, Dalits in India: Search for a common Destiny.

Radheyshyam Nirmal 2006. *Safai Kamgaron Ki Mukti Evam Punarvas Yojna Ki Sarthakta: Special study on Indore City*, Poorvadeva 12 (45-46) Rawat, Jaipur.

Harikishan Sanotoshi, 2009. *Daliton ke Dalit-Sthiti, Paristhiti Sambhawnayen*, Sasta Shitya Mandal.

Prem Kapadia 2006. *Dalit Utpeedan: Uttar Pradesh ki Dastaan',* Bhartiya Samajik Sansthan, New Delhi.

Bhagwan Singh, 2009. *Gandhi Aur Dalit. Bharat Jagran,* Bhartiya Gyanpreeth, New Delhi.

Jansatta, Daily-17-01-2013: New Delhi, *Pabandi ke Baad Bhi Sar Par Dhoya Ja Raha Hai Maila* (News from Roorkie).

Jansatta, Daily, *Government Request for time for the implementation of law against scavenging*, Supreme Court says, Government. Making False Promises, Jansatta, New Delhi Bureau.

R. Ravi Chandran, *Between class and caste*, EPW, March 26, pp. 21-25.

Scavenging profession: Between class and caste.

Vanvdiet Bas Spaargen 2005. Special Perspective on the Sanitation Challenge. New York. www.ncsk.nic.in/main_rep-3-3a3p.

# 11

# Sanitation and Hygiene Deficit in Karnataka

*Shaukath Azim*

Nobody denies that food, clothing and shelter are the vital needs of human life. These basic features depend on the adequate supply of water and sanitation. Water and sanitation are imperative for health and well being of people on earth. But the most indispensable need has been given least importance by most of the people in the globe. About half of the population in the world is living without access to safe sanitation. It is painful that more than half of the Indians are also struggling everyday to have safe drinking water and sanitation, primary education and health. In fact, majority of Indians have given least importance to sanitation. People hardly demand sanitation as their right. Indians are waiting since Independence to have independence in the use of sanitation. Even though Karnataka state is claiming that in IT and technology it is one of the developed states, its position in basic human services is lagging behind considerably, especially in water, sanitation, hygiene, electricity and roads. It is disgusting to view that almost half of the households in Karnataka lack toilet facility within their easy reach. Therefore, around three crore people of Karnataka do not have toilet facility within their premises. However, problem of safe sanitation and hygiene is not uniform throughout the state. Regional variation can be seen in the availability and access to safe and affordable sanitation facilities in the state. In this background the present study makes a modest attempt to study the magnitude of sanitation problem in the Karnataka. This chapter is based only on secondary sources.

*Sanitation is more important than Independence.*

**—Mahatma Gandhi**

> "Clean water and sanitation can make, or break human development. They are fundamental to what people can do and what they can become to their capabilities .....". (HDR, 2006:27).

It is a universal reality that food, clothing and shelter are the vital needs of human life. These basic features depend on the adequate supply of water and sanitation. They are imperative for health and well being of people on earth. It is also fundamental that 'human development of a country depends on access to drinking water, sanitation and hygiene and sanitation contributes to dignity and social development' (UN Water, 2008). Because 'Clean water and sanitation are among the most powerful drivers for human development. They extend opportunity, enhance dignity and help to create a virtuous cycle of improving health and rising wealth' (HDR, 2006:5). Thus, hygiene and cleanliness are part and parcel of every human being and 'everyone has the right to an adequate standard of living for themselves and their families, including adequate food, clothing, housing, water and sanitation' (UN Habitat, II). Further, access to sanitation has the potential to catalyse development and improve the quality of life by (1) ensuring the health of citizens and limiting the burden of treating preventable illness, (2) increasing access to education for all, (3) promoting economic growth in the poorest countries of the world (UN Habitat, 2008).

But the most indispensable need has been given least importance by some people on this earth. It is also distressing to trace that 'water and sanitation is the poor cousin of international development cooperation. While the international community has mobilised to an impressive degree in preparing to respond to the potential threat of an avian flu epidemic, it turns a blind eye to an actual epidemic that afflicts hundreds of millions of people every day' (*ibid.)*.

Therefore, overcoming the crisis in water and sanitation is one of the great human development challenges of the early 21st century (HDR, 2006). Delivering clean water, removing wastewater and providing sanitation are three of the most basic problems of the most developing countries of the world. Today, some 1.1 billion people in developing countries have inadequate access to water, and 2.6 billion lack basic sanitation (HDR, *ibid*.). Further, this Report stated that 'the US National Aeronautics and Space Administration will launch the Jupiter Icy Moons Project. Using technology now under development, a spacecraft will be dispatched to orbit three of Jupiter's moons to investigate the composition of the vast saltwater lakes beneath their ice surfaces and to determine whether the conditions for life exist. The irony of humanity spending billions of dollars in exploring the potential for life on the other planets would be powerful and tragic, if at the same time we allow the destruction of life and human capabilities on planet Earth for want of demanding technologies: the infrastructure to deliver clean water and sanitation to all. Providing a glass of clean water and a toilet may be challenging, but it is not rocket science (HDR, 2006:4).

Subsequently, 'Not having access' to water and sanitation is a polite euphemism for a form of deprivation that threatens life, destroys opportunity and undermines human dignity. Being without water means that people resort to ditches, rivers and lakes polluted with human, or animal excrement, or used by animals. It also means not having sufficient water to meet even the most basic human needs (HDR:5).

It is heartbreaking to examine that most of the people in rural areas of developing countries are ill with basic requirements. Consequently, they are prone to a number of diseases and health complications. Poor and marginalised groups are the worst sufferers of health and hygiene. Deprivation of water and sanitation has some multiplier effects. Some of them are: some 1.8 million child deaths each year as result of diarrhoea; the loss of 443 million school days each year from water-related illness; close to half of all people in developing countries suffering at any given time from a health problem caused by water and sanitation deficits; millions of women spending several hours a day collecting water.

## India and Sanitation

It is depressing that India's Total Sanitation Campaign (TSC) is half full and half empty. The second most populous country has failed miserably in fulfilling most of the basic needs of her citizens. It is painful that more than half of the Indians are struggling everyday to have safe drinking water and sanitation, primary education and health. Availability and accessibility of water and sanitation influence most the daily aspects of life. India's target oriented programmes have become futile in reaching the needy population. In fact, majority of Indians have given least importance to sanitation. People hardly demand sanitation as their right. Indians are waiting since Independence to have independence in the use of sanitation. It is extremely regretful that 'India is losing billions of dollars each year because of poor sanitation. Illnesses are costly to families, and to the economy as whole in terms of productivity losses and expenditures on medicines, health care and funerals' (UN-Water, 2008).

In more than six decades of Independence, our country has achieved about half of the sanitation coverage. Therefore, in simple mathematical calculation we require another five to six decades to reach total sanitation. While some states have already achieved the target and some are in near position to achieve it. However, according to WHO and UNICEF's Joint Monitoring Programme for Water Supply and Sanitation (JMPWSS), states such as Madhya Pradesh and Orissa will achieve this target only in the next century. Further, 17 states including Kerala, Haryana, Meghalaya, Himachal Pradesh, Punjab and most Union territories already reached the MDG target while Assam, Andhra Pradesh will achieve it in the next 10 years. States like Karnataka, Maharashtra, Tamil Nadu and Chhattisgarh will reach the MDG target in the next 25 years. It is very disheartening to note that Madhya Pradesh is expected to reach the goal in 2105 and Orissa only in 2160 going by the present state of sanitation and water facilities. In his latest Census highlights, the Registrar General and Census Commissioner, India, *Census* of India, 2011 revealed the availability of household amenities in India. Accordingly, 51.7 per cent of households do not have toilet facility within their premises. Wide disparities also found in the amenities. For instance, only 5.5 per cent of households of Kerala do not have latrine facility within their premises. But 80.4 per cent households of Odisha, 79.4 per cent of Jharkhand, 78.2 per cent of Chhattisgarh, 76.3 per cent of Bihar, 68.7 per cent of Madhya Pradesh do not possess toilet facility within their premises. Further, 59.4 per cent of households of India have bathing facility within their premises.

In this background, in the present study an attempt has been made to examine the status of sanitation and other related facility in Karnataka state.

**Sanitation in Karnataka**

Karnataka is a state located on south-west India. It has a geographical areas of 1,91,976 square kilometres. It covers 5.83 per cent of the total geographical area of our country. Thus, it is the eighth largest Indian state by area and ninth largest state by population. The state has three main geographical zones: (1) the coastal region of Karavali; (2) the hilly Malenadu region comprising the Western Ghats; and (3) the Bayaluseeme region comprising the plains of Deccan Plateau. In Karnataka 83 per cent of them are Hindus, 12.4 per cent are Muslims, four per cent are Christians, 0.8 per cent are Jains and 0.7 per cent are Buddhists.

**Table 1. A Profile of Karnataka, 2011**

| | |
|---|---|
| Population of Karnataka | 6,11,30,704 |
| Male population | 3,10,57,742 |
| Female population | 3,00,72, 963 |
| Density | 319 |
| Literacy | 75.61 |
| Male Literacy | 82.84 |
| Female Literacy | 68.45 |
| Literates | 4,10,29,323 |
| Illiterates | 1,32, 45,580 |
| Illiterates (Males) | 47,21,430 |
| Illiterates (Females) | 85,24,150 |
| Sex Ratio | 968 |

At the start of the 21st century, the violation of the human right to clean water and sanitation is destroying human potential on an epic scale. In today's increasingly prosperous and interconnected world more children die for want of clean water and a toilet than from almost any other cause. Exclusion from clean water and basic sanitation destroys more lives than any war, or terrorist act (HDR, 2006). Even though Karnataka claims, in IT and technology it is one of the developed states, its position in basic human services is lagging behind considerably, especially in water, sanitation, primary health, electricity and roads. This is evident from the information provided in Table 2.

**Table 2. Availability of Toilet Facility in Karnataka**

| *Region* | *Total Households* | *Number of Households having Latrine Facility with the Premises* | *Number of Households not having Latrine Facility within the Premises* | *No Latrine within Premises* | |
|---|---|---|---|---|---|
| | | | | *Alternative Source* | |
| | | | | *Public Latrine* | *Open* |
| Rural | 78,64,196 (100.00) | 22,34,534 (28.42%) | 56,29,662 (71.58%) | 2,72,968 (4.84%) | 53,56,694 (95.15%) |
| Urban | 53, 15, 715 (100.00) | 45,14,862 (84.93%) | 8,00,853 (15.06%) | 2,31,249 (28.87%) | 5,69,604 (71.12%) |
| **Total** | **1,31, 79, 911 (100.00)** | **67,49,396 (51.21%)** | **64,30,515 (48.79%)** | **5,04,217 (7.84%)** | **59,26,298 (92.15%)** |

*Source:* HH-Series Tables, Census of India, 2011.

It is evident from Table 2 that almost three-fourth (71.58 per cent) of rural households do not have toilet facility within its premises. It is disgusting to view that almost half of the households in Karnataka lack toilet facility within their easy reach. Therefore, around three crore people of Karnataka do not have toilet facility within their premises. As a result 92.15 per cent of them have to defecate in open places. Further, information provided in Table 3 reveals that only 22.0 per cent of the rural people have improved sanitation facility in their houses.

**Table 3. A Brief outline of Sanitation Facility in Karnataka**

| *Sl. No.* | *Sanitation Facility* | *Rural* | *Urban* | *Total* |
|---|---|---|---|---|
| 1. | Improved sanitation | 22.0 | 59.3 | 32.4 |
| 2. | Flush to sewer/septic/pit | 20.3 | 56.3 | 30.4 |
| 3. | Not improved | 40.7 | 78.0 | 67.7 |
| 4. | No toilet/open space | 76.8 | 26.3 | 62.7 |

*Source:* DLHS-3, Karnataka.

## Bathing Facility and Drainage Connectivity

Gloomy picture can also be seen in the facility of bathing and drainage connectivity. Almost one fourth of them do not possess this facility within their house or premises. It is also perturbing to underscore that 3.60 per cent of the urban households in the state do not have bathing facility within their premises. Most of the poor slum dwellers face this indispensable requirement of routine life (Table 4).

**Table 4. Households Having Bathing Facility**

| *Region* | *Total Households* | *Number of Households having Bathroom facility with the premises* | *Enclosure Without Roof* | *Number of households not having Bathroom facility within the premises* |
|---|---|---|---|---|
| Rural | 78,64,196 (100.00) | 49,85,101 (63.38%) | 12,63,205 (16.06) | 16,15,890 (20.55%) |
| Urban | 53, 15, 715 (100.00) | 48,74,674 (91.70%) | 2,49,269 (4.69%) | 1,91,772 (3.60%) |
| **Total** | **1,31, 79, 911 (100.00)** | **98,59,775 (74.80%)** | **15,12,474 (11.47%)** | **18,07,662 (13.71%)** |

*Source:* HH-Series Tables, Census of India, 2011

Information about drainage connectivity reveals that 'Open Indian Style' is visible in the state. Majority of rural households (87.26 per cent) do not have connectivity to their drainage. It is alarming to notice that only 12.61 per cent of urban households in Karnataka have closed drainage facility to their houses. And roughly the same percentage of households manages without any drainage facility (Table 5).

**Table 5. Drainage Connectivity for Waste Water Outlet**

| *Sl. No.* | *Region* | *Closed Drainage* | *Open Drainage* | *No Drainage* |
|---|---|---|---|---|
| 1. | Rural | 30,05,430 (87.39%) | 29,11,757 (63.82%) | 45,18,789 (87.26%) |
| 2. | Urban | 4,33,650 (12.61%) | 16,51,008 (36.18%) | 6,59,277 (12.74%) |
| | **Total** | **34,39,080 (100.00)** | **45,62,765 (100.00)** | **51,78,066 (100.00)** |

## Removal of Human Waste

One of the most hazardous aspects of human social life is removal of human waste/excreta by using brooms, tin plates and baskets from dry latrine and carrying it to disposal grounds some distance away. It is displeasing that the Census 2011 has given information about night-soil disposition in Karnataka. Development in science and technology is also not in a position to eradicate this horrendous task to night-soil removal by human. In fact, in 1970s itself the state of Karnataka passed a law to ban manual scavenging. It is terrible to know that still people are utilising the help of human only to remove human excreta in Karnataka. 7,740 cases have been reported in Karnataka as per Census 2011 (Table 6).

**Table 6. Night Soil Disposition in Karnataka**

| *Sl. No.* | *Region* | *Night Soil Disposed into Open Drain* | *Night Soil Removed by Human* | *Night Soil Serviced by Animal* |
|---|---|---|---|---|
| 1. | Rural | 9,328 (15.10%) | 2,052 (26.51%) | 13,388 (46.18%) |
| 2. | Urban | 52,474 (84.90%) | 5,688 (73.49%) | 15,607 (53.82%) |
| | **Total** | **61,802 (100.00)** | **7,740 (100.00)** | **28,995 (100.00)** |

*Source:* HH-Series Tables, Census of India, 2011.

Removal of night, soil by humans is found more in southern part of Karnataka. This problem is more found in capital of the Karnataka state Bangalore urban (3776) and then Bangalore rural (528) (Table 7).

**Table 7. Percentage of Night Soil Removed by Human by Districts**

| *Sl. No.* | *District* | *Night Soil Removed by Human* |
|---|---|---|
| 1. | Belgaum | 343 |
| 2. | Bagalkot | 167 |
| 3. | Bijapur | 109 |
| 4. | Gulbarga | 32 |
| 5. | Bidar | 21 |
| 6. | Raichur | 95 |
| 7. | Koppal | 0 |
| 8. | Gadag | 0 |
| 9. | Dharwad | 173 |
| 10. | Haveri | 229 |
| 11. | Bellary | 11 |
| 12 | Uttar Kannada | 0 |
| 13. | Yadgir | 0 |
| | **North Karnataka** | **1180 (15.24%)** |
| 14. | Chitradurga | 123 |
| 15. | Shimoga | 129 |
| 16 | Davangere | 101 |
| 17. | Udupi | 0 |
| 18. | Chikmaglur | 119 |
| 19. | Tumkur | 325 |
| 20. | Kolar | 543 |
| 21. | Bangalore | 3,776 |
| 22. | Bangalore Rural | 528 |
| 23. | Mandya | 167 |
| 24. | Hassan | 108 |
| 25. | Dakshina Kannada | 12 |
| 26. | Kodagu | 46 |
| 28. | Mysore | 19 |
| 28. | Chamarajanagar | 16 |
| 29. | Ramanagar | 299 |
| 30. | Chikkaballapur | 249 |
| | **South Karnataka** | **6560 (84.76%)** |
| | **Karnataka** | **7740 (100.00)** |

*Source:* HH-Series Tables, Census of India, 2011.

## Magnitude of Sanitation Deprivation in Karnataka

One of the perceptible problems pertaining to hygiene in the state is the continuation of rural and urban disparities. Whereas most of the urban areas inevitably have done to maintain cleanliness and hygiene, villages in Karnataka suffer from these provisions.

**Table 8. Sanitation Facility Karnataka**

| *Sl. No.* | *Sanitation Facility* | *Rural* | *Urban* | *Total* |
|---|---|---|---|---|
| 1. | Improved sanitation | 22.0 | 59.3 | 32.4 |
| 2. | Flush to sewer/septic/pit | 20.3 | 56.3 | 30.4 |
| 3. | Not improved | 78.0 | 40.7 | 67.7 |
| 4. | No toilet/open space | 76.8 | 26.3 | 62.7 |

*Source:* DLHS-3 in Karnataka.

## Regional Deprivations in Health and Hygiene

Economically, Karnataka is one of the developed states in India. This state is known for its progress in IT/BT sector. But this development largely confine to Bangalore only. Regional disparities are completely

**Table 9. Availability of Toilet Facility in Gulbarga Division**

| *Division/ Districts* | *Region* | *Total Households* | *Number of Households having latrine facility with the premises* | *Number of households not having latrine facility within the premises* |
|---|---|---|---|---|
| Bidar | Rural | 2,37,380 | 20,983 | 2,16,397 |
| | Urban | 76,141 | 51,822 | 24,319 |
| | Total | 3,13,521 | 72,805 | 2,40,716 |
| Raichur | Rural | 2,64,274 | 26,397 | 2,37,877 |
| | Urban | 95,063 | 47,929 | 47,134 |
| | Total | 3,59,337 | 74,326 | 2,85,011 |

*contd..*

*contd..*

| *Division/ Districts* | *Region* | *Total Households* | *Number of Households having latrine facility with the premises* | *Number of households not having latrine facility within the premises* |
|---|---|---|---|---|
| Koppal | Rural | 2,13,217 | 25,565 | 1,87,652 |
| | Urban | 46,179 | 22,366 | 23,813 |
| | Total | 2,59,396 | 47,931 | 2,11,465 |
| Gulbarga | Rural | 3,11,531 | 13,911 | 2,97,620 |
| | Urban | 1,53,714 | 1,04,881 | 48,833 |
| | Total | 4,65,245 | 1,18,792 | 3,46,453 |
| Yadgir | Rural | 1,61,665 | 6,938 | 1,54,727 |
| | Urban | 38,759 | 15,585 | 23,174 |
| | Total | 2,00,424 | 22,523 | 1,77,901 |
| Bellary | Rural | 2,91,383 | 35,296 | 2,56,087 |
| | Urban | 1,90,321 | 1,20,814 | 69,507 |
| | Total | 4,81,704 | 1,56,110 | 3,25,594 |
| **Gulbarga Division(HK Region)** | **Total** | **20,79,627 (100.00)** | **4,92,487 (23.68%)** | **15,87,140 (76.32%)** |

obvious in the state not only in economic field but also in human development aspects. Regional deprivations are also seen in the availability of sanitation facility. The problem of sanitation is not uniformly distributed in the state. Some districts have achieved almost complete sanitation, others performed dismally. For administrative purpose Karnataka state has been divided into four divisions. They are in Northern Karnataka, Gulbarga and Belgaum and in South Karnataka, Mysore and Bangalore. Information about Division wise disparities in sanitation same has been given in following Tables (*Source*: HH-Series Tables, Census of India, 2011).

**Table 10. Availability of Toilet Facility in Belgaum Division.**

| *District* | *Region* | *Total Households* | *Number of Households having Latrine Facility with the Premises* | *Number of Households not having Latrine Facility within the Premises* |
|---|---|---|---|---|
| Belgaum | Rural | 7,08,069 | 1,31,009 | 5,77,060 |
| | Urban | 2, 55, 756 | 1,85,216 | 70,540 |
| | Total | 9,63,825 | 3,16,225 | 6,47,600 |
| Bagalkot | Rural | 2,38,746 | 17,187 | 2,21,559 |
| | Urban | 1,16,631 | 49,626 | 67,005 |
| | Total | 3,55,377 | 66,813 | 2,88,564 |
| Bijapur | Rural | 3,07,984 | 15,516 | 2,92,468 |
| | Urban | 97,092 | 57,784 | 39,308 |
| | Total | 4,05,076 | 73,300 | 3,31,776 |
| Gadag | Rural | 1,37,799 | 12,732 | 1,25,067 |
| | Urban | 77,803 | 32,936 | 44,867 |
| | Total | 2,15,602 | 45,668 | 1,69,934 |
| Dharwad | Rural | 1,57,960 | 36,449 | 1,21,511 |
| | Urban | 2,14,094 | 1,75,642 | 38,452 |
| | Total | 3,72,054 | 2,12,091 | 1,59, 963 |
| Haveri | Rural | 2,54,181 | 71,774 | 1,82,407 |
| | Urban | 71,275 | 49,646 | 21,629 |
| | Total | 3,25,456 | 1,21,420 | 2,04,036 |
| Uttar Kannada | Rural | 2,26,803 | 1,14,752 | 1,12,051 |
| | Urban | 93,109 | 75,091 | 18,018 |
| | Total | 3,19,912 | 1,89,843 | 1,30,069 |
| **Belgaum Division** | **Total** | **29,57,302 (100.00)** | **10,25,360 (34.67%)** | **19,31,942 (65.33%)** |

*Source:* HH-Series Tables, Census of India, 2011.

**Table 11. Availability of Toilet Facility in Bangalore Division**

| *District* | *Region* | *Total House-holds* | *Number of Households having latrine facility with the premises* | *Number of households not having latrine facility within the premises* |
|---|---|---|---|---|
| Chitradurga | Rural | 2,82,019 | 53,839 | 2,28,180 |
| | Urban | 72,124 | 53,303 | 18,821 |
| | Total | 3,54,143 | 1,07,142 | 2,47,001 |
| Davangere | Rural | 2,72,929 | 81,363 | 1,91,566 |
| | Urban | 1,31,911 | 1,06,683 | 25,228 |
| | Total | 4,04,840 | 1,88,046 | 2,16,794 |
| Tumkur | Rural | 4,95,885 | 90,868 | 4,05,017 |
| | Urban | 1,40,509 | 1,15,953 | 24,556 |
| | Total | 6,36,394 | 2,06,821 | 4,29,573 |
| Bangalore | Rural | 2,07,628 | 1,55,366 | 52,262 |
| | Urban | 21,69,428 | 20,99,233 | 70,195 |
| | Total | 23,77,056 | 22,54,599 | 1,22,457 |
| Kolar | Rural | 2,26,245 | 57,664 | 1,68,581 |
| | Urban | 1,04,745 | 84,011 | 20,734 |
| | Total | 3,30,990 | 1,41,675 | 1,89,315 |
| Chikkaballapur | Rural | 2.20,309 | 50,677 | 1,69,632 |
| | Urban | 62,002 | 52,280 | 9,722 |
| | Total | 2,82,311 | 1,02,957 | 1,79,354 |
| Bangalore Rural | Rural | 1,62,398 | 1,22,643 | 39,755 |
| | Urban | 62,347 | 56,946 | 5,401 |
| | Total | 2,24,745 | 1,79,589 | 45,156 |
| Ramanagara | Rural | 2,00,171 | 56,142 | 1,44,029 |
| | Urban | 59,623 | 52,749 | 6,874 |
| | Total | 2,59,794 | 1,08,891 | 1,50,903 |
| Shimoga | Rural | 2,57,060 | 1,58,828 | 98,232 |
| | Urban | 1,45,079 | 1,27,301 | 17,778 |
| | Total | 4,02,139 | 2,86,129 | 1,16,010 |
| **Bangalore Division** | **Total** | **52,72,412 (100.00)** | **35,75,849 (67.82%)** | **16,96,563 (32.17%)** |

*Source:* HH-Series Tables, Census of India, 2011.

**Table 12. Availability of Toilet Facility in Mysore Division**

| *District* | *Region* | *Total House-holds* | *Number of House-holds having Latrine Facility with the Premises* | *Number of House-holds not having Latrine Facility within the Premises* |
|---|---|---|---|---|
| Udupi | Rural | 1,74,548 | 1,45,909 | 28,639 |
| | Urban | 71,765 | 68,899 | 2,866 |
| | Total | 2,46,313 | 2,14,808 | 31,505 |
| Chikmaglur | Rural | 2,15,334 | 1,16,556 | 98,778 |
| | Urban | 56,839 | 50,813 | 6,026 |
| | Total | 2,72,173 | 1,67,369 | 1,04,804 |
| Mandya | Rural | 3,54,049 | 97,526 | 2,56,523 |
| | Urban | 72,529 | 62,292 | 10,237 |
| | Total | 4,26,578 | 1,59,818 | 2,66,760 |
| Hassan | Rural | 3,39,911 | 90,891 | 2,49,020 |
| | Urban | 89,381 | 80,321 | 9,060 |
| | Total | 4,29,292 | 1,71,212 | 2,58,080 |
| D. Kannada | Rural | 2,20,806 | 1,94,578 | 26,228 |
| | Urban | 2,04,485 | 1,99,491 | 4,994 |
| | Total | 4,25,291 | 3,94,069 | 31,222 |
| Mysore | Rural | 4,01,655 | 1,08,475 | 2,93,183 |
| | Urban | 2,86,767 | 2,70,028 | 16,739 |
| | Total | 6,88,422 | 3,78,503 | 3,09,919 |
| Kodagu | Rural | 1,18,509 | 93,421 | 25,088 |
| | Urban | 19,794 | 19,205 | 589 |
| | Total | 1,38,303 | 1,12,626 | 25,677 |
| Chamarajnagar | Rural | 2,03,748 | 31,279 | 1,72,469 |
| | Urban | 40,450 | 26,016 | 14,434 |
| | Total | 2,44,198 | 57,295 | 1,86,903 |
| **Mysore Division** | **Total** | **28,70,570 (100.0)** | **16,55,700 (57.57%)** | **12,14,870 (42.32%)** |

*Source:* HH-Series Tables, Census of India, 2011.

It is evident from the Tables that availability of toilet facility is very poor in Gulbarga division. Only 23.68 per cent of the households possess toilet facility within their premises. More than 90 per cent of the rural parts of this region lack this basic facility. Some districts like Bangalore (94.84 per cent), Dakshina Kannada (92.65 per cent) households have better access to toilet facility in their premises, whereas Kodagu and Udupi have about 80 per cent access to toilet facilities.

## Missing Toilets in Karnataka

One of the major problems of unsanitary conditions in Karnataka is the increasing number of missing toilets at the time of physical verification. It was seen from the reliable sources that many toilets have been sanctioned to the people of BPL families with the provision of subsidies from the government. But at the time actual physical verification, most of the sanctioned toilets were found only on official records without any construction or structure. This was also raised by the Central government. The Union Ministry of Drinking Water and Sanitation (MDWS) has asked government of Karnataka as well as some other states to find out the reasons behind the enormous disparity in the claims of Karnataka government on rural sanitation coverage and recent data published by the census 2011. Though the Government of Karnataka claimed to have covered 63.87 per cent rural households under the Total Sanitation Coverage till 2011-12, the census figures showed that it reached only 31.90 per cent in the villages across the state.

## Why don't People Use Toilets?

Arghyam, a public charitable trust conducted ASHWAS participatory survey to ascertain the status of household water and sanitation in rural Karnataka in the year 2008-09. This Trust was set up with an endowment from Rohini Nilekani. Since 2005, Arghyam has been supporting efforts to address equity and sustainability in access to water and sanitation for all citizens. This survey also reported that 72 per cent of people of Karnataka do not have access to toilets, 21 per cent have toilets outside their house and only seven per cent have inside their house. ASHWAS listed some of the reasons for not constructing toilets in Karnataka. They are given in Table 13. Two-thirds of the people stated financial problem and about 29 per cent were not in position to construct the toilet for want of space in their house.

**Table 13. Reasons for not constructing Toilets**

| *Sl. No.* | *Reasons* | *Percentage* |
|---|---|---|
| 1. | Financial Problem | 59.00 |
| 2. | No Space | 29.00 |
| 3. | Don't want/not a priority | 06.00 |
| 4. | Cultural and Religious Reasons | 03.00 |
| 5. | Psychological Reasons | 03.00 |

ASHWAS, 2008-09.

ASHWAS Report also examined the problems people face during open defecation. People remarked that due to open defecation they can defecate only during late evenings or night. 21 per cent of them opined that it is unsafe to defecate openly and also they feel embarrassed during defecation.

**Table 14. Problems of Open Defecation (OD)**

| *Sl. No.* | *Problems of OD* | *Percentage* |
|---|---|---|
| 1. | Possible to go only in dawn/dark | 26.00 |
| 2. | Embarrassment | 21.00 |
| 3. | Unsafe | 21.00 |
| 4. | Uncomfortable | 16.00 |
| 5. | Unhealthy | 12.00 |
| 6. | Water Problem | 04.00 |

ASHWAS, 2008-09.

## Reasons for Backwardness in Sanitation

According to Human Development Report, 2006, six interlocking barriers come in the way of providing sanitation. These could be aptly applied to India and Karnataka. They are: national policy, behaviour, poverty, gender and supply barriers.

## The National Policy Barrier

Effective national policies are conspicuously absent for sanitation than for water. The state of a country's sanitation may shape its prospects for human development. And yet sanitation seldom figures prominently on the national political agenda (HDR, 2006). Karnataka state evolved various water and sanitation programmes. Prominent among them are: Swachcha Gram Yojana; Nirmal Gram Puraskar; Total Sanitation Campaign (TSC); Sachetena; Suvarna Jal; Swajaldhara; Jal Nirmal; ARWSP/National Rural Water Supply Programme. Even with these national level and state level sanitation programmes and policies, it has not been possible to achieve at least half of rural sanitation facilities in the state.

## The Behaviour Barrier

Attitude of the people matters most in the utilisation and provision of sanitary facilities. Toilet facility is not at all a priority to most of the villagers. Often we find people resorting to using/misusing only public roads instead of their own personal spheres. Further, participatory research exercises show that people tend to attach a higher priority to water than to sanitation and lack of clean water is a more immediate threat of life than the absence of a toilet (HDR, 2006). It is not enough if one or two households construct the toilet. Entire villagers should come forward to change their attitude towards age-old behaviour.

### The Poverty Barrier

Use of toilets is relatively less among poor than rich. Poverty remains a major constraint in gaining access to health and hygiene. Nearly 1.4 billion people without access to sanitation live on less than two dollar a day. For most of them, even low-cost improved technology may be beyond financial reach (HDR).

### The Gender Barrier

Women are scarcely consulted before evolving policies and programmes. In fact, satisfactory sanitation facilities are more required for women than men. Toilet is a topmost priority to women and girls than men and boys. But people attach least priority in involving women in decision making process.

### The Supply Barrier

Turning from demand to supply shows that progress is impeded not just by the absence of affordable sanitation technology, but also by the oversupply of inappropriate technologies, leading to mismatch between what people want and what governments have offered (HDR, *ibid*).

On the whole, progress made in hygiene and cleanliness is far from satisfactory in Karnataka. Poor implementation of sanitation programme, attitude of the public and public servants come in the way of total sanitation programme. There is an urgent need for social marketing and sustainable sanitation approach to the state. Social marketing focuses on influencing human behaviour to accept healthy behaviour. Sustainable sanitation highlights that in order to be sustainable, a sanitation approach is required to be socially suitable and economically feasible. Sustainable sanitation is participatory based approach. It differs primarily from the current conventional approach of wastewater management. The new approach not only recognises technology, but also social, environmental and economic aspects. It adopts holistic rather than top-down approach.

## References

ASHWAS: A Survey of Household Water and Sanitation Karnataka-2008-09, Arghyam, Bangalore.

C. Chandramouli (2011): Houses, Household Amenities and Assets among Female Headed Households, Highlights from census 2011, Registrar General and Census Commissioner, India, Census of India, 2011, Censusindia. gov. in. 2011.

District Level Household and Facility Survey (2007-08) Karnataka, (2010), IIPS, Mumbai.

Human Development Report 2006: Beyond Scarcity: Power, poverty and the global water crisis, UNDP, New York.

India's Sanitation for All: How to Make it Happen: Water for All Series 18 (2009), Asian Development Bank, Philippines.

Karnataka: Human Development Report 2005, (2006), Planning and Statistics Department, Government of Karnataka.

National Family Health Survey (NFHS-3), Karnataka 2005-06 (2008), IIPS, Mumbai.

Sanitation: A Human Rights Imperative, UN-HABITAT (2008), Geneva.

UN–Water (2008), Tackling a Global crisis: International Year of Sanitation, in India's Sanitation for All: How to Make it Happen: Water for All Series 18 (2009), Asian Development Bank, Philippines.

# 12

# Social Deprivation and Scavengers: A Case of Jammu City

*Vishav Raksha*

The present paper is based on the research study conducted among the scavengers residing and working in Jammu city. The interviews were conducted across the different religious groups they belong to, the different workplace they work at, namely, municipality, other than municipality and the private households, both male and female scavengers keeping in view that women work as scavengers in large number and also across different age groups. The paper highlights the kind of social deprivation scavengers face, because of the occupation they are involved in. Scavengers remain marginalised in Indian society even today despite the constitutional provisions which direct the state to promote their various interests including economic, educational and social interests. They remain marginalised because their community is still predominantly employed to carry out the country's basic sanitary services. While their economic and social problems are shared by other scheduled castes, it is the 'unclean and polluting nature' of their sanitary work that marginalises the scavengers. The nature of their employment causes even other lower castes to discriminate against them.

Social deprivation is the reduction or prevention of culturally normal interaction between an individual and the rest of society. This social deprivation is included in a broad network of correlated factors that contribute to social exclusion; these factors include mental illness, poverty, poor education and low socio-economic status. In Indian context, the core features of social exclusion include the denial of equal opportunities imposed by certain groups of society upon others which leads to inability of an individual to participate in the basic political, economic and social functioning of the society. Two defining characteristics of exclusion are particularly relevant, namely, the deprivation caused through exclusion (or denial of equal opportunity) in multiple spheres—showing its multidimensionality. Second feature is that, it is embedded in the societal relations and societal institutions—the process through which individuals or groups are wholly or partially excluded from full participation in the society in which they live (Hann, 1997).

The process of social exclusion has kept the poor, marginalised and deprived groups and communities away from the benefits of economic, social and human development. This sharply highlights the persistence of widespread inequality. India's low level of human development also reflects the extensive nature of human deprivations, suggesting a denial of rights and the absence of freedoms along critical dimensions of human life. Illiteracy, ill health, malnutrition, insufficient earnings, social exclusion and lack of decision-making—all these have to be viewed as a 'set of un-freedoms constituting human poverty' (Sen, 1999).

In India, social exclusion has been predominantly used in understanding caste-based discrimination. Caste-based occupational groups in India, like that of scavengers (including manual scavengers) constitute one such socially, economically, psychologically and politically marginalised section of the society. Excluded groups are often faced with double and triple discrimination. A *dalit* or *adivasi* woman faces discrimination on account of gender as well as caste, leading to increased vulnerability and exclusion from the process of development. For example, the male literacy rate in India is 82.14 per cent compared to the much lower female literacy rate at 65.46 per cent. This disparity is in itself alarming. However, it is the low rate of literacy among the SC and ST females at 41.9 per cent and 47.8 per cent respectively, which reflects the double disadvantage faced by the *dalit* and *adivasi* women. Similarly, specific *dalit* communities (for instance, communities involved in manual scavenging) are comparatively worse off than other *dalit* communities. It is, therefore, that this paper takes the scavenger groups to illustrate the point that specific *dalit* communities (as the scavengers) are completely worse off than other *dalit* communities, thus pointing to the fact that some excluded groups are marginalised even within the broad category of socially excluded and socially deprived groups and have much poorer developmental indice.

Scavengers are predominantly found in cities and towns, as the need for a special caste to remove night-soil and clean latrines is minimal in rural areas where villagers prefer to defecate in the fields. Officials in the 20th century have tended to use the term *bhangi* as a label for scavengers and sweepers, throughout the country. Although the name *bhangi* is now used for a widespread *jati* in Northern India including Jammu and Kashmir, but it is more associated with the occupational description. As scavenger is seen as someone who cleans latrines and removes nightsoil, so it becomes difficult to differentiate the scavengers and *bhangis*. More so, because even within one family, several members may be employed as municipal sweepers who clean roads and remove garbage, while others work as scavengers cleaning public and private latrines.

*Bhangis* have an occupation that has remained hereditary, because their tasks are dirty and they have to work in appalling conditions, especially during the monsoon season. The removal of nightsoil and refuse is viewed by the Hindu society as a very degrading occupation which constitutes a permanent state of pollution. As a consequence, scavenger and sweeper communities have been treated as untouchable, unapproachable and unseeable.

*Bhangis* also face isolation from other low caste groups. Owen Lynch (1969) in his study of the low caste *jatavas* in Agra noted that there was a definite opposition to marriage with *bhangis* which was only qualified by such provisos as the boy being well educated or having other qualifications. For *jatavas*, it was a case of 'marrying down' to associate with *bhangis*. In U.P., the *chamras* avoid social contact with the *bhangis*. In the old quarter of Jaipur, neighbourhoods can be found that are split down the middle. On one side of the road are the *meenas*, low caste Hindus and Muslims, and on the other are the scavengers.

For the present study on which this paper is based, out of the estimated universe of 4000 scavengers in Jammu city, it was decided to have five per cent sample for the purpose. This meant taking up a sample of 200 scavengers. The sample was selected keeping the strata in mind. The sample comprised of 78 men and 122 women as more women are in this job. Keeping the ratio of different religious communities, namely, Christians, Hindus and Muslims and the proportion of their participation in this work, 96 Christians, 82 Hindus and 22 Muslims were selected. As the age was divided in three groups namely, 18-30 years, 30-45 years and 45 years and above, the sample comprised of 71, 81 and 48 respectively. Finally, the fourth stratum of occupation was kept in mind and the sample selected was 90 who worked with municipality, 73 who worked in other than municipality organisations and 37 who worked on private basis.

## Scavengers in Jammu

Scavengers in Jammu trace their origin depending on the particular regional group that they belong to. They are mainly divided into two groups—one that traces its origin to regions like Sialkot which is now in Pakistan and they identify themselves as scavengers who belong to Jammu as they were present in the state much before the other group was brought. The other group is of the scavengers belonging to Punjab who were brought to Jammu in 1957 by the then Prime Minister of State of Jammu and Kashmir, Bakshi Ghulam Mohammad. The scavengers of the first group had gone on a strike and to handle the crisis situation, arisen out of that strike, these scavengers from Punjab were brought in. Initially, there were 70 families who were called to do the cleaning jobs. They were given the permit to enter the state and were provided housing facilities and were allowed only to do the cleaning jobs. Even now they have the right to do and apply only for scavenging job under CSR (Civil Services Regulation) Rule 35(B) as they are not considered the permanent residents of this state. To apply for any other type of employment, one needs to have a permanent resident's certificate because of Article 370 in this state.

Thus, one actually witnesses a clear-cut bifurcation of scavengers in Jammu city into two groups. One has a claim of belonging to the state, because its members have been born and brought up in Jammu and has a permanent resident's certificate. The other call themselves Punjabis, but also claim now to be people living since 1957 and their children now being born and brought up in Jammu. They do not have permanent resident's certificate thus losing their claim of belonging to the state and hence losing out on all other avenues of mobility and growth. Their children are not able to continue and get into higher studies. And some who have finished their high or higher secondary schooling are not able to get any state service employment.

Most of the scavengers belonging to first group are Christians and some are *balmikis*. These Christians are the ones who had converted themselves years ago when the missionaries came to Jammu and started schools and church. Majority of the second group of scavengers are Hindu–*balmikis* who are also known and called as *chuhras*. *Chuhra* is the caste name under which they fall under scheduled caste category. They speak Punjabi and have a long association with their Punjabi roots including, *Adh Dharm* movement. Their main concern is to get the permanent residence certificate, lack of which has deprived them of many opportunities which are available to their other fellow scavengers.

There is also a small third group comprising of Sunni Muslims who belong to Jammu and most of whom have migrated from Sunderbani area of Jammu division to the Jammu city. They do not associate themselves with the other two groups as one does not find them living in any of the localities where Christian and *balmiki* scavengers live. There is no inter-religious marriage or any other kind of association except the occupational similarity.

In Jammu city, there are scavengers working across both formal and informal setup. Formal setup includes most of the cleaning work done in public sphere. One of the main public agencies taking care of the scavenging and cleaning work is Jammu municipality. Along with municipality there are other public agencies like Banks, government offices, other offices, schools, hotels where work comes under public and formal category, but it is other than municipality work. In Jammu city, most of the houses have flush wet latrines but there are some houses within the old city, where there are still old dry latrines in use. In both these cases, the scavengers are employed to do the cleaning work on the private basis. Where there are wet latrines, women scavengers are employed to clean toilets clubbing it with the work of sweeping and mopping the house, washing clothes and to some extent even cleaning utensils. Where there are dry latrines, there are Indian flush seats used wherein water is poured and the scavenger cleans it off with a broom in the drain.

Social deprivation of this community can be broadly discussed around the network of conditions in which scavengers live, exist, work and survive in Jammu city. The conditions range right from occupational situation to different and limited alternatives of livelihood available to them, from the modern form of untouchability to the problem of social acceptance in other jobs and the kind of other jobs available to them. This also includes the educational opportunities for their children to the unclean unhygienic working conditions they have. One would realise that there are a number of reasons for them to still remain marginalised, deprived and excluded.

### Occupation and Unclean Work

There are a good number of young people doing this job as it is very difficult to change this profession. There are considerable number of old people who have spent their life doing this job and who want their children to take up other jobs, as they have experienced tough situation because of being scavengers. The young people are opting for this not out of choice but because of non-availability and non-acceptance in other areas of works. The attitude of the respondents towards the mobility out of their present jobs was equally divided. The negative attitude of half of the respondents could be attributed to the strong caste consciousness that they have imbibed and have been socialised with. The attitude that 'if we will not do this job then who will do it' is responsible for the feeling that it is difficult to move out of their job. More so, the belief in 'once a sweeper always a sweeper', or '*ek safaiwale ka beta safaiwala hi banta hai*' has also led to a negative approach towards mobility out of job. The other half of the respondents are the ones who have had some education and their children are doing some temporary jobs or have started small business, etc., who believe that it is possible to move out of this job. For them education is the tool that would take the next generation away from this job. Robert Deliege has also observed that, "the people among whom I lived bothered little about medical college or the Indian Administrative service, and would certainly prefer some help to send their children to the primary school or to get a loan in order to buy a bullock cart. Most people, besides, had never received any help from the government. Yet, they kept making efforts to better their lives: they became masons, factory workers, brick makers, bullock cart drivers, etc., all this without any kind of help at all. The official policies are mainly oriented towards government jobs, and do not stimulate private initiatives." (Deliege, 2003).

Many of them feel that their work is very exclusive one; nobody else in the society can work in place of them. Thus, they should be paid more for their work. They argue that the kind of job that they do is not less than any other job, rather it is a job without which the life goes out of gear. Many of them talk of the time when *safai karamcharis* and sweepers had gone on strike and the city's life was thrown out of gear. They also consider them to be indispensable and irreplaceable as nobody else would like to do the kind of job they do and this also becomes an important reason for them to demand a higher salary. The working conditions of these people include cleaning septic tanks and public toilets as well, which means their work still remains to be unclean and inhuman.

Another important issue that bothers them is that it was not possible to take off the tag of being a scavenger, so finding a clean job is next to impossible. In the present society, they believe it is very difficult to shun one's caste identity, but earning more money is the need of the day and they do not have many opportunities to do the same. More mechanisation will also not change the nature of their job. They felt that the job of sweeping, cleaning drains and removing human excreta from the public and private toilets cannot become clean even if more machines are brought in as it would only make it physically clean and hygienic, the uneasiness and discomfort that their job causes in the mind and psychological problems encountered due to the stigma attached with their job cannot be taken away by the machines. One good effort which can be seen in Jammu city like many other cities in India is the taking over of public toilets by agencies like Sulabh International. The newly constructed toilets offer much cleaner working conditions but the work still remains to be treated as a low job.

The kind of alternative jobs that they perform include working in a motor workshop, car repair centre, school science laboratories, beauty parlours, in different shops and such other places. But what needs to be seriously observed and addressed is the kind of job profile they have in these places. It certainly always remains that of cleaning, sweeping, tidying or clearing of the mess in a place like beauty parlour or school laboratory. It has been shown by many scholars that in case of migration to other cities, too, the problem for scavengers remains the same. As Shah and others (2006) put it "many Dalits, especially the younger generation, migrate to towns to escape from unclean occupations, but even there they find work mainly as road sweepers and drain cleaners. There seems little escape for them from social ostracism."

**Education**

Most of the respondents in this study have school going children, thus highlighting the fact that they have come out of the fear of sending their children to school where they will face tough humiliating situations because of untouchability. The entry of their children in schools thus in educational arena also gives them the confidence of the breaking the norm of their remaining uneducated and having no right to education.

It is worth mentioning here that schools where these children go to study are the ones which are identified as the schools catering to the children of scavengers as they are located around and nearby the area where these scavengers live. The upper caste parents avoid sending their children to such schools. Thus, these tend to become 'exclusive schools'. The convent schools where children of other upper caste people also study have separate sections for the scavengers' children. They are sometimes known as Hindi medium students. Many of the scavengers send their children to government schools because they cannot afford to pay the private tuition fees. In short, the assumption that discrimination in educational field and abolition of untouchability has taken place and all individuals are being treated at par, is not true.

Although there are a number of welfare schemes being run by the state but many children do not avail them as they have converted to Christianity and many do not want to take the scholarships as the amount is very little. Besides, this also becomes a reminder of their caste identity especially for the ones who go to government schools and are studying with other caste children. Besides, as many of them have come from Punjab and they do not belong to the state, this also keeps them away from reservation (not being the state domicile).

**Untouchability**

The signs of existence of untouchability are numerous in Jammu city. One such important sign is the segregated colonies in which they live; there are identified localities which are their inhabitant places. One does not find the scavengers constructing their houses, or living on rent in places other than the colonies where their fellow scavengers live. Another important symbol of untouchability is people walking away when any scavenger comes their way. People are conscious of the existence and the presence of scavengers in and around them and all their actions take place keeping this in mind so that they are not made a participant in any of the happenings.

With modernisation and change in the socio-economic conditions of the Jammu society, there has been an increase in the demand for the domestic helpers who can share and help in performing household chores. The scavengers have made use of this opportunity and to get a feeling that untouchability is now very less practised, they have entered the households of the upper caste people as domestic servants. They are performing the chores of cleaning the house, cleaning their vehicles, gardening, washing clothes, cleaning utensils, cleaning the bathroom, ironing the clothes and two of them even talked of helping in the kitchen with the cooking chores. But cooking and kitchen chores still remained to be the works that these people are kept away from and the most preferred work of the owners that they perform is of cleaning bathrooms. So, although in order to overcome the humiliation of untouchability and to get a psychological mental satisfaction that there is no more untouchability in practice, they have started working in the upper caste households as helpers, but their prohibition in the kitchen work and preference for cleaning the toilets again reinforces the ideology of untouchability practised by the upper castes against the scavenger community, although in a less severe manner. There are households in Jammu city, wherein the older practice of keeping separate utensils like cups, mugs, plates and tumblers is still practised, but there are some who evolved a refined practice of giving them water in plastic bottles and then not taking those bottles back. Thus, maintaining the *status quo* in keeping their used articles away. But some of the scavengers do not see this as an untouchability practice but feel that it is a modern way and upper caste people are so kind that even give their bottles away (they tend to even have ignorance about the fact that these bottles are disposable in any case). There is very clear cut unsaid rule that anybody who cleans the toilets and bathrooms cannot do the kitchen work involving cleaning utensils. They are even prohibited from entering the kitchen. There are some households where they wash utensils but that is done either outside the kitchen or in a corner in the kitchen. Although majority of the people in Jammu city have flush cleaned toilet seats but to clean even those seats scavengers are hired on private basis, for it is considered as dirty unclean work. Those who clean them do not enter the remaining area of the house. It shows that there is still some form of untouchability and physical distance which is being maintained by the higher caste people in Jammu city which these people have internalised, for they believe that allowing them to enter their homes and letting them work in their houses is good enough. For them perceiving anything more than this is not possible.

Although the public transport and public eating places have contributed towards abolishing untouchability, but in Jammu city people recognise the scavengers by the kind of dialect they speak and some other manifest features thus exercising the segregating practices of not sitting with them and not eating with them.

## Conversion

Almost all the Christians are the convert Christians among the scavengers in Jammu. Some had converted long back, some have recently converted. As already stated, there are scavengers in Jammu who have come from Punjab. These Punjabi Christian scavengers had converted long back in Punjab and Punjab has a long history of conversion as stated by various scholars (Jodhka, 2002). The ones who have come from the areas that fall in present Pakistan and who claim to be settled in Jammu since the days of Maharaja again report that they had converted since that time, especially with coming of Church—education, economic and financial interests made them convert to Christianity. But what is very important to note is that some of them had converted in the recent past which points to the fact that conversion is an ongoing phenomenon and quite a sizeable number of scavengers are converting to Christianity.

In Jammu, the Christian scavengers while speaking about their conversion argue that untouchability remains to be the main reason for their conversion. As upper caste Hindus would not allow them to be part of any religious celebration and temple entry was also restricted, they decided to convert to Christianity. For them Christianity has opened up a lot of practices which they otherwise were not able to follow. Now they have their own church to go to where they go for *Sunday mass* and on all other religious occasions as well. Although conversion has taken away some of the privileges that they could avail otherwise like the benefit of reservation, scholarship to their children, but the humiliation faced by them as Hindus was much greater, so they have given up on these facilities and have made a conscious choice of being Christians. On being asked whether they would come back to Hindu fold if they are given financial benefits, reservation and lot more, they very clearly declined and responded positively about remaining as Christians.

One very important aspect of the social life of these scavengers is the recent political awakening that has taken place. They have frequent meetings and conferences which have political objectives. They are very well organised at their locality levels. There are leaders of every locality who are very conscious of their democratic rights and the political power of voting. They have a *safai karamchari* union whose head is a very conscious and politically active person. They have political presence not just in the political scenario of Jammu and Kashmir but they are also participating in the *Adhikar Yatras* associated with *Adh Dharm* movement of Punjab. These scavengers are aware of the benefits that have been given to them by political leaders. There is a municipal corporator who has been instrumental in getting contractual jobs to many of them. He is seen as a mediator between them and the municipality and he had won the election because of the votes of these people. Another very important reason that has brought these people together is the whole question of identity arising from the permanent resident question. The scavengers who have come or rather were brought from Punjab and have been living in Jammu for the past fifty years do not have a claim to government jobs and other benefits as they are not considered permanent residents of the state. This has led to a movement wherein they are pressurising government to give them the permanent resident status. This also has led to a division among them, i.e., of Jammu scavengers who are permanent residents and Punjab scavengers who are not permanent residents.

To sum up, it can be argued that the scavengers as an occupational community are an important constituent of our society, who perform an important task. This study, which was taken up as an academic pursuit, has ended up becoming an important chain in creating public awareness about their plight. In the process of understanding their mobility it became very clear that mobility is very low as they continue to perform their tasks accepting them as their caste roles without any resistance. Many of them continue to do the unclean job because alternative occupation are either not available or are not remunerative and secure. Practice of untouchability continues to pervade life of these people and this continues even when post-independence India claims to have undergone radical changes. All this points to the fact, that this community remains to be socially deprived. The scavengers of Jammu city need to be brought into the mainstream by putting in some efforts like creating public awareness and by motivating them to organise themselves to fight injustice in order to make their presence felt and have participation in all fields, be it political, economic and social. And finally, the state government has to take the responsibility of bringing them to the core from the margins with more initiatives of inclusive policy.

## References

Berreman, G.D. 1979. *Caste and Other Inequities:. Essays on Inequality*. Merrut: Folklore Institute.

Briggs, G.W. 1920. *The Chamars*. Calcutta: Association Press. (Reprinted Delhi: BR 1975).

Chaplin, Susan, E. 2002. 'Scavengers: Still Marginalised' in Ghanshyam Shah (ed.). *Dalits and the State*. New Delhi: Concept Publishing Company.

Charsley, S R and G K Karanth. 1998. *Challenging Untouchability: Dalit Initiative and Experience from Karnataka*. New Delhi: Sage Publications.

Charsley, S. 1996. 'Untouchable: What is in a name?' in *Journal of the Royal Anthropological Institute*, 2(1).

Chatterjee, Partha. 1989. *Caste and Subaltern Consciousness* in Ranajit Guha (ed.) *Subaltern Studies*, VI, New Delhi: Oxford University Press.

Chauhan, B.R. 1967. *A Rajasthan Village.* Delhi: Vir Publishing House.

Deliege, R. 1996. *'The World of the Untouchables: Paraiyars of Tamil Nadu.'* Delhi: Oxford University Press.

——— 1999. *The Untouchables of India.* New York: Berg.

———2002. 'Is there still untouchability in India?' Working paper No. 5, *Heidelberg Papers in South Asian and Comparative Politics*. South Asia Institute, University of Heidelberg.

——— 2003. Caste without a system: A study of South Indian Harijans in M. Searle Chaterjee and U. Sharma (ed.). *Contextualising Caste: Post Dumontian Approaches.* Jaipur: Rawat Publications.

Fuller, C. (ed.). 1996. *Caste Today.* Delhi: Oxford University Press.

Ghani, G.R., 2005. *A study of the Economic and Sociological Conditions of the Scavenging Community in the Kashmir Valley.* Unpublished Ph.D. Thesis: University of Kashmir.

Gupta, Dipankar (ed.). 2004. *Caste in Question: Identity or Hierarchy?* New Delhi: Sage Publications.

Haan, Arjan. 1997. *Poverty and Social Exclusion: A Comparison of Debates on Deprivation* Working Paper No. 2, Poverty Research Unit, Brighton: Sussex University.

Jodhka, S.S., (2002). Caste and Untouchability in Rural Punjab in *Economic and Political Weekly*, XXXVII (May 11, 2002) 19. pp. 1813-1823.

Judge, Paramjit Singh and Bal, Gurpreet. (2009). *Mapping Dalits,* Jaipur: Rawat Publications.

Krishna, Gopal. (2003). 'Plight of Scavengers in India' in *IMC India – Plight of Scavengers in India.* (india.indymedia.org/en/2003/02/3339.shtml)

Lynch, Owen. (1969). *The Politics of Untouchability: Social Mobility and Social Change in a City of India,* Delhi: National Publishing House.

Mahar, J.M. (ed.) 1998. *The Untouchables in Contemporary India.* Jaipur: Rawat Publications.

Moon, Vasant. 2001. *Growing up Untouchable in India: A Dalit Autobiography* translated from the Marathi by Gail Omvedt. New Delhi: Vistaar Publications.

Pathak, B. 1991. *Road to Freedom: A Sociological study on the Abolition of Scavenging in India.* Delhi: Motilal Banarasidas Publishers.

Poddar, Bhagirath. (2001) *The Untouchables in Modern India,* New Delhi: Sarup and Sons Publishers.

Raksha, Vishav. (2012) *Untouchability and Social mobility: A Study of Scavengers,* New Delhi: Kanishka Publishers.

Ram, Ronki, (2004). 'Untouchability, Dalit Consciousness, and the Ad- Dharm Movement in Punjab', *Contributions to Indian Sociology,* 38 (2004) 3. pp, 323-349.

Ramaswamy, Gita. (2005). *India Stinking: Manual Scavengers in Andhra Pradesh and their Work*, Pondicherry: Navayana Publishing.

Ravan, Darshan Ratan. (2010). *Ambedkar se Vimokh Safai Kamgar Samaj-Upekshit, Kaaran aur Mukti*, New Delhi: Aadhas Samvaad. (Hindi)

Sachchidananda. (2001). *People at the Bottom: A Portrait of the Scavengers,* New Delhi: Concept Publishing Company.

Searle-Chatterjee, M. 1977. 'Conjugal Roles and Social Network in an Indian Urban Sweeper Locality.' *Journal of Marriage and the Family.* Vol. xix, No. 2.

——— (1981). *Reversible Sex Roles: The Special Caste of Benaras Sweepers*, Oxford: Pergamon Press.

Searle-Chatterjee, M and U. Sharma (ed.). 2003. *Contextualising Caste: Post-Dumontian Approaches.* Jaipur: Rawat Publications.

Sen, Amartya. 1999. *Development as Freedom*, New Delhi: Oxford University Press.

Shah, Ghanshyam et al. (2006). *Untouchability in Rural India*, New Delhi: Sage Publications.

Shyamlal, (1984). *The Bhangis in Transition,* New Delhi: Inter-India.

Sharma, U. 2002. *'Caste'*. New Delhi: Viva Publications.

——2003. 'Berreman revisited: Caste and the Comparative method.' in Mary Searle-Chatterjee, and Ursula Sharma (eds.) *Contextualising Caste: Post-Dumontian Approaches*. Jaipur: Rawat Publications.

Thekaekara, Mari Marcel. (2003). *Endless Filth-The Saga of the Bhangis*, Bangalore: Books for Change.

Thorat, Sukhdeo and Paul Attewell. (2007). 'The Legacy of Social Exclusion: A Correspondence Study of Job Discrimination in India', *Economic and Political Weekly,* Vol. 42, No. 41 Oct 13-19, pp. 4141-4145.

Vivek, P.S. 1998. *Scavengers: Exploited class of city professionals.* Mumbai: Himalaya Publishing House.

Zaidi, Annie. (2006). 'India's Shame', *Frontline,* 23 (September 2006) 18. pp. 9-22.

# 13

# Situation of Sanitation with Special Reference to Rural Odisha

*Saroj Ranjan Mania*

Social development and sanitation go hand-in-hand since without attending the conditions relating to public health, no society can be attributed to be developed or civilised in true sense of the term. It is now considered that the provision of sanitation is a vital development intervention, without it ill health dominates and makes life stressful. Increased access to sanitation and improving hygienic behaviours play a significant role in inhibiting various diseases. In the context of India, despite the inflow of lot of resources over the last quarter century for sanitation, the situation is still challenging. Moreover, providing environmentally—safe sanitation to millions of people having a preponderance of rural mass is an up-heal task in a populous country like India. Though government is optimistic to achieve MDG target but still it will be significantly challenging due to its realistic gap in rural India. Apart from this, rapid urbanisation is also putting stress on urban sanitation system since most slum pockets are not linked with city's sanitation infrastructure which is shocking but true.

India is second largest populous country in the world having more than 70 per cent rural inhabitants for which it is called "India lives in villages". Moreover, 25 out of every 100 rural mass are having access to sanitation facilities but there is intense disparity amongst the states with regard to access to sanitation facilities. It is reported that less than 10 per cent rural households in Madhya Pradesh use toilet as compared to over 80 per cent in Kerala or 60 per cent in Assam. In case of Haryana more than 60 per cent rural households possess electrical and electronics gadgets like television and fridge etc., at home. whereas less than 30 per cent rural households are having toilet facility. Hence, it may be inferred that the habit of using toilet is more of an attitude than affordability.

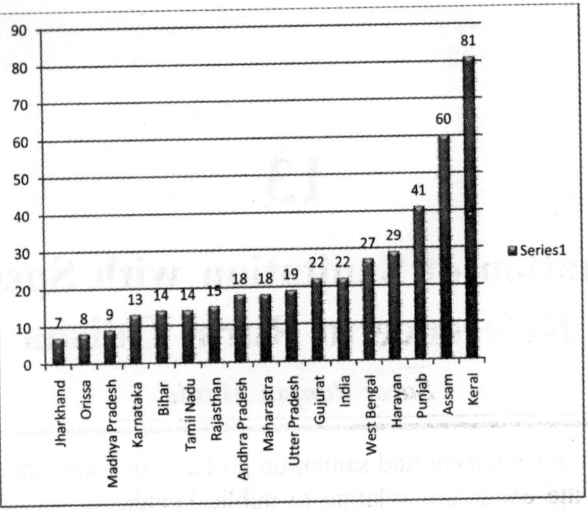


**Fig. 1. Percentage of Rural Household with Toilet Facility by States, 2001.**

*Source:* Census of India, 2001.

## Situation in Odisha

When one looks at the situation of sanitation in the state of Odisha, it depicts a greater challenge and opportunity. With a total population of 4,19,47,358 (2011 Census), the state ranks 11th in size in India and covers a geographical area of approximately 1,55,700 square kilometers comprising of 30 districts; 314 CD Blocks; 6,234 *gram panchayats* and 1,34,850 habitations. The human development indicators of the state are very low as compared to other states. As reported by SRS-2009, the IMR in Odisha stands at 65/1000 live births which is higher than the national average of 54/1000 births. About half of the state's population is hanging below the poverty line. However, the dismal depiction pertaining to its socio-economic reflection may be attributed to the composition of its population and habitation in different agro-climatic zones.

## Tribal Scenario

Here about one-fourth of the total populations belongs to ST category from 62 types of tribal communities including 13 primitive tribal groups. Most of them stay in inaccessible forest and hilly terrains. Their socio-economic condition is abysmally low. They lack to have proper fooding, shelter and clothing. Due to poverty they are not literate in the true sense and also lack the awareness and drive to send their wards for the formal schooling. As a result, the literacy rate is very poor and the same of the tribal women is alarmingly low. They are mostly away from the mainstream. In this backdrop, they do not realise sanitation as a necessity for healthy living. Similarly, about 17 per cent of the state's population belongs to scheduled caste category of which a distinct majority depicts

an inclined socio-economic situation in the graph. Hence, when about 40 per cent population of the state reflects a deplorable socio-economic situation; its average growth rate depicts an inclined picture despite candid attempts from the remaining relatively fortunate mass.

It is well reported that consumption of safe driving water, proper sanitation and adoption of correct hygiene practices play a significant role in maintaining good health of people. But people those abode at a hilly terrain, with poor infrastructure, low level of literacy and awareness, stressed with poverty, make a mechanical living without aspiring for safe drinking water or better sanitation. It is revealed that usually the tribal people fetch drinking water from nearby streams, ponds and *chuas* which must be contaminated as per the prevailing standard. They do not have any option but follow the age old practice and trend to collect water for consumption.

## Rural Scenario

Apart from the tribals, there is another section of population in this state, those who live in coastal zone adjourning to Bay of Bengal. Here majority of rural habitations are relatively developed, the people are educated and have sustained income source from various means. But here due to proximity to different water bodies, people in the costal rural areas prefer open defecation as an attitude rather than the use of toilet. They have understood the utility of toilet but they go the neighbouring fields, riverbeds and defecate behind bushes. Usually, the rural folk go jointly or in small groups during early in the morning and in late-afternoon taking tobacco paste called *gudakhu* or smoking *bidi*. This is a usual habit. Besides, going outside the home for the purpose provides an opportunity to gossip during the process.

Though these activities hamper human dignity, still they move out for the purpose as an attitude despite having capability to setup a toilet or already having at home. There are instances, you may find some villages have been covered under TSC in pen and paper, but in case of a physical verification you may not find or you may find shortfalls in number as compared to the record. Besides, there are many instances where you may notice that the toilets constructed for sanitation purposes are being used as animal sheds or for the purpose of storing agricultural produce etc.

Apart from the attitudinal issue, the other factors responsible for the unutilisation of toilet is lack of water source at the toilet. There are instances people say, what is the use of taking a bucket of water to the toilet for the purpose and it may not be sufficient to properly flush out which require additional water from home. Instead, they go to their nearby field without any such hindrance and complete the work without any such problem. This shows that lack of water connection to the toilets is also a pertinent point for the unutilisation of home toilets by the rural people.

Thus, the factors which stand as impediments in achieving the target of sanitation mission and that need special attention for the purpose have been reflected as follows:

(i) Hilly terrain zones having low water table;

(ii) Forest areas having lack of water source;

(iii) Poverty, illiteracy and low level of awareness;

(iv) Meager household land holding to construct toilet;

(v) Lack of proper implementation and sincere verification of the programme;

(vi) Despite affordability, attitude and habit inhibit its use/ construction;

(vii) Along with the hardware job (installation of toilet) the software (IEC, BCC or motivational activities) should be taken up regularly to change their age old habit;

(viii) The rural children in the schools may be motivated for discarding open defecation on health ground;

(ix) Construction of toilet along with water-taps may be considered since without water source to the latrine some people do not prefer to use it on various counts; and

(x) Different cross sections of the rural community like children, youth, women and old people, etc., should be motivated separately by experienced counsellors to change their habit and to sensitise them about the short comings of open defecation to their life, property and environment.

Finally, it would be fruitful if the government machineries recognise the reality of the situation and design appropriate measures to address ground reality. For this challenging issue, it has to establish holistic partnership and link up with civil society organisations, CBOs and PRI members, etc., to facilitate the process through advocacy programmes, motivational campaigns for achieving the desired result. This should be taken as a mission to achieve since the Supreme Court of India has also ruled that both water and sanitation are part of the constitutional right to life (Article-21). The court has stated that "the right to access to clean drinking water is fundamental to life and there is a duty on the state under the said Article to provide clean drinking water to its citizens; (*Andhra Pradesh Pollution Control Board II* Vs. *Prof M.V. Naidu and others (Civil Appeal Nos. 368-373 of 1999*).

In this light, this forum gives us a moral platform to act hand in hand with the government machinery and non-governmental organisations, so as to awaken the society, to realise the importance of the use of toilet and to distance from varied health hazards.

# 14

# Sociology of Sanitation and its Key Challenges

*B.N. Srivastava*

## Introduction

The expression 'Sociology of Sanitation' is broad enough to embrace subject as diverse as the conditions that affect health of human society. To keep the habitation clean and livable is a major human responsibility towards the society. Sanitation, therefore, continues to be a critical component of Sociology. 'Action Sociology' is one of the major initiatives of Sulabh Sanitation and Social Reform Movement launched by Dr Bindeshwar Pathak since 1970. The Sulabh Sanitation and Reform Movement is a well-organised institutional attempt to change society through social reform, education, persuasion and pressure and restore human dignity to the underprivileged people, especially to thousands of scavengers who still physically clean and carry human excrement. Dr Pathak has identified the problems, work on them and find solutions.

He carried and conceptualised the term 'Action Sociology' and brought to the fore the issue of relevance of sociological knowledge in understanding and solving the problems of society. His idea of 'Action Sociology' is much broader in its out-reach and goes beyond the previous sociological constructs of 'Applied Sociology' and 'Sociology in Action'. In that sense, he has innovated and improved upon the older action-frames in the discipline of sociology. Unlike conventional sociologists who rallied round the concept of 'Applied Sociology' and 'Sociology in Action', Dr Pathak conceived the idea of Action Sociology.

## What is Action Sociology

The idea underlying the concept of 'Action Sociology' is to provide it in an action-orientation and make it reach to people who are awaiting to enjoy the fruits of progress and prosperity. Sociological investigations and researches, howsoever profound and scholarly, are of little relevance, if they are concerned mainly with critical explication and analysis of the social phenomenon. No society values sociological knowledge which treats the life of a common man as something alien and apart. Society values such knowledge as is worthy of producing worthwhile social results. The real knowledge is that which entails the seeds of inspired action and illuminated service. Accordingly, the real sociological knowledge is one that could be converted into action. The value of sociology is the value of its practical contribution to society.

For a better description 'Action Sociology' is one that is intimately linked with life and is useful as a guide, an inspirer and a path finder. It is a sociology that is interested in full circle of human existence and not merely in segments. It is a sociology which is meant not only to interpret the society, but also to better it by pursuing ideas through their practical conclusions. It is a sociology which advocates ideas that are socially relevant and feasible in terms of practice and action. It is a sociology that hates abstraction and loves action. And finally, it is a sociology that is enlivened by the principle of thought and action operating in a balanced existence.

'Action Sociology' in the context of Sulabh Movement is concerned with social issues connected with human misery and degradation, particularly of those who are backward, un-resourced and disadvantaged. It means action and actual work for the betterment of society and the upliftment of the downtrodden. It is a means finding appropriate approaches for planning and programme execution, which may entail acceptable and affordable solutions based on scientific experimentation and intervention into ground-level social realities.

## Challenges of Action Sociology

In conformity with the above conceptualisation of 'Action Sociology', 'Action Sociologist' is one who plunges into action arena and shows good results. He is not the one who gives suggestions and refrains from 'action'. Action Sociologist is an 'interventionist' who gets into the heart of the solution and plays the fire-fighting role. In order to demonstrate his convictions about his notion of Action Sociologists, Dr Pathak personally intervened to change the deplorable condition of manual scavengers, the most degraded among the so-called untouchables in the Indian society. He did not talk of solutions for others to put into practice, he took up his solutions, applied them with full conviction, sincerity and vigour, produced viable results and showed to the people that his ideas were fruitful and feasible.

## Centre for Action Sociology

Dr Pathak founded the Sulabh International Centre for Action Sociology which enjoys the backing of a large number of distinguished Indian sociologists. The Centre, right from its inception, has been engaged in a relentless pursuit of scientific enquiry into such critical areas of wider social concern that agitate the minds of a large number of political leaders, policy planners, administrators, academicians and voluntary social workers.

The Sulabh Centre for Action Sociology has already organised seminars workshops in the past to explaining chisel the concept of Action Sociology and determine its boundaries. The general consensus that emerged conceived action sociology as one associated with the interventionist activities of the sociologists seeking to help the disadvantaged sections of society. It is concerned with practical aspects of working with underprivileged and disadvantaged sections of society. It has to concern itself with ensuring the involvement of sociologists in all stages of development. It was held that sociologists rooted in the life experiences of the people having courage to respond to the various social problems and possessing intellectual capacity to build new models are needed to strengthen the field of Action Sociology. Sociologists have to be action oriented and intervention for change has to be their primary responsibility. They have to be the catalysts in the process of change.

## Sanitation Critical Component of Sociology

Sanitation has many linkages, most important among them being water supply and safe and hygienic disposal of human waste. Sanitation broadly covers human excreta, waste water, solid waste and even personal hygiene etc.

Insanitation has wide-spread effects, water sources get polluted, incidence of disease rises, affecting billions of people all over the world, labour force is affected, productivity of industry and agriculture falls putting stresses on budgetary resources needed for development and strengthening the economy. Invariably people who are unserved with basic facilities of water supply and sanitation are the poor ones. They lack not only the means to have such facilities but also need guidance how to minimise the ill effects of insanitary conditions in which they live. Poverty breeds diseases and disease breeds poverty. High rate of child mortality encourages couples to have more children, resulting in increase in population. The infrastructural facilities like water supply, safe disposal of human waste, solid waste and waste water disposal are not able to keep pace with the growth of population. Due to rapid urbanisation nearly half the population in towns live in slums, pavements and shanty townships. Their health and physical well-being are threatened by inadequate sanitation. They are the ones who resort to open defecation and suffer most from the vicious cycle of ill health, lowered productive capacity and hardships in a deteriorating environment. The women and children are the worst sufferers. The women have to get early in the morning before dawn to attend to the nature's call and similarly after sunset. They are subjected to harassment and even molestation by rogues and anti-social elements. Sanitation is, therefore, a basic condition for development, an input to raise production; otherwise all that is sought to be gained through economic reform will be lost for want of toilets.

## Sanitation through the Ages

The problem of scavenging, or night-soil disposal is a product of civilisation; during the stone-age when man was leading a wild life, there was no question of scavenging. It is only when he settled and habitations grew in size, the problem of scavenging arose. If one were asked to identify a single aspect that accounts for fascination that India has held for a span of more than 5000 years, perhaps it is the system of sanitary practices followed by the people in the country. In this chapter an attempt has been made to trace out the history of this cultural behaviour from the early stages till today.

The Indus Valley Civilisation marked the beginning of Indian protohistory which flourished 5000 years ago. The town planning was elaborate and seems to have been the work of experienced architects. There was an efficient drainage system linked with household latrines and bathing pool in the town. The first invaders, the Aryans, came from Iranian plateau. It was they who destroyed, in about 1500 BC, the cities of the Indus Valley. They seem to have descended the course of the Indus to its estuary—which was then at a higher latitude than it is today and then settled in the region between the Indus and the Ganges, gradually advancing eastwards along the fertile Ganges valley. This invasion has incalculable consequences for India, since it brought with it the Sanskrit language, the no toilets inside the house and the people have to go outside for attending to the nature's call. The same conditions prevailed during the post Vedic period. It was compulsory to go to river or pond for bath after open air defecation.

In the 6th century BC new invading forces reaching the north-west of India: the Achaemenians, first under Cyrus (559-29), then under Darius (521-485), conquered Bactria, Gandhara, Arachosia and the Indus valley, turning all these regions into Satrapies. For two centuries they remained provinces of the Persian empire. During this period hygiene and sense of sanitation was unknown to the people. They used to go outside for attending nature's call.

The end of the Persian domination was brought about by yet another invasion, that of the armies of Alexender the Great in 326-5 BC. Although short-lived, this invasion brought a wave of Greek influence into north-western provinces from the Indo-Greek kingdoms of Sogdiana and Bactria. This period conceded with the Mauryas. According to Megasthenes nobody was allowed to defecate in the open in Pataliputra. In about 80 BC the provinces of the north-west passed from the domination of the Greek *satrapies* to that of the Sakas (Scythians). In the first and second centuries AD the Kushans, built up a powerful empire stretching from the Oxus to the Ganges plain embracing both the Hellenised states and the Aryan territories. During this period the cities were well planned with proper drainage system. People used to go to the nearby fields and groves for nature's call.

In the 5th century when India was at last unified under the national dynasty of the Guptas, the White Huns from Bactria appeared at the frontiers. Their attacks were repulsed, but did much to weaken the power of the Guptas. During Guptas the Indian civilisation was at its peak. There was no open defecation in the city. There was a very high degree of civic sense. The buildings were very clean with every house having sewage system.

In about the year 1000, Muslim forces reached the Indus valley. They spread slowly eastwards, gradually overthrowing the Indian kingdoms they attacked. During the Medieval period people used to defecate in the open. There was no civic sense amongst the people. The kings and queens in the palaces used to have their own toilets which was cleaned by the war captives. There was no drainage in the towns. People were afraid to come out of the house during day time.

Mughals came to India in 1526 and remained in power till 1857. There was a total absence of social awareness about the values of community sanitation. This aspect was overlooked. The system of scavenging assumed the form of a profession. Bucket privies were designed and constructed by Muslims for their women in Purdah which were cleaned by captives.

Lastly, Britishers took over the reign of governance in India. They set up army cantonments and civil lines and a large number of people were employed to do sweeping and scavenging work on a regular basis.

By the time the British came and ruled India (1772-1947), John Harrington had developed the flush toilet in 1596 in Britain. Sewerage was first introduced in London in 1850, in New York in 1860 and in India in Kolkata in 1870; yet after 138 years, of 7933 *towns*/cities only *929* towns are covered by sewage system and that, too, partially because of the heavy cost of construction and maintenance and enormous quantity of water required to flush human excreta. Septic tanks need more water to flush (10 litres per flush) and gas pipe is needed to allow exit of gases and intake of gas to help bacteria survive to degrade excreta. When septic tank fills up it has to be cleaned. Decomposed sludge, raw human excreta and water have to be manually cleaned, needing the services of scavengers. After two years, another trenching ground is required for further decomposition before it can be used as fertiliser. This found favour with only 30 per cent of the urban population and was hardly adopted in rural areas. The reason was that the construction and maintenance were too expensive and too much water was required. Developing countries could not afford it. Hence, the problem could not be solved either in urban areas or in rural areas. So culture and lack of affordable technology played a major role in the continuance of the practice of defecation in the open.

India had and has two basic problems in the field of sanitation: (I) Defecation in the open – according to 2011 Census, 116 million households have no toilet within the premises and 123 million households or 626 million people resort to defecation in the open; (II) There is the sub-human practice of cleaning human excreta manually by the people called scavengers since the last 4000 years. Till today (2011 Census) about 1.3 millions houses have bucket previes cleaned by thousands of scavengers and animals.

When Mahatma Gandhi came to India from South Africa to lead the freedom movement, his attention was drawn towards the problem of defecation in the open and the prevalence of manual scavenging. In 1901, when Mahatma Gandhi attended the Calcutta Conference of the

Congress, he himself cleaned the night-soil and urged others to do likewise. Further, Gandhi recommended two practices; firstly after defecation, to cover the human excreta with soil, lest it becomes a source of diseases and pollute the environment, a method which he called *"Tatti par Mitti"*, soil upon night-soil; and secondly, to use trench latrines for defecation. He also said that the system of manual scavenging should be abolished and the scavengers should be treated at par with others, so as to bring them in mainstream of the society.

Mahatma Gandhi had special concern for cleanliness and one of his dreams was to end the practice of manual cleaning of human excreta. About clean sanitation he once said he wanted independence later and a clean India first. And secondly, he said, "I may not be born again but if it happens, I would like to be born in a family of scavengers so that I could relieve them from this sub-human occupation. During Gandhi's life time some attempts were made but they were palliative in nature and the dream of Mahatma Gandhi remained unfulfilled.

### Commission/Committees

After independence the problem of sanitation came to the forefront. The widespread phenomenon of open defecation and the inhuman practice of manual scavenging remained grim. The central and state governments set up a number of commission/committees like Barve Committee (1949), Backward Classes Commission (1955), Malkani Committee (1957), Committee on Customary Rights under Prof Malkani (1966) and Pandya Committee (1968-69). Similar committees were also constituted at the state level in the states of Uttar Pradesh (1955), Haryana (1969), Kerala (1971) and Karnataka (1976). These committees/commissions confined itself to give recommendations for improving the living and working condition of the scavengers, but none of them gave any suggestions for liberating scavengers from the inhuman practice of manual scavenging and rehabilitating them in other dignified occupations, or demolishing the existing dry latrines and converting them into sanitary ones. There was no proposal from any quarter for eradicating this system by any legislative, or executive order, or by suggesting an alternate to manual scavenging. In the earlier Five Year Plans the entire allocation was earmarked on sewerage only.

### Bihar, Gandhi Celebration Committee and Birth of a New Technology

It was in 1969, that Dr Bindeshwar Pathak joined the Gandhi Centenary Celebration Committee, Patna, as social worker which involved extensive tour of villages in Bihar. Besides deep studies in Gandhian thought of compassion and humanism, the job also exposed him to the problems of scavengers who were target groups for the committee to serve. Soon after joining the Gandhi Centenary Celebration Committee a storm started brewing in Dr Pathak's mind on seeing the pathetic condition of scavengers who carried human excreta on the head, generation after generation. Imbued with the determination to devise and develop an appropriate alternative to replace the obsolete and obnoxious system of manual scavenging, he carried-out extensive studies and research. He studied a large number of toilet deigns which could possibly replace the manually cleaned bucket privies. Eventually, he came across a book titled *Excreta Disposal for Rural Areas and Small Communities* by E. G. Wagner and J.N. Lanoix (WHO, Geneva, 1958). He got the clue to the riddle and invented a low-cost two-pit pour-flush water-seal toilet system, which proved a viable and most effective alternative to replace the pit privies which required manual scavenging. The Government of Bihar recognised the Sulabh Technology and applauded its work, to begin with, in the two districts, namely, Arrah and Buxar. Sulabh's seminal work propelled the WHO, the Government of India and the UNICEF to convene a high level seminar in Patna in 1978 to examine the implications of the Bihar experiments. The seminar recommended that 'two-pit pour-flush water-seal latrine with on-site disposal system is the most appropriate low cost technology to be introduced on a large scale in the urban areas as the system meets the technical, social and cultural needs of the country.'

When Dr Pathak entered on the scene of sanitation, the situation was dismal in India, both in urban and rural areas and only few towns had provision of sewage system, a small number of people were using septic tanks and only two systems were prevalent on large scale, i.e., defecation in the open and manual cleaning of human excreta by a class of people called 'scavengers'. At that time there was no proper survey of the houses having safe and hygienic toilets. After his intervention in the year 1969, the situation has changed, but even today 626 million people defecate in the open and bucket toilets are still cleaned by thousands of scavengers daily. Dr Pathak while addressing these two problems, developed two technologies, viz., one for individual households as discussed above and the other is public toilets for places where people congregate in large number like market, hospitals, railway stations, bus stand etc.

Therefore, his key challenges were:

1. Providing affordable sanitary toilets to the masses;
2. Installation of community toilets at public places including slums;
3. Liberation of scavengers from the demeaning task of manual scavenging wherever they exist;
4. Completing the work of conversion of dry latrines into sanitary ones thus liberating manual scavengers fully;
5. To impart training to the liberated scavengers in vocational trades so that they can stand on their own, earn their livelihood and may not revert to their hereditary profession;
6. Rehabilitation of scavengers in other dignified occupations;
7. Imparting quality education to the wards of scavengers.

The achieving of these objectives requires a large scale mobilisation of both governmental and voluntary efforts and above all the involvement of the people.

**Central Sector Scheme for Conversion of Dry Latrines Based on Two-pit Low Cost Sanitation Technology**

It was in the Sixth Five Year Plan a scheme for the conversion of existing dry latrines for the liberation and rehabilitation was introduced under "Machinery for Implementation of PCR Act" at Dr Pathak's initiative in 1980-81. The scheme is in operation in an amended form in all the states where the system of manual scavenging still exists and achieved tangible results.

**Dr Pathak Inspired by Gandhi**

Dr Pathak was deeply inspired by the Gandhi's ideology because the *Brahmin* in him had already developed a sense of revulsion against the discriminatory and dehumanising caste practice of Hindu social order. He followed Mahatma Gandhi's philosophy for the eradication of untouchability and the emancipation of scavengers.

**Undesirable Job of Scavengers**

The hereditary occupation of the scavengers has been scavenging; removing night-soil and cleaning of latrines, removal of filth, dead cattle, sweeping of houses and roads. The job of scavengers is not only undesirable, polluting and tedious but also low paid. They suffer from the worst form of untouchability. And are kept at the lowest rung of the caste structure. In the 1931 census, the number of *Bhangis*, *Chuhras*,

*Halekhar, Hari, Lalbegi, Mehtar* and *Paki* was 19,57,460. They were also spread over the areas which are now in Pakistan. The 1941 census data on populations of castes and tribes were presented on a somewhat modest scale since their compilation was restricted due to World War II. In pursuance of the national government's policy after independence to discourage community distinctions based on caste, race, etc., the 1951 census, which was the first census after independence, was not caste-based census and hence figures of scavengers are not available: The 1961 census was also not caste-based but separate enumeration of Scheduled Castes and Scheduled Tribes was done in the context of development programmes for their upliftment. The number of sweepers and scavengers in 1961 census was 35.32 laks out of which 8,02,400 were scavengers. The number of sweepers and scavengers as recorded in 1971 census was 50.28 lakh, but no information was collected about the number of scavengers engaged in manual scavenging. During the subsequent censuses the information regarding the number of scavengers was not collected. The number of scavengers based on the rapid survey to identify scavengers undertaken by the state governments in 1992 was 7, 70,338. The number of scavengers rehabilitated up to 2006 was 4,27,870 and the number of those rehabilitated from 2007 to 2010 was 78,941. The Government of India has estimated that the number of manual scavengers as per census 2011 in 4041 statutory towns /cities may be of the order of 61,944. The Ministry of Social Justice and Empowerment has decided to undertake a fresh survey to identify the number of scavengers who are still engaged in manual scavenging. The survey is in progress.

## NGO Without Parallel

The Sulabh International Social Service Organisation, a non-profit voluntary organisation, founded by Dr Pathak in 1970 has demonstrated, in partnership with local governments, the success of low cost twin-pit water-seal toilet technology throughout the country and abroad. So far, more than 1.2 million individual household toilets have been constructed, or substituted for existing dry latrines by Sulabh and 8000 community toilets have been installed on 'pay and use' toilets at important places all over the country, out of which 200 are linked with biogas plants. Thus, more than 10 million people use these facilities every day. The census figures of 2011 shows that the sanitation coverage in the country has increased to 46.9 per cent, 30.7 per cent in the rural areas and 81.4 per cent in the urban areas. This has brought down the practice of open defecation from 73 per cent in 1990 to 49.8 per cent in 2011. This was the contribution of Dr Bindeshwar Pathak in fulfilling the dream of Mahatma Gandhi.

As a social spin-off Sulabh has been able to liberate 1, 20,000 scavengers from their forced profession. A key to the success of Sulabh lies in implementing the programme for the liberation and rehabilitation of scavengers from the sub-human occupation of manual scavenging. They have trained more than 8000 liberated scavengers in market oriented trades and occupations through vocational training centre set-up by them at various places.

## Importance of Education

As part of rehabilitation programme Sulabh has been running Sulabh Public School since 1992. Dr Pathak has been of the view that education holds the key of any major change and development and is essential for improving the condition of the traditionally oppressed scheduled caste communities.

With the objective of imparting quality education, Sulabh Public School, a premium English Medium School, was set up in Delhi in 1992. The school aims at preparing children from the weaker sections of society for a better life by bringing quality education within the reach of boys and girls from scavenger families. The school is recognised by Directorate of Education, Government of Delhi and provides education up to tenth standard. Apart from academic activities, co-curricular activities are regularly organised at the school to promote social integration among students. To avoid perpetuation of segregation that characterises the special schools for the scheduled castes, the school is open to the children of families from non-scavenging communities also. Children from scavenger families are provided tuition fee waiver apart from free uniforms, books and stationary.

## Vocational Training

Sulabh has also been running a vocational training centre for wards of scavengers. The centre at New Delhi in Sulabh campus, which was started in 1992, now offers training facilities in eight trades, i.e., audio-visual repair, beauty care, computer application, dress designing, electrical, embroidery, tailoring (cutting and sewing), shorthand and typing. Course contents and training methods follow the pattern of Industrial Training Institutes. So far more than 8000 boys and girls have undergone different vocational training courses.

The Sulabh International Social Service Organisation has been engaged in liberation of scavengers for more than four decades. The experience gained in the liberation programme shows that the liberation is not enough and to make it more effective, this has to be combined with and followed by a programme of their training and rehabilitation. The scavengers are trained in market-oriented trades so that they engage in activities which give them financial support. With this end in view it was in the 80s that Dr Pathak launched a programme for their training and rehabilitation. The training and rehabilitation programme was launched at Patna in 1985 in which the scavengers and their wards were given training in market-oriented trades. 3000 scavengers were trained at Patna. A similar type of training centre was set up at Jambhol in Maharashtra.

### Nai Disha: A Novel Idea towards Assimilation with Rest of the Society

As an earnest of its concern for the downtrodden scavenging class, a project "Nai Disha" has been launched at Alwar and Tonk in Rajasthan for imparting vocational training to under privileged women scavengers who were earlier doing the dirty job of cleaning latrines. They are being trained in various trades such as sewing, embroidery, beauty care etc. to enable them to earn their livelihood by alternate means and lead a life of dignity.

In the first batch twenty eight women were educated and trained in food processing, beautycare and tailoring. They are now being paid a monthly stipend of 2500 rupees so that they do not return to their earlier profession. In the last few months these women have not only gained education to receive their stipend through monthly account payee cheques, but have also learnt to successfully market the goods they produce. The end goal is to make them economically independent as this is the only way to eliminate the evil of scavenging from the very root. The products manufactured by these women have been approved by the Hotel Ashok, an ITDC five-star hotel of Delhi, with a formal agreement for purchase of the products in the offing. Another batch of 28 scavengers is now recently undergoing training in this Centre. Now Alwar is scavenging free. Sulabh has set up another vocational training centre for 225 liberated scavengers at Tonk in Rajasthan. The women scavengers liberated are undergoing training. Now Tonk is also scavenging free.

### A New Lease of Life

The women who have undergone training at the centres have acquired self-confidence. In fact, they have boosted their morale and they now know how to write name and sign cheques. They have opened savings accounts in the bank and operate it. The vocational training centre at Alwar is a unique case of women empowerment.

The initiative in imparting training to the liberated scavengers in market–oriented trades through vocational training centres has yielded laudable results. The liberated scavengers are now settled in dignified employment, trades and occupations. Their social-economic status has gone up and they are now engaged in producing their own products like garments, embroidery, pickle, *papads* etc. and sending it to the market for sale. Their goods are absorbed locally and are used by the persons belonging to all communities. This attitudinal change among the people towards them is remarkable as at one point of time when they were engaged in manual scavenging the people looked at them with contempt. But now they are using goods, articles, eatables prepared by them gladly and treat on par with others. Another instance of attitudinal change by way of illustration is that those who have been trained in beauty trade in the vocational training centre have started their own Beauty Parlor and now touch the face of those ladies belonging to upper castes at a time of make-up, massage and they gladly accept this.

## Visit to UN at New York

The liberated scavengers who have been rehabilitated by Sulabh have acquired confidence and brought into the mainstream of the society. In July 2008, they were invited to participate in a cultural show organised by the U.N. at New York as a part of the observance of the International Year of Sanitation 2008. This event was widely applauded.

## Applauded by President and Prime Minister

On return from New York, they were blessed by the President of India and Prime Minister in a special audience given to them.

## No More Untouchable

These Dalit women were allowed to enter the local *Jagannath* Temple in Alwar for the first time and dined with the same upper-caste people who did not even let them enter their houses earlier as they were treated as untouchables. The fact is that they performed Puja with Vedic Brahmins and also dined with them.

The *Dalit* women also performed rituals with upper caste Hindus at the *Vishwanatha temple* in Varanasi. Amidst ecstatic shouts of '*Har Har Gange*' the women also took a dip in the Ganges and chanted hymns along the *Dashashwamedh Ghat*, deemed to be the most pious bank.

### Feeling Empowered

"It's an out of this world experience for us. We want to stay here as long as we can. This day will remain memorable for us. We now feel we have really joined the mainstream", said one of the liberated scavenger. She added, "Sharing" a platform with the upper caste is really a privilege mingling with upper-castes, an out-of-this world experience".

### Attitudinal Change

It is important from two points of view; one is that such places have helped the liberated scavengers in bringing them in the mainstream of the society and the other is indicative of attitudinal change among the people. The attitudinal change is of considerable relevance as at one point of time when they were engaged in manual scavenging, the people looked at them with contempt. But now they are using goods, articles, eatables prepared by them gladly and treat them on par with others. They have been now absorbed in the mainstream of the society. This achievement is of immense satisfaction.

After Gandhi, Dr Pathak is the man, more than any other in India, who has championed the cause of upliftment of the untouchables as mission of his life for more than four decades. He has been working relentlessly to keep the ecosystem clean and bring the marginalised sections of the society in the mainstream. His contribution in abolishing the inhuman practice of manual scavenging as a true action sociologist is seminal and unparalleled in the sense that he not only tackled effectively the social evils but provided its categorical solution through a low-cost toilet technology and developed a self-sustaining sanitation system across the country.

# 15

# Challenges for the Total Sanitation Campaign in North-East India: Reviewing the Case of Tribal Villages in West Tripura

*Sharmila Chhotray*

## I

The paper sets out to examine the challenges of the Government of India initiated Total Sanitation Campaign in Tripura, a sociologically neglected research area. The second smallest state in Northeast India (10,491,69 sq. km), Tripura is bordering largely with Bangladesh on the west and with Assam and Mizoram in the north and east. While the government report projects their 100 per cent success stories of its implementation on these territories in major districts of Tripura, a private group called East-Wind Communications (EWC) based in Agartala, evaluates the programme of the Sanitation Department of the State Government and reveals different social realities.

This paper, therefore, evaluates the challenges for the giant flagship sanitation programme of the Government of India that promises for a clean and healthy environment in the backward villages of West Tripura. Through various secondary literatures, largely the study reports and situational analysis, this paper projects the challenges for the TSC and the failures of government agencies which evaluated the impact of the campaign. Therefore, finally an attempt to present the problems, consequences and actions to be taken as measures concerned with poor health, hygiene and sanitation in rural villages are discussed.

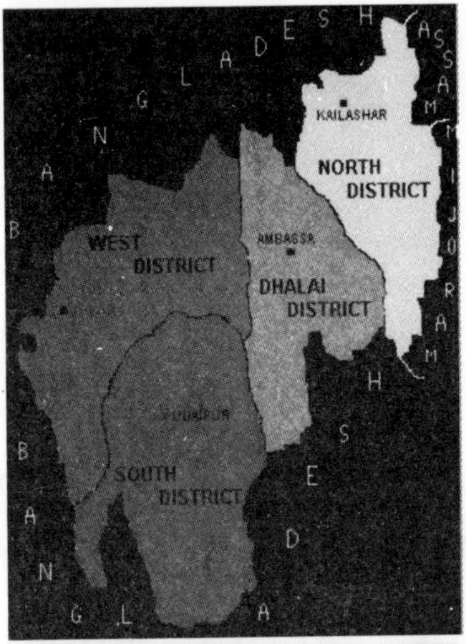


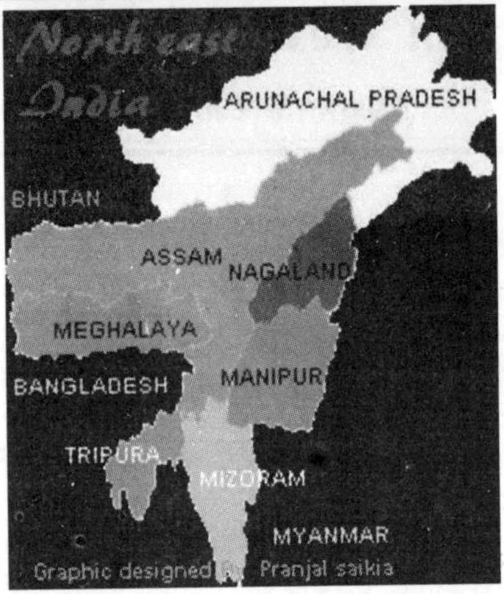


*Source*: tripurainfo.com.

## Total Sanitation Campaign in Urban and Rural Tripura

Sanitary condition and social progress are complimentary to each other. This is reflected within the process of urbanisation and modernisation of any society with urgent requirements for protection and improvement of urban people's health and living conditions. The same is applicable in rural villages as well. The Sanitation Mission Statement for implementation and achievement of the TSC in Tripura states that "all cities and towns in Tripura will be totally sanitised by

2015 so as to ensure good public health standards, human dignity and privacy for all citizens", various government reports present a successful case. As compared to an all India Report of the TSC, analysis presents a successful picture of Tripura. Let us discuss different achievements in TSC in Tripura. According to the government reports as mentioned by Snehlata and Anitha (2011) in their situation reports, the component wise achievement of the TSC in Tripura in present time are presented in the following table.

**Table 1. Component wise Achievement in TSC in Tripura**

| *Component* | *Percentage of Achievement* | *Percentage of Success as per India grand total* |
|---|---|---|
| Individual Household Latine IHHL | 83.49 | Above 75 |
| School sanitation) toilets and Hygienic Education SSHE | 71.07 | Between 50-75 |
| Sanitary Complex | 109.31 | Above 75 |
| Anganwadi Centres | 82.32 | Above 75 |

*Source:* Data excerpts from a comparison table across different Indian states www.ddws.nic.in dt: 01:01:2010.

The above table indicates 75 per cent achievement in providing importance for IHHL and indicates the mind-set of the people and their care for the environment. For Tripura as also Goa, Kerala and Mizoram are geographically very small, the IHHL access and usage could be easily implemented.

Similarly, the literacy rate (94 per cent) and decentralisation of powers to local institutions must have been given for a better implementation. The sanitary complex component among ten other states as Snehalata and Anitha have reported, Tripura has a coverage of above 75 per cent which clearly puts forth the fact that this state is focusing more on sanitation coverage. School toilets coverage in Tripura is in the category of 50 per cent to 75 per cent coverage which implies that the state government has realised the need for construction of school toilets with increased awareness regarding education of school children and its repercussions on the society as a whole. Similar attention is also given to the promotion of Self Help Groups and *anganwadi* across the state for empowerment of women groups. Tripura has been also awarded with 46 *nirmal gram purskar* in 2007 for achieving total sanitation.

A similar extensive rapid assessment report of the TSC prepared by the Department of Drinking Water and Sanitation of the Government, reports that West Tripura district has an average performance for sustainable sanitation.

The strategic draft prepared by the Urban Development Department (2010), is yet to be implemented by the Urban Local Bodies. According to the draft, in 2001, Tripura was declared free of the practice of manual removal of night-soil, subsequent to the Government of Tripura's Order on Prohibition of Manual Scavengers and Construction of Dry Pits with effect from 1 July, 1999. Substantial improvements in sanitation have occurred since then on account of the implementation of the Total Sanitation Campaign. As a result urban Tripura is better positioned than the rest of urban India in sanitation provision with only 2.5 per cent to 3.5 per cent of the population defecating in the open as compared to a national average of 18 per cent. When it comes to treatment and disposal of human waste, however, no single town has Sewerage System and Sewerage Treatment Plants (STPs). Around 23 per cent of urban households are yet to have access to adequate modern sanitation facilities.

I

## Challenges to the Total Sanitation Campaign: Reviewing the Study Report (2012-2013) of East-Wind Communications, Agartala

The TSC started functioning with a goal of achieving 100 per cent sanitation coverage all over the district by the end of September 2003 for improving the quality of life of the tribal people and provides privacy and dignity to women. The Government Report of the TSC's evaluation has equal positive improvement in South Tripura in 2001. Out of total targeted 1,03,273 BPL families, 83,541 families have been covered with sanitary toilets and out of total targeted 44,116 APL families, 21,087 number of families have been covered with sanitary toilets. Different models have been designed for different locations, cost, availability of water, flood prone areas using local materials for constructing the toilets.

An on-going baseline survey of the TSC in three most backward blocks in West Tripura district (Mandai, Lefunga and Hazamura) has been conducted by a public relation company based in Agartala, the East-Wind Communications (EWC). Largely to revise the status of 'sanitation related issues' in particular, the 'sanitation awareness' among different *gram panchayats* of these three blocks, EWC has just begun the survey and awareness programme in the rural villages. The methodologies they have adopted are observation, meetings, group discussions and interviews with local administrations, village committees and the stakeholders-villagers, for making an impact assessment of the TSC project. The baseline survey conducted by East Wind Communications to understand the below mentioned objectives of their assessment, has something else to offer.

- To identify, critically access and summerise the present status of sanitation related awareness among the community members within the project area;
- To conduct a comparison among the different villages so as to formulate are specific strategies for implementing the TSC project properly;
- To formulate the communication matrix fixing the exact message to be conveyed by the project staff, considering the socio-economic and cultural situation prevailing in the project area;
- To identify the misconceptions regarding sanitation related issues of the community members;
- To explore alternative and effective ways for implementing the TSC programme.

The above objectives of the study are part of the ongoing project of EWC. Interestingly, the Government of Tripura did not outsource the tender to any non-profitable organisation (local NGOS) to access the TSC implemented by them since 1999. Therefore, this study report is not offering an objective holistic situational analysis of the TSC in Tripura.

The data collected from seven villages namely: Dinokobra, Harbang, Khangari, Thaiplockpheng, Ashigarh, Bodhjangnagar, Borkathal, with household ranging from 300-800 in total and a population varying from 1000 to 2500, EWC has gathered data based on knowledge, attitude, behaviour and practices issues related sanitation of the villagers *vis-à-vis* the practice of health, hygiene that are dependent upon the geographical inaccessibility, environmental vulnerabilities and socio-economic factors. The survey encompasses questions related villages knowledge regarding the necessity of a toilet, water usage, comfortability, awareness among children, hygienic sense and drainage system.

## The Paradox of Achievement

It is evident from the field study that Total Sanitation Campaign related knowledge and practice has been similar among tribal and non-tribal across villages. People either from APL or BPL are equally unaware about sanitation and hygiene. The place of defecation at the dwelling units are pond side, vegetable garden or road side bush and other areas which are not frequented by villagers. This has been a 100 per cent open to field response in many villages. In almost all villages there is a least number of sub-health centre, in every village five-seven *anganwadi* centres, one to two basic level school and 10 per cent to 20 per cent of villagers are given toilets only. In almost all villages, despite the TSC being implemented, its only 10 per cent of villagers have handed over the cement slabs, plastic toilet pans to both BPL and APL families. However, in Thaiplockpheng village and Bhagvan Chowdhury Para of Lefunga block no villager is given a sanitary slab. Most of the families are without a proper sanitary facility in their house or there is no provision of community toilet in the villages. Therefore, most of the villagers are used to open space defecation. This common phenomenon of the communities across villages affects the health and hygiene situation causing various waterborne diseases.

Apart from the proper supply of slabs or pans, villagers are not sufficiently paid for the construction of the cemented toilets in their residential area. Even if they are being paid with a meager amount of rupees 3000 for cement, brick, iron rods, they were told to manage the rest of the expenses from MGNREGA work. This cannot be only taken as a mockery at the government officials, but it is a horrifying retrenchment of human rights. The allocated fund is not being spent and the negligent TSC actors being in the government sector and non-government sector. This is a matter of corruption and persistent deplorable affair of the tribal life of health and hygiene. Paramount problem arises after the distribution of the slabs. For example, on the one hand latrine slabs are given but not being informed about the proper usage of the sanitary or even the necessity of the proper sanitation in the house.

Similarly, to understand a sense of hygiene in different *gram panchayats* within a project area is different. Although there is a high literacy rate in Tripura villages and urban centers, but the knowledge of hygiene and sanitation is very low.

Paradoxically, *anganwadi* centers in villages are having at least one sanitary toilet but no schools have got one. This is a threat to girl students which results to their highest dropout from school. Absence of sanitary latrine is not only posing a serious problem for women and girl children, but for also ailing old family members and physically challenged people.

The most severe problem is acute water crisis for better sanitation in villages. Here comes the problem of unavailability of sufficient water. The tube wells are mostly remained dysfunctional. While drinking water has been a scarcity in these villages, water for using in toilet is a major crisis. To quote a tribal of Harbang village with regard to the accessibility of water for different household purpose, water resources are very poor. The only river *Garmarani* is a natural water resource which is again flowing one mile away from the village and on the other hand some small waterfalls become usable only during rainy season. EWC observes that 'the source of drinking water is either government installed hand pumps, or household tube-wells. Access to water is more acute especially by the rural women who often travel about a kilometer or more to fetch water. Even in majority the running tube well platforms are found broken and people are not aware of chemical and bacteriological contamination. Availability of water, therefore, is found to be the biggest challenge for the people at Lefunga, Mandai and Hazamura block in West Tripura'. This important provision for any community, whether large or small, is grossly neglected in the villages of West Tripura district. However, situation is not completely bleak with regard to the initiative in water harvesting method. One villager in his house has started harvesting water and a farmer from Thaiplockphang has made a sanitary toilet without any government aids. Therefore, it is not lack of sufficient efforts by the villagers; it is the inadequate dissemination of information and training for improvement of quality life among the villagers.

## The Need of Hour

Sanitary condition and social progress should be coexisting and Tripura as a Northeastern state should never be bereft of its social progress due to the ignorance or indifference on the part of the tribal's or donor, neglect. The impact of public health policies is uneven in rural and urban areas. EWC group recommends that measures for an effective TSC in targeted blocks of West Tripura through the following initiatives which are the needs of the hour:

- **Water scarcity:** The acute crisis of water for drinking and sanitation purpose in all household should be given immediate attention. Rain water harvesting is the only alternative method for coping up with water crisis of high hill people to store water for cleaning purpose. Deep water tube well and its maintenance and proper usage need to be provided at earliest.

- **Poor infrastructure:** Houses, roads and transport in the geographically inaccessible areas of tribal areas have been the hurdles of proper participation of the villagers and the policy implementers. The habitations in highland areas make the supply of raw materials for sanitation toilets from low land are miserable. The space for building up the sanitary toilets is immense, but to fetch the latrine pan/slabs to the people live in high lands and in disconnected *kachcha* roads has been troublesome. The supply of materials for sanitation program can be highly expensive if helicopter would be the only medium. Thus, no development can be achieved unless communication and transportation facilities are created. This situation, the poor infrastructure facilities of their life, drives people away to participate in any community development programme.
- **Dissemination of public awareness:** Through IEC-based campaign and the strategic actions like sensitisation programs should be led by local village committees, youth clubs and school teachers, and SHGs, feel Manas Paul and Ishika Basu of EWC. Thereby better health among school children in all villages is mandatory who would be the future of our clean environment. Lack of consciousness of personal hygiene and sanitation, both of which help to prevent disease among a mixed ethnic population of Hindu, Christian and Muslim people in rural areas. A strong awareness program to NGOs in the area whose participation in developmental activities is extremely less.
- **Lack of rural health centers/hospitals:** Using unhygienic pond water and insufficient safe drinking water by the tribal living in high hillocks and deep forest is a major challenge when there is no a health center or health care staff in PHCs. This is a general situation across Tripura as there are only two state hospitals in Agartala (the capital city) and in South Tripura district.
- **Gender insensitivity:** Women/girls are the main victims of poor basic sanitation facilities. The success or failures of such programs have high impact particularly on health, education and the promotion of gender equality. Girls and women may also be more vulnerable to diseases associated with poor sanitation than counterparts. The more women of families are aware of basic hygienic toilets; the children will be more informed about the health.

To conclude the paper, it is evident that proper sanitation facilities that leads to have healthy life of human beings is qualitatively absent in one of the backward regions of north eastern states of India. The need for action based sociology has been more crucial in these areas rather than the implementation of TSC or just building sanitation infrastructure in every household. This can only be add-on to the national human developmental reports. Therefore, some immediate action plans need to be addressed in order to implement another TSC through public-private or more preferably private-private partnerships. External support agencies like Sulabh International can play a leading role through collaboration with local private groups like EWC in addressing and solving the lack of basic access to water, establishing hygiene awareness programs, facilitating community participation, developing community based construction teams and implementing as well as monitoring the projects for a healthy environment/community. Apart from the urban sanitation improvement, it is the agrarian community which is hardly benefitted from the continuous flow of financial aid in the context of development.

## References

*Cencus Report 2001 and Department of Tribal Affairs, Tripura*. [Online at: http://sas-space.sas.ac.uk/3408/1/B24]

*Health, Hygiene and Sanitation in Latin America c1870 to c1950.*

[Online at: http://www.plosmedicine.org/article/info:doi/10HYPERLINK "http://www.plosmedicine.org/article/info:doi/10.1371/journal. pmed. 1000365". 1371/journal.pmed.1000365]

Means, Philip Ainsworth, *Sociological Background of Sanitation Work in Peru*. [Online at: http://www.ncbi.nlm.nih.gov/pmc/articles/PMC1353662/pdf/amjphealth00077-0033.pdf]

Report of Department of Drinking Water Supply-Progress and Achievements: Success Story of Total Sanitation Campaign Implementation in South Tripura.

TALBOT, Marion (1996), Sanitation and Sociology, *American Journal of Sociology*, Vol. 2, No. 1 (Jul. 1996): 74-81.

*Tripura Urban Sanitation Strategy: A Draft, Prepared by the Urban Development Department, Government of Tripura*. [Online at:http://www.urbanindia.nic.in/programme/uwss/slb/Drafts_SSS per cent5Csss-Tripura.pdf]

# 16

# Public Health in Action: An Approach through Community Mobilisation

*Vishesh Kr. Gupta*

The unsatisfactory health condition of the economically and socially deprived sections of the communities is caused by unequal distribution of income, goods and services. Their vulnerability makes it difficult for them to achieve satisfactory health status since they are continuously affected by poor social policies and programmes, unfair economic arrangements and decades of economic and social deprivation. Their health condition can be substantially altered only by a social determinants approach, which improves their daily living conditions, help to tackle inequitable distribution of power and resources and adequate state policies to address their multiple development challenges adequately. It is heartening that now in all health forums, the social determinants dimension of health is well recognised. Millennium Development Goals are very important move in that direction, but unfortunately "we have only two years left and still about one-fourth people still live in extreme poverty. More than forty per cent people lack access to safe drinking water. About thirty-forty per cent people have no regular access to reliable energy services, about forty per cent adults cannot read. Until we do not make significant progress on these critical areas, health will remain a distant dream for millions of people all over India. Perhaps it was the result of this situation, Shri Jairam Ramesh, former Minister at Centre, gave a statement about the need of more toilets then temples.

**Problem Statement**

Reaching out to the unreached is a global challenge and of a larger concern in India with one third of its population, constituting 250-300 million, living in remote, difficult and vulnerable areas and whose basic needs are not fulfilled. Despite several achievements and efforts, the 60 years of development plan has not changed the lives of almost one third of India's population. The continuing poverty of the rural poor is mainly due to structural constraints in improving their livelihood and securing their well-being in terms of parameters of health, education and gender equity. Available qualitative and quantitative data clearly show extremely uneven health and development progress in various parts of the country. Even within the states that are doing reasonably well, there remain regions where little has changed since independence.

Health is an important factor in development and is closely related to socio-economic and other factors. India is undergoing a dramatic demographic, societal and economic transformation. However, the health status of the citizens of India still lags behind and the health gains in the country have been uneven. Although there has been substantial advances in life expectancy and disease prevention since the middle of the 20th century, the Indian health systems provide little protection against financial risk, and most importantly there is widespread inequity in the health status of the population. It is now clearly indicated that the poor have much higher levels of mortality, malnutrition and fertility than the rich.

We were greatly encouraged to launch this initiative due to the prevailing climate of partnership being created by the government in view of their own concern regarding the extremely uneven health and development status of the country. We can focus on the strengths of Village Councils. Their multi-faceted approach, individuality and problem-solving capabilities may be encouraged. The functions being envisaged and performed by the Councils in the field of health and development are:

- Preparing area plans and allocating resources,
- Making the government health infrastructure accountable to panchayats,
- Empowering zila parishads to appoint and dismiss doctors, and
- Involving and mobilising the community and encouraging community participation, in order to meet the health and development needs of the area.

If the first three above stated functions of the Councils are facilitated at the earliest, many of the health problems in the rural areas can be tackled at the primary level itself.

This situation permeated right to the grassroots where district officials were looking for effective partnerships between the government health and development infrastructure, NGOs and the private sector to optimise the health infrastructure and improve the health and development status of the people.

This opened up an enormous potential for involving people and elected village leaders, many of whom were women, in a process of transformation of the village development scenario. The other major factor, which helped us to realise this goal, was present either in nascent or developed form from among some motivated local NGOs, who were willing to work hard with communities with a considerable degree of commitment to experiment with this innovative approach to development.

While taking up this important step, we realised that in a sub-continent as diverse as India, centralised planning for health, does not make sense—socially, economically, politically, culturally, demographically and topographically. Given the uneven terrain, it is hopeless to do centralised planning and implementation for the whole country. Besides this wide spectrum of situations, it is naive to expect people to participate in a programme which does not involve them in its conceptualisation, planning and implementation. Far off central ministry or state secretariats are as alien to an ordinary villager as is the UN Headquarters to a commuter in Delhi. On the other hand, if we opt for decentralised planning and implementation, we open up enormous possibilities.

**Partnerships**

It is also being realised that decentralisation opens up a range of possibilities, such as school teachers becoming motivators and health educators, local healers and our local festivals giving us ready-made *fora* to plan, discuss and implement the programmes as well as to educate the people and local panchayats and youth clubs becoming active partners in our effort. We have often been surprised by the incredible potential of these partnerships. Perhaps we should not be, since for centuries the communities of people have been organising massive events around their aspirations and needs. We need to get our health and population programmes linked to this energetic normal day-to-day life of our communities all over the country. This will mean initiating a process of give and take; by joining their momentum and not the other way around. We need to be bold, energetic and creative in meeting this challenge of implanting on existing local health traditions, not uprooting them and transplanting our 'hybrid' ideas, but implanting them with some local solutions.

Needless to point-out that convergence of services was the essence of the community development model that India had adopted in the early fifties. Somehow, this got displaced by target-oriented selective models due to the pressure and influence from multiple external funding agencies, despite the earlier model having paid rich dividends towards self-sufficiency in food grains as well as in creating an early infrastructure in health, education and other social sectors. A selective approach has created a situation where holistic public health and family welfare have been left with very little space, with no additional resources and with a large unmotivated defunct infrastructure, in many parts of the country. Currently we are in a situation where the people are crying out for treatment of malaria; kids are dying of diarrhoea due to unsafe drinking water and we say our mandate ends at Polio. We are working on the health and population front to help people lead a happy and healthy life and not just wage a battle against one particular disease. It is cynical to talk about micro nutrients, while not bothering about minimum wages or unequal wages between men and women.

Our experience of several years in many parts of the country has taught us that critical aspects like infant mortality, maternal mortality and fertility are directly linked to the socio-economic status of women; their literacy, age of marriage and gainful employment. It is, therefore, clear that there will be very little impact on the health and population front if we do not ensure gradual but comprehensive development of other related sectors. The unparalleled opportunity that has been given to us to empower more than lacs of elected panchayat leaders, almost half of whom are women, so that they can turn around decades of underdevelopment, must be availed of in full measure.

**Policy Environment**

Given the fact that during the last few decades, the country has failed in its effort to reach out to the people living in vulnerable areas, it was realised that unless many facets of inequity among its population are addressed, which greatly impairs successful outreach of social, economic and political benefit to a large sector of our citizens, this may not be possible.

Inequity that affects the health sector in India could be broadly categorised as follows :

1. Economic
2. Political
3. Social
4. Gender Issues
5. Locational Problems

India realises that a paradigm shift in the prevailing situation of inequity is only possible if there is a change in the fundamentals of legal, social and political rights of the poor and under-privileged. The situation in India is also complicated by the fact that we are an extraordinarily heterogeneous nation with people from a variety of cultural and ethnic backgrounds. Being a democratic pluralistic nation, it is impossible to thrust a particular view of social transformation quickly and assertively upon the population. It is essential for the country to carry its people along in major decisions of social, economic and political development, which means a long and sometimes frustrating consensus building process. In this overall background, we need to look at the issues of equity and health in India.

**Planning and Implementation**

Following the various parameters outlined above, we may identify different pockets in the country in which to initiate the concerned project. While identifying these locations, it was ensured that they sufficiently represented the social, economic, political, geographical, and ethnic diversity of the country. Broadly, these locations are in the physically challenging areas like the remote mountains and deserts. Areas mainly inhabited by the indigenous people and heartland India, where social, economic and gender status are polarised and the feudal infrastructure has still not been dismantled. Our premise was that the experience of working in these diverse areas would give us enough experiential learning to upscale similar initiatives in most of the country's vulnerable pockets.

While finalising the approach to our work in these pockets, it was felt that we should;

(1) Go in with an open mind and develop the project depending on the local basic needs as expressed by the people;

(2) Utilise the existing government infrastructures to the optimum level;

(3) Build local health and development skills and expertise;

(4) Launch sustainable initiatives, in terms of financial as well as human resources;

(5) Ensure that on the whole it not only affects the health and development status of the people, but ensures permanent capacity building in the community.

One of the critical elements of the project was to identify local partners in the voluntary sector, who may not have tremendous experience, but are motivated and are also rooted in the local community. Your state level Sulabh Institution can play an instrumental role in this process.

**Thrust Areas**

The thrust areas of work taken up under this programme can be classified as follows:

- Health
- Community Development
- Community Organisation
- Environment
- Women's Empowerment

Over a period of time a marked change has been seen in the above mentioned areas in all the Sulabh projects. However, all the projects are at different stages of achievement due to difference in the time of their initiation and considerable variations in local situations, geography, culture, political scenario and law and order situation.

**Health Interventions**

Since the beginning, health interventions were used to develop a rapport with the community so as to ensure their fullest participation in the overall development process for the area. Health interventions were mainly used as an entry point. From the baseline in most of the project area, it was apparent that those areas did not have any access to quality health care. In such projects, the main emphasis during the initial phase was on provision of curative services. Curative services were provided by a team comprising village health workers, a trained supervisor and a medical doctor.

**Community Organisation**

All the projects have before taken effective steps to organise people's groups at different levels in the project villages. These groups are mainly in the form of women's groups (Mahila Mandals), youth groups and farmer groups. The formation of these groups has ensured a comprehensive relationship between the project and the community. In most of the projects apart from these groups, there are also village health committees where representatives from different groups come together and decide the future plans and strategies for health and development related work to be undertaken in the villages. This process has also ensured that the community has a say in the decision making process. This has also given the community a strong feeling of ownership and has enhanced their involvement in all stages of the project.

Some of the positive outcomes of these processes are:

**Mobilisation of Village Committees:** Village communities can be mobilised at various levels, i.e., villages, blocks, panchayats, etc. and who are aware of and making efforts for improving their conditions.

**Formation of Social Action Groups to Optimise Government Resources**: In most of these areas, it was found that the existing large government health infrastructure was not operating optimally. Subsequently, over time the local communities had lost faith in it and the facilities were being hardly utilised, except for dire emergency and occasional preventive health work. Keeping in view the large amount of government expenditure that is incurred on maintaining these facilities, it was necessary to ensure that they were operating at an acceptable level of performance. They needed sometimes to bridge critical gaps that exist in the government systems, organising events for them to complete their preventive activities like immunisation, or re-orienting the government functionaries, so that they can effectively meet the local needs.

**Effective Linkages with Panchayats:** The projects have been able to establish good working relationships with local panchayats with the result that health has become an important aspect of panchayat activities. The micro plans being developed by local panchayats are more relevant and available to the local needs. Panchayat members are also functioning as effective change agents.

**Capacity Building:** The process of capacity building involved vocational training, training for other income generation activities, more effective utilisation of locally available resources and entrepreneurship development. To make relevant information available to local villages many projects have set up Village Information Centres to meet information needs of remote difficult areas.

**Income Generation :** These include:

- Vocational Training
- Promotion of Local Crafts
- Entrepreneurship Development
- Collaboration with Government

The trend towards collaboration with the government is increasing. The following activities are the project's mainstay:

**1. Health:** Immunisation programmes, family planning programmes, health camps, workshops (as government resource persons), referrals.

**2. Sanitation and Drinking Water:** Linkages with CAPART, DRDA, and Block Offices and Panchayats.

**3. Direct Benefits under Various Government Schemes:** e.g., maternity, Ayushmati, Vatsalya, old age pension, adolescent girls, Rashtriya Parivar Yojana, Indira Awas Yojna, Jawahar Rozgar Yojna, etc.

**4. Training:** Involving capacity building of Panchayat Members.

**5. Recognition of the Projects by State Governments:** As seen by handing over of PHCs (Arunachal, Orissa, etc.), training of animators (NLM) and direct financial support to projects for specific activities.

**Sustainability**

Sustainability is an essential feature of any projects from the very beginning, conscious efforts were made to select sustainable interventions. Some of these efforts are in the direction of :

- Sustainable income generation programmes
- Emphasis on human resource development
- Strengthening local panchayats
- Developing linkages with government and other agencies.

The health impact of the project can be summarised as:

- Increased health awareness reflected by reduced time lag between onset of symptoms and reporting to health functionaries;
- Increased utilisation of available government health services;
- Significant improvement in antenatal care, natal care and post-natal care;
- Reduction in mortality, especially due to communicable diseases like diarrhea, malaria, acute respiratory infections (ARI), as well as due to pregnancy and associated complications;

- Effective diseases surveillance leading to prevention of epidemics from taking place;
- Significant reduction in health expenditure as the quality health services including labouratory services are available within a reasonable distance and reasonable cost.

**Follow-up and Lessons Learned**

In a large, complex yet vibrant country like India, promoting health is a challenging task, but given the size of the population of the country it also holds the key to dramatic change in global health situation.

Happily, the solutions to these complex problems clearly exist in many innovative successful experiments within the country itself. It is a matter of concern that a large part of the existing health structure of the government within the country is operating in an unimaginative manner, which does not inspire confidence about their ability to cope effectively with the current problems and future challenges. Restructuring and revitalising the sector is an urgent need.

Success has been shown over the years through an overall improvement in the various health and development indice of India's underserved communities living in difficult and remote parts of the country.

# 17

# Environment, Sanitation and Health: Some Issues

*V. Chandrasekhar* and *A. Karuppiah*

Science and technology have increased the ability of man to harness and exploit the natural resources for his benefit and created complex and multi-dimensional problems. The rapid depletion of non-renewable resources and the exploitation of natural resources beyond the limit, destruction of the ecosystem, biosphere, flora and fauna due to industrial pollution are the important issues today in India. Unregulated industrialisation and urbanisation combined with the capitalist economic development models lead to ecological disaster. The degradation of environment would affect the human life and their entire ecosystem.

India witnesses the lower level of gross national product (GNP) and per capita income, population explosion, higher infant mortality and lower expectation of life at birth. While life expectancy has increased in India over the past decades (64.19 years) in comparison with developed nations (above 80 years). In the developed countries, it is less than six out of thousand children born, who die immediately after the birth and vast majority of them survive through childhood and adulthood but in India, it is 47/1000 birth die. The developed countries enjoy good water supply and sewerage systems and the incidence of water related diseases has been reduced. By contrast, in India, 72 of the 1000 babies born fails to reach their fifth birthday. The major killers are gastrointestinal infections, pneumonia, pre-term birth complications, diarrhea and malaria.

Eighty per cent of all the diseases are caused by water, sanitation and environmental pollution. Ill-health of this kind would impose economic costs reducing the availability of labour, impairing the productivity of employed workers and capital goods, wasting current resources and impending the development of natural resources. The low health status and the loss of human potential in India can be attributed to the lack of safe drinking water supply and sanitation facilities. The most recent UNICEF survey indicates that about 783 million people are without adequate safe drinking water supply and 665 million people (72 per cent) lack sanitary facilities in India. 626 million people practise open defecation and only 31 per cent of Indian population have access to sanitation facilities.

Only 21 per cent of rural population in India have adequate sanitary facilities against 54 per cent in urban areas. 84 per cent of rural population have access to better water supply against 96 per cent in urban areas. In many villages in India, women spend many hours every day to fetch water from far-off places for their families' survival. The number of water facets per 1000 habitants would be a better measure of health than the number of beds in a hospital.

## Environmental Problems

Non-renewable resources in India cannot sustain the infinite growth of industrialisation. The non-renewable resources are getting depleted at a rapid rate and the renewable resources have to be used widely to protect the environment.

Population explosion in India (1.22 billion) places higher demands on natural resources. Growth of population (1.312 per cent) today is an important contributing factor to the rapid depletion of resources, as the use of resources increase with the increase of population. Population pressure (382 persons per sq. kilometer) on land may lead to over exploitation and soil degradation with the excessive use of fertilisers and pesticides which in turn would disturb the ecosystem. Unemployment and the meager resources force the rural people migrate to urban areas resulting in socio-economic, environmental and health problems. These migrants are forced to live in huts with unhygienic conditions which later develop into slums causing environmental hazards. In Tamil Nadu alone, there are about 2,88,66,893 people live in slums. Thus, the population pressure (20,000 persons per sq. kilometer) in cities makes it more difficult to provide safe and sufficient water supply and sanitation facilities.

Exploitation of forest and energy sources are other important factors for the environmental degradation. Deforestation affects the equilibrium of fragile environment and the livelihood of the poor. In India, forest area is getting depleted by 367 sq. kilometer compared with 2009. The adverse consequences of indiscriminate deforestation affect the climate, geography, atmosphere and cause floods, landslides, soil erosion, silting of canals, reservoirs, etc. Now, there is a greater need to protect the forest resources in order to create good environment which ultimately is connected with good health.

Apart from the depletion of resources, environmental pollution is considered to be the extreme gravity of global situation. Industrial pollution has far-reaching effects on the health and well being of human beings. The industrial effluents, wastes, smoke and dust poison the land, air and surface as well as ground water to the point that they pose a threat to the survival of human, plant, animal and marine life. Besides, the direct effect of the environmental pollution leads to bio-accumulation and bio-magnifications in aquatic food chain. Modern agricultural and horticultural practices also cause pollution of environment because of the nitrate toxicity from the heavy application of chemical fertilisers and pesticides. Irrigation adversely affects the water quality due to chemicals entering the streams and rivers for which chemical treatment become necessary.

Atmospheric pollution caused by industrial plants is further exacerbated by the automobiles in cities accounting for a high proportion of population at risk for lung cancer, respiratory diseases and cardio-vascular ailments.

## Development and Environment

The rapid depletion of natural resources and environmental degradation could be attributed to the development models that are inequitable and wasteful. There is a greater need for radical rethinking of the rationale for the developmental strategies. Technology in the West has involved the mechanisation of many functions with high energy input. Developed countries with this kind of technology cannot provide a model for developing countries which are in need of the employment creating and energy conserving technologies. Hence, the adoption of Western models are misguiding and unlikely to contribute to an improvement in the quality of life (QOL) in developing countries.

Development planning in India gives high priority to economic criteria and fails to incorporate the environmentalist's concern. Even the environmentalists have ignored the environment in the construction of development theory. Both planners and administrators need to possess vision and display a capacity to think clearly and plan ahead in their efforts to construct a suitable development model. Preservation of environment need not be at the cost of development rather both should go hand in hand. Both are inseparable expressions manifesting the capacity of man to improve his quality of life. As a matter of fact, the conservation of environment should coincide with the development strategy. People should not only aim to conserve our resources but also to enrich them so that they can be safeguarded for the future generation as our heritage. Hence 'development without destruction' should be our goal.

## Social Culture and Development

The analysis of environmental crisis must take into account its interacting variables. Therefore environmental problem should not be treated as just those resulting from the detrimental and irrational use of resources. This is to be viewed as a problem of under development and advocates a holistic approach which requires the contributions of natural, physical and social sciences.

It is not the mere scientific breakthrough that has revolutionised the health of the people by eradicating small pox, cholera and other epidemics but the political will and social participation. Public resistance and lack of community cooperation are the practical obstacles to be removed. Change of attitude and acceptance of fresh values should start at the grass root level.

In the process of obtaining cooperation and participation of the community the choice of technology plays a vital role. Appropriate technology in water supply and sanitation programmes should be scientifically sound, technologically feasible, economically viable, socially and culturally acceptable and environmentally compatible.

Technology which is imposed independent of social context cannot be easily accepted by the people. However, scientific knowledge must be transferred into socially useful goods and services in accordance with social demands. The adoption of technology and programmes may be easier, if they are need-based, endogenous, self reliant, economically sound and based on structural transformation. Above all these, people must be mentally prepared to avail the services rendered through relevant educative processes.

It is obvious that there is a bridge between the development agents and the people they intend to serve in the transfer of information, skills and attitudes. Development agents, most often, operate at a different conceptual level and in a different framework from the people. Hardly, there is any consideration given to the local environment and indigenous culture that are more crucially functional. Utilisation of traditional culture and religious practices as variables are ranked higher in correlation with development process. The premise underlying such a strategy is that culture is a living entity, functionally adaptive to social change and is a vanguard of such a change.

Many planners have taken up the banner of culturally rooted development strategies and efforts are made to tailor the development's potentially attractive benefits to the dimensions of traditional rationalities. The crux of the culture-development strategy is to identify the most efficient and effective means of introducing new skills, knowledge and attitude within the existing cultural patterns, social institutions and values, so that development takes place in a more meaningful and harmonious fashion. The long cherished cultural pathways of interaction, established roles, value incentive systems and the established social institutions must be utilised as levers for positive development enhancing human survival.

Religious aspects of culture in India in which the sense of personal hygiene is deeply rooted in the form of customs and norms are the essential avenues for the development strategies. The indigenous models of socio-economic organisation, politico-legal systems and patterns of leadership that are integrated into the life of community, offer the greatest potential for people's participation in development.

Placed in a structural-functional framework, the entire range of cultural elements, cultural norms and motivational resources could be identified, mobilised and used to carry the message of personal as well as community health to the collective heart of the people with age old credibility. It is essential to identify the two important parameters of culture if our development programmes are to be successful. The first one is 'soft culture', that is, cultures and customs that we could change easily and influence immediately; and the other parameter is 'hard culture' which is intimately associated with deep-rooted beliefs and religions that may create antagonism in the community unless approached cautiously. Development through the traditional fabric of culture is guided by the principle that cultural elements would assume traditional legitimacy to participate in development. Thus, culture can be viewed as a foundation than a barrier to development. Hence the cultural factors are to be revitalised and marshaled for the intellectual nourishment.

## References

United Nations, Department of Economic and Social Affairs (UN DESA) (2011).

http://envfor.nic.in/assets/redd-bk3.pdf

http://en.wikipedia.org/wiki/Deforestation

http://www.indiaonlinepages.com/population/slum-population-in-india.html

http://www.trendsindia.org/?p=1

http://www.indiaonlinepages.com/population/india-current-population.html

*Children in urban world,* UNICEF 2012.

http://en.wikipedia.org/wiki/List_of_countries_by_population

# 18

# Displacement and Environment: A Study in the Migrant Camps of Jammu City

*Hema Gandotra*

The present paper is an attempt to address the issue, of environmental problems faced by a community after displacement. The paper will specifically focus on the Kashmiri Pandit migrants who got displaced in 1989-90 and were settled in the various camps in Jammu city and will try to analyse the environmental problems, particularly health, water and sanitation problems faced by the community after displacement.

Environmental health relates to the impact the environment can have on a population. Environmental health programmes include technical inputs related to water, the disposal of excreta and solid waste, vector control, shelter and the promotion of hygiene. As such water and sanitation programmes contribute only in part to the overall environmental health of a population. The success of an environmental health programme largely depends upon how the component parts relate to each other and water and sanitation can be considered as the foundation of such a programme. The term 'sanitation' is often taken to refer only to the disposal of human excreta. The concept of 'environmental sanitation' refers to the hygienic disposal of human excreta, solid wastes, wastewater and the control of disease vectors. There is a growing recognition that water and sanitation needs should not be looked at in isolation, but should form part of a holistic programme attempting to address the total environmental health needs of an emergency-affected community. The aim of a water and sanitation programme in an emergency is to attempt to modify the environment in which the disease-carrying organisms are simultaneously most vulnerable and threatening to humans. Modifying an environment to make it less favourable to disease-carrying organisms such as flies and rats (referred to as vector control), or minimising the areas of stagnant water around a populated area by means of good drainage, can play a significant role in reducing the transmission cycle of a number of diseases.

Human-caused and natural disasters expose populations to considerable health risks by disrupting their established patterns of water use, defecation and waste disposal. Displaced populations are often accommodated in camps where population densities are considerably greater than the most densely settled rural areas. It is vital, therefore, that they follow sanitation practices which reduce the risk of major outbreaks of diarrheal disease; control of defecation practices can play a large part in this. Invariably, this means the use of latrines and improving personal hygiene. Whilst some displaced populations are already familiar with latrines and others are able to adapt to their use without much difficulty, many displaced people are not familiar with them. Their arrival in a densely populated camp will force them to realise that their old habits pose a sudden threat to their health, and will require them to change their life-long defecation practices.

Lack of proper sanitation is a major concern for India. Statistics conducted by UNICEF have shown that only 31 per cent of India's population is using improved sanitation facilities as of 2008. It is estimated that one in every ten deaths in India is linked to poor sanitation and hygiene. Diarrhea is the single largest killer and accounts for one in every twenty deaths. Around 450,000 deaths were linked to diarrhea alone in 2006, of which 88 per cent were deaths of children below five. Studies by UNICEF have also shown that diseases resulting from poor sanitation affects children in their cognitive development. Without proper sanitation facilities in India, people defecate in the open or by rivers. One gram of faeces could potentially contain 10 million viruses, one million bacteria, 1000 parasite cysts and 100 worm eggs. The Ganges river in India has a stunning 1.1 million litres of raw sewage being disposed into it every minute. The high level of contamination of the river by human waste allow diseases like cholera to spread easily, resulting in many deaths, especially among children who are more susceptible to such viruses.

A lack of adequate sanitation also leads to significant economic losses for the country. A Water and Sanitation Programme (WSP) study on the economic impacts of inadequate sanitation in India (2010) showed that inadequate sanitation caused India considerable economic losses, equivalent to 6.4 per cent of India's GDP in 2006 at US$ 53.8 billion (Rs 2.4 trillion). In addition, the poorest 20 per cent of households living in urban areas bore the highest per capita economic impacts of inadequate sanitation. Recognising the importance of proper sanitation, the Government of India started the Central Rural Sanitation Programme (CRSP) in 1986, in hope of improving the basic sanitation amenities of rural areas. This programme was later reviewed and, in 1999, the Total Sanitation Campaign (TSC) was launched. Programmes such as Individual Household Latrines (IHHL), School Sanitation and Hygiene Education (SSHE), Community Sanitary Complex, *anganwadi* toilets were implemented under the TSC. Through the TSC, the Indian Government hopes to stimulate the demand for sanitation facilities, rather than to continually provide these amenities to its population. This is a two-pronged strategy, where the people involved in this programme take ownership and better maintain their sanitation facilities, and at the same time, reduces the liabilities and costs on the Indian Government. This would allow the government to reallocate their resources to other aspects of development. Thus, the government set the objective of granting access to toilets to all by 2017. To meet this objective, incentives are given out to encourage participation from the rural population to construct their own sanitation amenities.

Water is the single most important provision for any population; people can survive much longer without food than they can without water. In an emergency situation, the provision of water should be looked upon as a dynamic process, aiming to move from initially providing sufficient quantities of reasonable quality water to improving the quality and use of the available water. Adopting such an evolutionary approach will go some way to helping people derive the greatest benefit from the intervention. For example, displaced people who are living in a camp for the first time may find their normal washing practices inadequate for their current densely populated living conditions. The provision of bathing facilities, and encouraging people to use them more frequently, may have a significant impact upon their environmental health in helping to prevent the spread of skin diseases. People will always use the available water facilities if there are no alternatives; if they do not, they will not survive. Hygienic excreta disposal, on the other hand, is not fundamental to immediate survival needs.

Whenever a community gets displaced, the discussions among the social scientists generally revolve around the issue of loss of identity, socio-economic conditions of the displaced community, the health problems which generally include the problems related to the change in weather, loss of socio-cultural fabric etc. But there is hardly any discussion on the issue of environmental sanitation and water programmes and similar was the situation in case of Kashmiri Pandit migrants. One would find a bulk of literature on the issue of preservation of identity among the Kashmiri Pandits but hardly finds any literature on the problems of sanitation and water among these Pandit families after displacement. More than 50,000 families migrated during 1989-90 and around 38,000 families got registered with the relief organisation and these families were accommodated by the government in emergency at different places and were later put up in the different camps of Jammu city.

# 19

# Movement towards the Green Pilgrimage: Mapping Environmental Sanitation Issues in Kumbh Mela at Prayag

*Ashish Saxena*

## Background

In recent years, there has been a spectacular growth in public consciousness about the forms of environmental degradation in India. With an amazing but welcome rapidity, this awareness is being translated on the one hand into substantial media coverage, and on the other into the creation of new government departments concerned with different aspects of environment management. All over the world, people from local to global level have been directly victimised by the depletion of natural resources due to the short-lived developmental activities initiated by the modern forms of state apparatuses are organised themselves to raise the voice against the over exploitation of natural resources. Although the voices were inaudible in the initial period, later on it got appreciation once the external agencies like media, civil society and social activists took this issue very seriously into the public discourse. Because of this combination of voices gave birth to institutionalisation of social movements by articulating the need for restoring our natural resources and adopting alternative views of development and modernisation. Departing from the conventional categorisation of social movements based on ethnic, class, gender differences, new social movements of this kind of voyage, new discourse in the public domain attracted voice of the people from different parts of the world regardless of class, creed, colour or gender for a common cause called protection of our environment.

Ecological modernisation theory perhaps puts forward a radical transformational phase as the way modern society grapple with the environment question. In so doing, the institutions of modern society, such as the market, the state and science and technology, need to be radically transformed in tune with the environmental crisis, but not beyond recognition.

Religion is one of the most important facets of Indian history and contemporary life. It may not be wrong to say that religion has been, and continues to be, a matter of absorbing interest for many in India still today. In former centuries, no aspect of life was set apart from religion. All social relations were inevitably and legitimately suffused with religious ideas and acts. The possibility of religion in a modern world can be felt through altered functioning of religion. The marketisation of religion by religious gurus performing miracles and fascinating public, the involvement of religious organisations in the building up of hospitals and schools, working for the victims of natural disasters, etc., and politicisation of religion by the outburst of fundamentalists reflect the altered character of it. Modern forces have certainly influenced folk culture and traditions in developing countries like India, but they have not as yet lost their vigour. References to modern objects, events and experiences find their way into folklore through the usual process of reworking traditional items, the composition of new pieces, and even the merger of new types. Thus in contemporary India, the impact of modernisation has led to the emergence of new religions, revivals and reforms within the great traditions. In modern societies, with their complex fabric of social differentiations, not only among religion, but other groups and social activities, there appears a proliferation of rites (Saxena, 2009). It is believed that during this auspicious astrological moment, the waters of the Ganges have the ability to wash away layer upon layer of karmic debt. Millions of Hindus have already started pouring into the northern Indian city of Allahabad for the *Kumbh Mela* festival. Such a large-scale event poses unfathomable challenges for organisers, especially when it comes to sanitation.

Those pilgrims who stay for the whole month (known as *Kalpwasis*) live in conditions that are more difficult than those they experience at home. They live in rudimentary tents without heating, often without sanitary facilities, sleeping on the ground and experiencing night-time temperatures approaching zero centigrade. The event is also very crowded, and again this contrasts with life in the villages from which the pilgrims come. The crowds make walking to the bathing areas difficult and on days that bathing is judged particularly auspicious in terms of Hindu traditions, it can take several hours to walk a kilometre or so. Another striking feature of the event is its noise level. A vast array of competing loudspeakers broadcast religious discourses, songs, announcements and other administrative information throughout the day and night.

Even if enduring hardship is integral to the act of pilgrimage and even if such hardships do not deter pilgrims from attending, these various circumstances—unsanitary conditions, severe cold, dense crowding and intense noise—are all those that would be expected to be bad for well-being. But are they? We ask if, in the light of social psychological research identifying associations between involvement in social group-related activities and well-being, participation in this mass gathering could impact well-being positively. Thus, against the dysfunctionality of crowd of *Mela* as source of nuisance, mismanagement and cheats, this work humbly tries to explore the functionality of historical Prayag *Kumbh*. It is observed that religious *Mela* has a spread-effect of maintaining sanitation through collective participation. It is emphasised that socialisation of good sanitation practices to the pilgrims can be instrumental in carrying it further at far flung areas of diverse India and making clean and green India.

## Sociology of Sanitation and Its Association with Kumbh Mela

Keeping in view the emergence of the discourse of Sociology of Sanitation in India by Sulabh International Centre for Action Sociology, present paper tries to develop an inter-linkage between environment, religion and polity. In Durkheimenian framework, one can observe Sociology of Sanitation as a shift from profane to sacred elements. Locating the issue of sanitation, L. Dumount rightly states that the Indian society is homo-hierarchicus resting on the religion with caste system having an element of 'pure' and 'impure'. Even M.N. Srinivas, too, speaks about 'purity and pollution', having bearing on caste interactions. His concept of '*sanskritisation*' has an inherent notion of sanitation for lower caste members. If one goes philosophically on the issue of sanitation of soul, one finds that 'secularisation' reflects decline in the religious intolerance and accommodation of diverse religious practices for healthy society. The doctrine of Hindu religion also focuses on sanitation with the purification of ones '*paap*' in the lifetime. Thus, sanitation of body and soul as a precondition for attaining *moksh* after death and for once re-birth. Even, performing once duties in the holy pilgrimage is deeply embedded in religio-philosophical matrix of Indian psyche. At this juncture the pilgrimage of '*Prayag Kumbh*' becomes crucial. The paper locates issues of 'sanitation' in the pilgrimage of '*Prayag Kumbh*'. Here emphasis is on 'power of sanitation' as an ideology and an instrument of maintaining sanctity and religious purity.

In the present paper an attempt has been made to observe the emergence of the environmental discourses and transition of sanitation issues owing to the famous *kumbh mela* at holy *Sangam Nagri*, Allahabad. To refer MacLean (2003), historically speaking, the *kumbh mela* was applied to Allahabad's extant *magh mela* in the 1860s by *Pragwals* (river *pandas* [priests] of Prayag [Allahabad]) working upon and within the limits imposed by the colonial state and its discourses. This process was inadvertently aided by the British, and the resulting *mela* was affirmed by *sadhus* (Hindu holy men) and pilgrims. The "ageless" *Kumbh mela* in Allahabad was, therefore, made by a combination of actors, responding to the aggrandisement and growth of the modern state, particularly its infrastructure, administration and preference for well-controlled, predictable, orderly and traditional manifestations of religion. In this sense, the making of the Allahabad *kumbh* is not merely another example of an invented tradition; indeed, had it been suspected of being invented in any sense, it would not have been accommodated by the British to the extent that it was. The Ist phase of the understanding can be restricted to the colonial interventions wherein the *kumbh* in Allahabad offers a complex illustration of how Indian actors, working with and reacting to British orientalist assumptions, cast a major cultural and religious event. In carefully constructing a religious festival, they created for themselves a sphere in which they could enjoy some autonomy in the atmosphere of an increasingly repressive colonial state, despite post-mutiny promises of freedom (Oldenburg, 1989).

The first mention of a *Kumbh Mela* in British administrative reports that have been able to find, however, is in the closing discussion of an 1868 report about pilgrimage and sanitation controls. In this light, the application of the *Kumbh Mela* tradition to an existing religious festival the Magh *Mela* can be seen as an attempt by *Pragwal*s to expand the fame of their *tirtha*. The environment of the later nineteenth century was not a favourable one for Allahabad's pilgrimage priests, a time when, recovering from an anti-*Pragwal* campaign after the rebellion, the *mela* was assailed with an aggressive missionary presence (Bayly, 1975). The new government, despite promises of religious freedom, not only defended missionary labours at the *mela,* but also voiced strong objections to pilgrimage on sanitary grounds, debating the wisdom of disallowing *melas* altogether. In addition, there were optimistic predictions that pilgrimage in India would, "as it did in Medieval Europe," soon "die out or decrease as the minds of the people become more enlightened and as their information is increased, as other modes of education prevail and as trading customs alter" (MacLean, 2003). The demographic of pilgrims had changed in the nineteenth century from being princely and extremely wealthy to a more prosperous peasantry, with the result that, instead of relying exclusively upon princely patronage (which had, with the princes themselves begun to decline), places of pilgrimage had to adapt to suit their new clientele. In 1868, the district magistrate of Allahabad noted that at the Magh *Mela* "the attendance consisted chiefly of the middle and lower classes of people and no Rajas attended this year as they generally have done and their absence has affected the profits of *Pragwals* and the traders. For increasingly prosperous villagers, attending the *mela* was a means of expressing their status. Not only did pilgrimage still carry the aura of the elites, who, in former times, were the only ones who could afford to embark upon what was an expensive and dangerous enterprise, but establishing ties with a priest at a major pilgrimage centre gave enterprising peasants the opportunity to document their family and property. Lineages could be claimed and inscribed into *Pragwal* registers, as claims to land ownership, which could be used as evidence in court cases should any dispute ever arise (Fusfeld, 1974).

Hostility directed towards the minorities has been a feature of the *Kumbh Mela*, especially after 1966 when the VHP first appeared on the scene and was permitted to organise the 'religious conference'. In 1966, the main plank of the VHP had been the unity of the Hindus through the popularisation of the three cults of Mother India, Mother Ganga and Mother Cow. In 1978, the conversion of Hindus and the threat to Hindu ethos as posed by, for example, secular historiography were made the focus. And now in 1989 the VHP is flexing its muscles (See Navalakha, 1989).

## Locating the Emergence of Environmental Sanitation and Health Issues

Although, the first mention of a *Kumbh Mela* in British administrative reports that I have been able to find, however, is in the closing discussion of an 1868 report about pilgrimage and sanitation controls.

Contemporarily, The United Provinces *Mela*s Act, 1938 is vested with the power to impose tolls, taxes and fees under section five in *mela* areas—tolls on any vehicle or animal entering, or person bringing goods for sale into such areas. Without prejudice the office-in-charge may allot sites for the following in particular—religious societies of persuasion, *kalpbasis*, market places, latrines, urinals and rubbish heaps, recreation and entertainments. Even the United Provinces *Melas* rule miscellaneous, Oct. 16, 1940 says that a person suffering from plague, smallpox or other infectious diseases shall not enter the *mela* area. The Officer-in-charge shall order any person found within *mela* area suffering from an infectious disease either to leave the *Mela* or to enter the infectious disease hospital within a fixed time.

As reflected in local and national newspapers (*Times of India*, December 2012 and *Amar Ujala* December 2012), recently in 2013 for *kumbh mela*, the Indian government set up a special administrative body about a year ago that is responsible for the smooth-running of the festival. But the people who make it work are the cleaners. They're the lowest paid, and they're working round the clock. There are thousands of street cleaners, then there's a smaller group that cleans the water. There are lots of different camps of holy men, and they all want to take their dips first, because they want the water to be clean. People take dips in the water every day, but when the holy men take their dips, it attracts big crowds—people want to dip at the same time with the holy men. The dips are staggered—there's always a half hour gap between each dip, so the cleaners can go into the waters and clean. They don't use chemical products; they fish out any objects left behind, like the flowers people take with them to bathe. It seemed, the weak links were water and sanitation—water leakage, not enough taps.

Recently, in the run-up to the festival, around 35,000 single-seat latrines, 340 blocks of 10-seat toilets and 4,000 urinals looked on-site. They're linked by a 165 kilometre network of plastic pipes which carry the waste to pits, which themselves are reinforced by brick. It'll be interesting to see how many new latrines and pits the administration will have to build, as what they've built so far may not be enough. People do not always use the toilets, particularly children—they just go in the open air. There are 9,000 sweepers, whose job it is to sweep away faeces into the pits. Waterborne diseases and a cholera outbreak are real risks. We hope to carry out research that will help the administration prevent the impact of waterborne diseases. Even the area of the *mela* is also on the rise: from 1,495.31 hectare and 11 sectors in 2001 to 1936.56 hectare and 14 sectors in 2013 (official website of *Kumbh mela* 2013).

According to national newspaper reports, arrangements provided 5,000 gallons of purified drinking water every minute; 8,000 buses which shuttle pilgrims in and out of the festival area that spread over 300 acres; 16,000 outlets and 6,000 poles which provided electrical facilities; 6,000 sweepers and sanitation employees who worked round the clock to maintain health standards; nine pontoon bridges which spanned the Ganges at intervals. Although, the Indian government set up a special administrative body about a year ago that is responsible for the smooth-running of the festival, but the people who make it work are the cleaners. They're the lowest paid, and they're working round the clock. There are thousands of street cleaners, then there's a smaller group that cleans the water. Further, agitated over high levels of pollution and shallow water in the holy Ganges, the Shankracharyas, seers and *dandi swamis*, along with all the *akaharas*, are all set to boycott the *Shahi Snan* on *Mauni Amavasya* which was scheduled for February 10, 2013. These saints threatened that if the situation remained unchanged, they will not bathe in the next *Shahi Snan*.

By going through the factors responsible for the failure of Ganga Action Plan (GAP), the parliamentary standing committee on science and technology, environment and forests has doubts if the prime minister's mission of cleaning Ganges by 2020 will be accomplished. Our vision is that in 12 years' time, every camp at the *Kumbh Mela* will be green, and every pilgrim will be reminded that it is the sacred duty of every Hindu to protect the environment.

It is reflected that the role of religious ideology and socio-religious leaders, too, have become active players towards generating environmental sanitation. In conclusion, it is urged that the 'size and complexity' of the *Kumbh Mela* is inspirational for inter-disciplinary research in a number of complementary fields of urban studies and design, religious and cultural studies, environmental science and public health, technology and communications. There is a need to bring the issue of 'Right to Sanitation' and also *sulabhisation* of pilgrimage sites. Needless to mention that environmental sanitation is the growing concern of the hour.

## References

Bayly, C.A. 1975. *The Local Roots of Indian Politics*, Allahabad, 1880-1920. Oxford: Clarendon Press.

Fusfeld, Warren E. 1974. "The Kumbh *Mela in Allahabad: Networks of Communication in Nineteenth Century North India."* Master's thesis, University of Pennsylvania.

Ghurye, G. S. 1964. *Indian Sadhus*. Bombay: Popular Prakashan.

Gordon, Richards, 1975. *The Hindu Mahasabha and the Indian National Congress*, 1915 to 1926, Modern Asian Studies, Vol. 9, No. 2 (1975), pp. 145-203.

MacLean, Kama, 2003. *Making the Colonial State Work for You: The Modern Beginnings of the Ancient Kumbh Mela in Allahabad*, The Journal of Asian Studies, Vol. 62, No. 3 (Aug., 2003), pp. 873-905.

Navlakha, Gautam, 1989. *A Show of 'Hindu Power'*, Economic and Political Weekly, Vol. 24, No. 13 (Apr. 1, 1989), p. 658.

Oldenburg, Veena Talwar, 1989. *The Making of Colonial Lucknow,* 1857-1877. Delhi: Oxford University Press.

Sax, William, 1987. "*Kumbha Mela.*" In Encyclopedia of Religion, edited by Mircea Eliade. Vol. 8. New York: Macmillan.

Saxena, Ashish, 2009. '*Religion, Caste and Community: Identity Substantiation through 'Maile' Congregations among the Dogras of Jammu and Kashmir (India)*' in '*Politics and Religion*' Center for Studies of Religion and Religious Tolerance, Serbia, Issue No. 1/2009 Vol. III.

# 20

# Qualitative Research Methodology and its Application in Health Research

*R. Shankar*

## Qualitative Research Methodology

Qualitative research is one of the two major approaches to research methodology in social sciences. Qualitative research involves an in-depth understanding of human behaviour and the reasons that govern human behaviour. Unlike quantitative research, qualitative research relies on reasons behind various aspects of behaviour. Simply put, it investigates the why and how of decision making, as compared to what, where, and when of quantitative research. Hence, the need is for smaller but focused samples rather than larger random samples. From which, qualitative research categorises data into patterns as the primary basis for organising and reporting results.

"Qualitative research methods also began at the margins of acceptable science". From Freud on, Carl Rogers (1942:1951) Piaget ... Mary Ainsworth (1979). Qualitative research approaches began to gain recognition in the 1970s. The phrase 'qualitative research' was until then marginalised as a discipline of anthropology or sociology, and terms like ethnography, fieldwork, participant observation and Chicago school (sociology) were used instead. During the 1970s and 1980s qualitative research began to be used in other disciplines, and became a dominant-or at least, significant-type of research in the fields of women's studies, disability studies, education studies, social work studies, information studies, management studies, nursing service studies, human service studies and others.

In the late 1980s and 1990s after a spate of criticisms from the quantitative side, new methods of qualitative research have been designed, to address the problems with reliability and imprecise modes of data analysis. An intelligent way of differentiating Qualitative research from Quantitative research is that largely Qualitative research is exploratory, while Quantitative research is conclusive. Quantitative data is measurable while Qualitative data cannot be put into a context that can be graphed or displayed as a mathematical term.

Data are not inherently quantitative, and can be bits and pieces of almost anything. They do not necessarily have to be expressed in numbers. Frequency distributions and probability tables don't have to be used. Data can come in the form of words, images, impressions, gestures, or tones which represent real events or reality, as it is seen symbolically or sociologically (*If people believe things to be real, they are real in their consequences*—the Thomas Dictum). Qualitative research uses unreconstructed logic to get at what is really real—the quality, meaning, context, or image of reality in what people actually do, not what they say they do (as on questionnaires). Unreconstructed logic means that there are no step-by-step rules, that researchers ought not to use prefabricated methods or reconstructed rules, terms and procedures that try to make their research look clean and neat (as in journal publications).

It is, therefore, difficult to define qualitative research since it doesn't involve the same terminology as ordinary science. The simplest definition is to say, it involves methods of data collection and analysis that are nonquantitative (Lofland and Lofland, 1984). Another way of defining it is to say, it focuses on "quality", a term referring to the essence or ambience of something (Berg, 1989). Others would say, it involves a subjective methodology and yourself as the research instrument (Adler and Adler, 1987). Everyone has their favourite or "pet" definition. Historical-comparative researchers would say, it always involves the historical context, and sometimes a critique of the 'front' being put on to get at the 'deep structure' of social relations. Qualitative research most often is *grounded theory*, built from the ground up.

Ethnomethodology Harold Garfinkel 'ethno' refers to the stock of common sense knowledge available to the member of society and 'methodology' methodology refers to the methods which actors use in different settings to make their meanings understandable to others. These methods ensure the successful accomplishment of every day communication and activity.

### What is Ethnography?

It may be defined as both a qualitative research process or method (one conducts an ethnography) and product (the outcome of this process is an ethnography) whose aim is cultural interpretation. Ethnographer generates understandings of culture through portrayal of what is called an emic perspective, often described as the 'insider's point of view.'

### Methods of Qualitative Research

1. Participant-Observation
2. Ethnography
3. Photography
4. Ethno methodology
5. Dramaturgical Interviewing
6. Sociometry
7. Natural Experiment
8. Case Study
9. Unobtrusive Measures
10. Content Analysis
11. Historiography
12. Secondary Analysis of data

### Qualitative Research and its Application on Health

The theme of the workshop is 'Qualitative research methodology and its application in health research'. I attach great importance to the word 'quality', therefore, I explain what I have in mind in some detail.

The well-being or quality of life of a population is an important concern in social sciences especially in sociology and political science. There are many components to well-being. A large part is standard of living, the amount of money and access to goods and services that a person has; these numbers are fairly easily measured. Others like freedom, happiness, art, environmental health, and innovation are far harder to measure. This has created an inevitable imbalance as programs and policies are created to fit the easily available economic numbers while ignoring the other measures, that are very difficult to plan for or assess.

Debate on quality of life is millennia-old, with Aristotle giving it much thought in his Nicomachean Ethics and eventually settling on the notion of eudaimonia, a Greek term often translated as happiness, as central. The neologism liveability (or livability), from the adjective 'liveable', is an abstract noun now often applied to the built environment or a town or city, meaning its overall contribution to the quality of life of inhabitants.

Understanding quality of life is today particularly important in health care, where monetary measures do not readily apply. Decisions on what research or treatments to invest the most in are closely related to their effect of a patient's quality of life.

## Measuring Health Related Quality of Life (HRQOL)

The measures often used in the study of healthcare are 'quality-adjusted life years' (QALYs) and the related 'disability-adjusted life years' (DALYs); both equal one for each year of full-health life, and less than one for various degrees of illness or disability.

Another method of measuring quality of life is by subtracting the *"standard of living"*, according to the technical definition of the term. For example, people in rural areas and small towns are generally reluctant to move to cities, even if it would mean a substantial increase in their standard of living. One can, thus, see that the quality of life of living in a rural area is of enough value to offset a higher standard of living. Similarly, people must be paid more to accept jobs that will lower their quality of life, night jobs, ones with extensive travel all pay more, and the difference in salaries can also give a measure of the value of quality of life.

There is a growing field of research concerned with developing, evaluating and applying quality of life measures within health related research. Many of these focus on the measurement of health related quality of life rather than a more global conceptualisation of quality of life. They also focus on measuring HRQoL from the perspective of the patient and thus, take the form of self completed questionnaires. A number of groups and agencies around the world have tried to develop ways of assessing quality of life.

QALYs are controversial as the measurement is used to calculate the allocation of healthcare resources based upon a ratio of cost per

QALY. As a result, some people will not receive treatment as it is calculated that cost of the intervention is not warranted by the benefit to their quality of life.

No system of healthcare research can be considered in isolation. For instance, the health status of people at any given time will depend upon several factors. Health status depends upon social and economic factors, such as the organisation of the home and family, equality or otherwise of the sexes, social stratification, general conditions of work and poverty, which increases proneness to disease while decreasing the capacity to combat it.

Health is closely related to nutrition and depends upon factors as the quality and adequacy of food supplies, dietary habits and culinary and food preservation practices. Healthcare system is obviously related to the technology of medicine and to our knowledge and ability to deal with the mal-functioning of the day.

Health is closely related to the spread of education among the people because of individual's understanding of health, his capacity to remain healthy and his ability to deal with illness are all conditioned upon the level of his education. Some of these factors fall within the sphere of health services and I hope these will be discussed in some detail in this workshop. I agree that the ultimate decisions in health are essentially political.

The concept of Medical Sociology is gaining importance of late and the need for studying Hospital as an institution is felt at all levels. The conducive and cordial atmosphere in the hospital, the accommodative relationship between the professionals and the patients would go a long way in building a healthy society. Hospital is also a social matrix where all kinds of social processes take place. Hence an analysis of Hospital as an institution is of immense value.

Anaemia is a common problem among the pregnant woman. A scientific study is essential to assess the condition of anemia in pregnancy. Because the women suffering from anemia in pregnancy are affected by physical, social and psychological profiles which indirectly creates problem in the family.

It is a tragic fact that in the very act of giving birth, of achieving motherhood, nearly half a million women die every year the world over. Many more who escape death, survive with serious ill health and a host of pregnancy and child birth related complications. It is the women in the developing countries who face the gravest risks. These women die of neglect and ignorance and due to inaccessibility of required services. During the last two decades the concerned and combined efforts of the countries, the UNICEF and WHO in particular, have brought down the infant mortality rate, all over the world, and more significantly in the developing countries.

Female education can be expected to reduce desired family size for a number of reasons, ranging from greater autonomy in defining fertility goals to enhanced receptiveness to modern social norms, reduced dependence on sons for social status and old-age security, and the higher opportunity cost of time for educated women.

Healthcare is one of the most important of all the human endeavours to improve the quality of life of the people. It implies that provision of conditions for normal physical and mental development and functioning of human being individually and the group. It provides a wide spectrum of services including primary healthcare, integration of preventive and curative health services, health education, protection of mothers and children, family welfare and the control of environmental hazards and communicable diseases. Healthcare facilities in rural areas in India are provided through Primary Health Centre (PHC) started as a part of national rural development scheme. The primary health centers function as the first anchor against disease and ill health in rural areas. It is close to the people and offer adequate medical care services to meet the basic health needs of the people.

Old age is a period of decline in human life. The decline in the physical vitality and psychological performance. This makes them weaker and incapacitate to lead a routine way of life. In this situation, the family members of the aged consider them as a burden. Thus, they are often discarded and ill treated by their kith and kin. The prevailed situation in the family compelled them to join the old age home. As a social security measure to tackle the problems of aged under Social Welfare Administration many effective programmes are being launched. One such effort is old age home to care and concern the aged under the grey revolution. The homes for the aged are started both in the Governmental and Non-Governmental sectors. The role of Non-Governmental sector is extensively high than the former one. Even in the home for aged, the life pattern experienced by the old age varies from person to person or organisation to organisation. But still sustained efforts are being taken by such sectors to improve upon the well-being and the quality of life of the aged.

Study of the elderly has been accorded an important place not only among biologists or psychologists, but also among the sociologists due to its sociological relevance. Because it is society which bears all the consequences of the process of aging sections of society. In the early days, the old age section of society enjoyed high social status and power in family as well as in society as such. But they do not have the same advantages today. This can be assumed that it is due to the demographic as well as socio-economic changes that accompany the transition of societies from agriculture and rural to industrial and urban production and distribution system prevailing not only in India but worldwide. Earlier the survival of old people in the society or family were neither considered and treated as problem nor waste on the part of their family. Instead the elders enjoyed by serving them and treated Godly. The social values such as *Karma* and *Dharma* also expected them to take care of the aged and keep them happy during the declining age.

But the dynamic industrial environment altered every institution whether occidental or oriental. Hence there is a great need for alternative institutions which can act as substitute institution for the old ones. The older people expect their welfare or care through these alternatives.

Today in this era of globalisation, Trusteeship concept of management entails ploughing back part of an organisation's profit into community initiatives. Meaningful and welfare driven initiatives make an impact on the quality of life of a large section of marginalised people. From this stems the organisations' social involvement far beyond business.

Modern education, urban influences, mass media and above all the emergence of materialistic individualistic outlook had the tendency to alter traditional kinship and family organisation towards nuclear family norms, with declining authority of aged.

It is very difficult to imagine the quality of life in slum areas. For instance, during rains, the whole area will be flooded and pathways become swampy and the entire area will be the suitable breeding place for mosquitoes, exposing the slum dwellers living in the area to all sorts of the diseases. During the floods, their thatched sheds will be badly disturbed. Quality of life in slum is deteriorated greatly and unfortunately it is underestimated as well as misrepresented. The lack of income constraints them to access facilities which are available in urban areas. The multi-dimensions of poverty, apart from lack of income, but lack of assets, lack of power, lack of legal rights, lack of resources/ contacts necessary to secure political advantages, lack of access to education and a very poor quality of housing in which most low income groups have to lie and the tremendous health burden this brings with it, especially where healthcare provision is also inadequate. All dimensions of the deprivation have been created a kind of frustration in their life. Yet, when the urban development programmes intervene in the cities, where majority of the slum dwellers feel they may be evicted at any moment and may loose the relationships which have been maintained years together.

New discoveries in biotechnology through agriculture, horticulture, medicine, chemical industry, criminology, control of environmental pollution and immunology (Defence mechanism) are going to change our life in the course of time. The findings of human genome project, quite comparable to the feet of landing on moon, have given new vision and impetus to our life. Disease causing genes have been identified. For many genetic diseases gene therapy has been formulated. All human beings, irrespective of race, caste, creed, etc., possess 99.90 per cent same genome. Predisposition of an individual to disease can be predicted. Biodegradable plastics have already come into the market. Seeds with essential amino acids are available. Golden brown rice has been developed with vitamin—A which can solve the problem of malnutrition among children.

Plants have been engineered for vaccine and antibody production against diarrhea. Scientists have been developed CT-B and heat liable entrotoxin-(LT-B) in potato. In tomato Hepatitis-B surface antigen has been developed which can cure liver disorders (Edible Vaccines) against Streptococcus mutants, which cause dental decay. Plant bodies have been developed. Large quantities of insulin are available through recombinant DNA technology. Tissue Plumage Activator (TPA) is being made available in large scale to dissolve blood clots. For early detection of AIDS, P24 Ag is employed immunologically. Useful chemicals like alkaloids, single cell proteins, etc., are obtained through plant culture. DNA fingerprint employed in forensic department as a proof to nab criminals and this evidence is acceptable in any court of law.

High power computers and micro array techniques are going to revolutionise our life in future. However, there are also eruptions like bioethics, legal issues, biosafety, cloning, anti-GMF association against GMO and GMF. Biological warfare, an advent of biological resolution, also is another problem, threatening the existence of human race, which one has to bear in mind amidst lofty credentials and achievements borne out of current development of biotechnology. Developing countries depend upon achievement of biotechnology in view of burgeoning population, which badly is in need of food and shelter. Whatever may be the thinking of modern revalidation in biotechnology (gene revolution), it is going to change our way of life in the days to come.

The concept of quality of life is as diversified as variations in populations and across cultures. Tracing its evolution to medical epidemiology and implications in the healthcare and management profession it has broadened its horizons to encompass a wide range of perspectives and disciplines. From a macro perspective nations- states speak about the quality of life indice and criteria and base their development plans on the basis of such indice for the people, while on a micro level social scientists and researchers in related disciplines express concern about the quality of life of smaller groups, communities, families and individuals. While itself is again relative in the sense that a particular indicator of well-being or prosperity for a particular population or community may not be so for another community or social group.

Quality of life denotes things, which are valued, thereby, people with different life styles stress different things, societies in different stages of development will emphasise different qualities, and differential need satisfaction will result in different things being held as crucial. The quality of life depends upon the degree of satisfaction of human needs; needs defined by the material and impersonal resources an individuals has and can master; needs related to love, companionship and solidarity; and needs denoting self actualisation and obverse of alienation. It involves both job-related well-being and family related well-being.

Today, all the social institutions like family, education, career, health, politics and entertainment, etc., are having the impacts of the "communication revolution" that is taking place in the country which made quality to the human life.

Today, all the social institutions have the impact of mass Communication and Information technology and the quality of life has much improved in all these institutions. At the sametime, many sociological problems are emerging out of the growth in Communications, which has its own problems in all the social institutions. Though Communication has brought Speed, Efficiency, Non-Polluting environment the sociological problems life Jobless society due to Computer revolution, Social problems emerging out of the impart of Mass Media's, Cyber Crime, etc., are prices given for quality of human life.

Quality of life today depends on many developments in the society including science and technology. Yet our policies are always selective and not people oriented. State health services are confined to the towns and cities which account for hardly 20 per cent of the population. Healthcare system is gradually shifting from state to private sector, which is naturally business oriented and not service oriented. There is an increase of "star" hospitals which are luxurious, catering to the needs of rich and the state health policy is very much ignorant of it. This leads to a new colonisation within the society. The innocent people are not only ignorant but silently witnessing the events with pain in their heart.

Medicinal plants are considered as natural medicines created by the 'Nature for human medicines'. For every diseases of man, medicines are available in the environment. It is our responsibility to identify the medicinal plants and to use them. Man is suffering from various types of diseases due to his negligence of the utilities for these wonderful medicines. About 25,000 medicinal plants are used as herbal medicines throughout the world. The reason for the chronic and acute illness of man is the excessive and prolonged use of synthetic drugs. Human body is Nature's Creation. Hence nature medicines are conducive to this body when it is ill. Having realised the dangers of inorganic farmings, man is returning to natural or organic farming, similarly in order to protect his health, man has to return to natural herbal medicines. The practical medical know–how of indigenous practice has been derived from centuries of experience by using various herbs and other substances to cure a variety of illness. Primarily, the use of herbs is guided by experience but their use is yet to be systematically recorded and documented (Ali, 1994). The practice of utilising medicinal plants for medicines is as old as 5,000 to 4,000 BC. Greeks have given enormous information about medicinal plants. Many factors make up the balance of nature. All lives depend on water, air and minerals. Since it is natural and good for health it is ideally suited for all body conditions. Children are the building rocks of society. Their survival and well being are very important for the development of the nation in future.

There is an increasing research interest on infant mortality. As a result, the knowledge pertaining to health issues and medical therapy have become expanded. But there is no corresponding improvement in the status of child health. The average health conditions of a child in India is no better than the average health of a child in the Third World.

The data pertaining to infant mortality in Tamil Nadu indicates positive results as compared to many other states in India. However, it does not mean that the infants who manage to survive are healthy. In fact, most of the surviving children are either undernourished or not given adequate medical care and attention.

Quality of life cannot be considered from health aspect in isolation. It is, however, obvious that quality of life will have to be an integral part of wider programme to improve the standards of living of the people and will have to be linked to programmes of abolishing poverty, larger production and better distribution of food (including proper storage and improved dietary and culinary practices) and basic education.

It is the adoption of this comprehensive approach that will facilitate and promote a broader conception of quality of life many approaches to "quality of life" some describe, others analyse and few focus on any one aspect of quality of life and study analytically. Its purpose is to introduce social scientists to look at quality of life from a broader perspective than they were hitherto exposed almost exclusively to medical sociology point of view. It is addressed particularly to emerging sociologists who intend to understand the value loaded concept of quality of life to gain insight and understanding of it. Such understanding is not possible without comprehension of the structural changes in the social institutions and their operation. The studies reported in this, represent a connected set of facts and oxioms in reference to which the sociologists may analyse and orient their thinking and communicate their thoughts and attitudes in respect of quality of life.

This workshop is an attempt to provide this essential foundation for broadening the formation of qualify of life. To serve this need, at least as a beginning—is the basis and background from which this has emerged. This workshop has been organised under the auspicious of the ICMR, if it achieves in some measures, the aim of the sincere efforts put into this will have been worthwhile.

'Qualitative research methodology and its application in health research' had brought experts from various disciplines like sociology, psychology, economics and health education. It is a welcome sign that the philosophical frame work of 'Quality of Life' is now being seriously questioned in several aspects and by several individuals and scholars including the medical sociologists. It will obviously take some time for a clear-cut outline for alternative or alternatives to emerge.

But the large-scale questioning of the concept and the continuous debate that are now taking place around some of its aspects auger well for the future. The Department of Sociology has, therefore, to highlight some of the important factors for ponder. The organisers of this workshop; their main objectives are to stimulate further thought in redefining Qualitative research methodology and its application in health research. I have strong reason to believe that this deliberation of the workshop will cause a new outlook and new direction of thinking.

But where do we go from here? The situation in India is different from that in north bloc countries. This is a difficult task. But the only possible solution is beyond a committed bond of de-classed intellectuals and emerging leadership from the young budding sociologists.

## Bibliography

Bhatia, Jagdish C and John Cleland, *Self reported symptoms of gynaecological Morbidity and their treatment in South India*, Studies in family Planning, 1995; Vol. 26, No. 4.

Bose K, Chakraborty F., Asian Pacific Journal of Clinical Nutrition, Delhi, 2005; 14(1): 80-2.

De Silva, M., '*Prevalence and consequences of iron deficiency anemia in pregnancy*'. Paper presented at a Consultative Meeting on 'Anemia in pregnancy', November 29-30, Colombo, 1993.

Family Welfare Programme in Tamil Nadu Year Book, Demographic and Evaluation Cell, State.

Family Welfare Bureau, Directorate of Medial and rural Health Services, 1990; Madras.

Fourth World Conference on Women, Beijing, Country Report; Government of India.

Department of Women and Child Development, Ministry of Human resource Development, 1995.

Health for all by 2000AD - Problems, approaches and challenges, GOL, Ministry of Health and Family Welfare, New Delhi, 1983.

India's Family Welfare Programmes towards a reproductive and child health approaches, Population and Human resource Operation Division, South Asia Country Report- II, 1995.

I.C.M.R. Nutrient Requirements and Recommended Dietary Allowances for Indians. National Institute of Nutrition, Hydrabad, 1992.

ICSSR and ICMR, Health for All, An Alternative Strategy, Indian Institute of Education, Pune, 1981.

NCAER, Household Survey of Medical Care, 1991, Survey of Primary Health Care, 1994.

Winkvist A, et al., Division of Epidemiology, Department of Public Health and Clinical Medicine, Umea University, Sweden, 2002.

World Development Report, Investing In Health, 1993.

# 21

# Sociology of Sanitation

*Ms Preeti Singh*

It is my privilege to have this opportunity to represent HUDCO in such important forum.

As you all know that we have gathered here today to deliberate on the important subject of 'Sociology of Sanitation—Environmental Sanitation, Public Health and Social Deprivation'. This topic has become more important and relevant as the time left out to achieve the Millennium Development Goals to cover 50 per cent of population by the year 2015, is nearing.

We all are also aware of the fact that the sanitation is a State subject in our country and 74th amendment in the year 1992 empowered the ULBs with responsibility of public health, sanitation, conservancy and SWM.

The sector as such is not commercially viable but is economically viable. It requires high capital cost and there is operation and maintenance cost involved. The funding, therefore, needs combination of grants, loans and tariff collection to make it happen. This is the reason why government of India is also providing viability gap funding. I would be covering the financing aspect in sanitation sector particularly sharing HUDCO experience.

HUDCO is one of the premier organisations to finance such type of projects with long term repayment period. HUDCO finances up to 90 per cent of the project cost as loan to the government agencies and up to 70 per cent for private borrowers. The repayment period is from 10 to 20 years. In our organisation, sanitation is considered as priority sector which includes sewerage, water supply, drainage and solid waste management also.

HUDCO has always acted as extended arm of the government of India in executing the sanitation projects by routing the GOI grants for the allocated purpose under various programmes like VAMBAY, Basic Sanitation, Night Shelter, Integrated Low Cost Sanitation etc.

At HH level for weaker section of the society under ILCS programme about Rs 400 crore of GOI subsidy and 500 crore of HUDCO loan have been released for completion of 28 lac individual toilets in 1538 towns.

At city/ ULB level, HUDCO has so far funded 547 sanitation projects to various state *parastatals* (water supply and sewerage/drainage boards), urban local bodies and private agencies. The project cost involved is about 85K CR (Rs 84,774.73 crore) and loan commitment of more than 27 K CR (Rs. 27,420.65 crore). These include 431 water supply schemes and 71 sewerage schemes.

The charging for water supply, sewerage and drainage was generally done indirectly as improvement charges or part of property tax.

In 1993, government moved towards national policy of full cost recovery in water supply and sanitation sectors. HUDCO propagated:

- Collection of advance or registration charges for water supply and sewerage connections. This reduced the requirement of loan and indicated the willingness of the public for the service.
- Metering was advised even in domestic connections against the flat rates so that the wastage could be reduced.
- The telescopic tariff was advocated so that minimum amount is available to all categories at reasonable rates.
- Cross subsidisation was done by charging higher for industrial and commercial connections.
- For sewerage in addition to connection or registration charges flat rate per month or percentage linked to the water supply charges were propagated.

The cash flows of projects were insisted with tariff revision to cover the debt burden. HUDCO has been instrumental in rationalisation of tariffs in many states (Kerala/Odisha) with 70 to 100 per cent increase initially. Further, there was commitment to go far incremental increase of 10 to 15 per cent per annum or over four to five years to have DSCR of at least one.

As there was risk of non-compliance of such commitments, the State governments guarantee as security and budgetary provision as repayment mechanism were kept in place to cover the default.

Later on, due to non-availability of the guarantee the proposals were funded against equitable mortgage (125 per cent) of alternate property and escrewing of identified revenue streams (150 per cent).

The other mechanism of funding was raising money from the market through bonds. The pooled finance concept of raising money from the market for small and medium towns for infrastructure funding was mooted by USAID under the FIRE-D Programme. This aspect of funding mechanism has drawback of interest burden starting from the day money is raised. The delay in project implementation affects the viability.

Directly raising money from the foreign institutions is also an alternative for cheaper funds. HUDCO experience is not good in this as there are commitment charges on not availing funds at stipulated period. The currency fluctuations in long repayment duration adversely affect the viability. The swapping arrangements and hedging for covering the risk involves cost.

HUDCO is supporting the other mechanism of funding of creating a dedicated pool of revenue by the state (with percentage of VAT/ GST and undertaking by the State to furnish the amount in case of shortfall) to raise the loan against the same. The ULBs pose their proposals with this as repayment mechanism.

In some states, the chief ministers have their own schemes of improving water supply and sanitation position, here 30 per cent of project cost is borne by the state and out of the 70 per cent cost to be borne by the ULB, the state government guarantees 75 per cent of loan repayment with interest from budgetary provision, hence only 25 per cent of repayment with interest is the responsibility of the ULB.

HUDCO also funds private agencies but ROI is marginally high, funding percentage is less and security is more stringent (mortgage 150 per cent with other securities like PDCs, collateral etc.,) to safeguard the public money.

Apart from loan assistance HUDCO has a programme (*Sajha Swachhata Abhiyan*) since 30.01.2006 for subsidy to fund construction of community toilets. Rs three crore have been disbursed for 22 projects. The scheme has 50 per cent subsidy provision (ceiling on cost per seat of Rs 40,000 maximum subsidy per districtis Rs 50 lacs). The balance funds could be from MPLAD or MLA funds. The provision of loan is also there to meet higher cost.

Under Corporate Social Responsibility HUDCO is doing night shelter schemes, community toilets, also trying to fund purchase of mobile toilets for *Kumbha mela*.

It is suggested that the government can direct profit making corporates to spent the amount available under CSR (corporate social responsibility) for developing community toilets to cover the population having no access at least for another two years 2013 and 2014.

In the end, I would like to assure that HUDCO is there to support the government in enabling both public and private sector borrowers for taking up Total Sanitation proposals in the country.

# 22

# Sociology of Sanitation: Forwarding Indian Sociology

*Hetukar Jha*

## Introduction

A national workshop on 'sociology of sanitation' was held in New Delhi on January 28 and 29, 2013. It was organised by Sulabh International Centre for Action Sociology and Sulabh International Social Service Organisation. The eminent founder of both those organisations, Dr. Bindeshwar Pathak, proposed in the inaugural session of this workshop in the presence of a large number of sociologists/social scientists, social workers, Lok Sabha Speaker and rural Development Minister (Government of India), that sociology of sanitation should be developed and included as an important field of study/research and teaching from secondary to higher level of education in our country. This idea seems to have evolved in his mind in the course of his struggle that began in the 1960s. Here, it is not necessary to discuss the details of how he confronted the years of tribulation, the account of which has already been brought to light (*I have a Dream*, Rashmi Bansal, New Delhi, Westland Ltd, 2011). I would like to draw the attention of scholars to two incidents that occurred in the town of Bettiah (north Bihar) in1969 in his presence.

The first incident relates to the torture of the bride of a scavenger who was forced to clean the latrine immediately after her arrival. The second incident was more shocking. Bansal (*Ibid*: 10-11) narrates it in the following words:

"A bull charged towards a young boy in the market place. At first, several people rushed forward to rescue him. Then someone shouted,

"This boy is from the scavenger colony"! And suddenly the crowd dispersed." What was more awful? The ferocity of bull's attack or the reaction of the people in the crowd? Dr. Pathak's conscience, it seems, was deeply moved by the telling experience of the manifestation of inhuman mindset of people before his eyes. I think, this prompted him to dedicate his life to the mission of Mahatma Gandhi for liberating the *bhangis* (scavengers) from their occupation of cleaning night-soil. And, thus, began his innovative strategies and efforts which are now too well known to be repeated. Sulabh Movement is a visible reality today. At the national level, its coverage is wide, and at the international level, its recognition is remarkable by all means.

However, the problem of *bhangis* seems to be multi-dimensional involving not only the question of individual and collective dignity, but the historical conditions of their existence in different regions of the country. Dr. Pathak, I am sure, realised it well that it is a socio-historical and cultural problem and, therefore, the most effective means to end the tyranny of the decadent forces, and practices of our society has to be that of cultural innovation and change.

It may be said here that the problem of sanitation is related not only to that of scavenger community across the country, but also to the widely prevailing practice of open defecation. Dean Spears throws significant light on this issue (*The Hindu*, Kolkata, March 14, 2013). Children in India are shorter in height on average than those of Africa even though people are poorer. This is 'Asian Enigma'. Spears observes on the basis of research that it is the effect of the wide spread open defecation. Faeces contain germs and exposure to these germs due to open defecation generally causes changes in the tissues of intestines which prevent the absorption and use of nutrients in food. It may be mentioned that more than half of all people in the world who defecate in the open live in India. No country measured in the last decade has a higher rate of open defecation than Bihar. Twelve per cent of all people worldwide who openly defecate, live in Utter Pradesh (*ibid*). Spears asserts that the high rate of open defecation does account for high rate of stunting and considers sanitation to be our emergency not only for health but also for the economy (*Ibid*). No wonder, "Members of Parliament, civil society organisations and campaigners from India, Pakistan, Bangladesh, Nepal, Bhutan and Sri Lanka, marched towards the SAARC secretariat in Kathmandu" demanding "Right to Sanitation for All" (*The Hindu*, Kolkata, March 20,2013).

It may be pointed out here that Dr. Pathak's Sulabh Movement has remained active for eliminating the practice of open defecation by creating and maintaining a large network of the system of Sulabh latrines in the country. However, the existence of *bhangis* and the prevalence of the practice of open defecation seem to imply a crisis of our cultural order. It seems necessary, under the circumstances, that different socio-economic and cultural conditions as well as consequences of this crisis should be ethically examined from the point of view of Indian civilisation as a whole. This is a time consuming and arduous task that requires the pursuit of appropriate cultural means for the generation and communication of knowledge that can change the age old practices and habits of people at large in the context of sanitation. Sociology of sanitation as a part of Indian sociology would, I am sure, prove to be one of such means. The historic-sociological studies and research from the points of view of the present crisis would, hopefully, equip the people of future generations with the knowledge of the practices, habits, manners, beliefs, etc., to be pursued and internalised in place of those which have been weakening our society so far both morally and physically. I welcome the proposal of Dr. Pathak quite enthusiastically. However, for sociology of sanitation to emerge and flourish, it seems imperative that its theoretical *corpus* should be recognised and enriched continuously. I would like to suggest the following themes in this context to be considered relevant to the field of sociology of sanitation.

## Issues and Themes

In the first conference of Indian Sociological Society (1955), D.P. Mukerji delivered the presidential address in which he urged the Indian sociologists to consider the study of the traditions of this country as their foremost task for promoting the discipline of sociology in India. He also asserted that even for changing a particular tradition, it is necessary that the tradition should be studied thoroughly. The assertion of D.P. Mukerji implies that efforts of changing a particular tradition, considered irrelevant or retrograding or inhuman, without understanding it in the totality of space and time could hardly be effective. Considering this view, I think, it is necessary that the tradition of scavenging and the tradition of scavengers should be thoroughly studied. One has to explore how scavenging was practised in different periods and in different regions; how the need of people (caste-wise, class-wise and religion-wise) was defined in this context and how it did relate to environment.

Further, regarding scavengers, it seems important to identify their communities in different regions of the country and then examine each such communities in terms of how it emerged in history; which socio-political forces were responsible for its emergence and continuity; how the cleaners of filth were placed at the bottom by the producers of filth, etc. Besides, more important is to study the *bhangis*' world-view, their perception of themselves and other communities; their customs, practices, their gods, their rituals, their beliefs, etc., all from their points of view. In this context, folk tales, ballads, proverbs, folk songs, etc., existing in their oral tradition should be analysed. Different normative and descriptive texts of ancient and medieval eras should also be consulted in this context.

Another issue relevant to the sociology of sanitation is one of dignity. What is the concept of dignity in our culture and how it has varied from region to region and from time to time? Here, more important is to consider the dignity at the collective level, that is, collective dignity, caste and community dignity. What was the role of *brahmanic* and Lokayate ideologies and traditions in this context?

The concept of shame (*lajja* or *laaj*) should also be considered for socio-historical research in this field. The behaviours and manners causing the feeling of shame have to be explored. Norbert Elias in his famous work, *The Civilising Process, The History of Manners and State Formation and Civilisation* (Basil Blackwell, 1995), observed that change in the feeling of shame played a decisive role in civilising process in European world (*Ibid*: XII). Historic sociological investigation into the changes in the meaning and understanding of shame form the points of view of the norms suggested explicitly or implicitly in this context by the *shastras* of brahmanic tradition and the literature (oral as well as written) of *Lokayata* tradition would hopefully throw much light on how the class-wise, caste-wise and gender-wise association of the feeling of shame and the manners of defecation has been changing in history. Further, it will not be out of place to explore the changing relationship of man and environment in our history in the context of the habits related to defecation. Rabindranath Tagore once pointed out that in Indian culture environment is not perceived as an object of control and exploitation, rather, it is supposed to be a sacrosanct part of our culture. How this attitude to environment changed effecting the rise of the practice of open defecation, deserves to be rigorously examined. Another issue that appears to be important for socio-historical inquiry is that of purity. How is purity defined and what are the contexts of its operation? Which ideology gave rise to the idea of purity? How, and under which socio-economic conditions, caste level purity or pollution came to prevail? Which philosophies (idealist or materialist) promoted the practice related to purity and pollution? How could physical touch come to be viewed as radiating spiritual pollution? Which ideological systems were opposed to such notions and how did they work against thinking in terms of purity and pollution at any level? There are many such questions which deserve to be critically examined for understanding the nature of existence of *bhangis* under varying ideological and socio-political systems. In this context, one should depend more on field-view or descriptive sources for understanding what actually happened in society.

So far, I have dealt with the themes relevant to sociology of sanitation for research and studies at the higher level. The literature already available in this context may be used for teaching as well. However, for promoting the theoretical base of this field of sociology, rigorous research into the traditions regarding the issues, discussed has to be undertaken.

The students of primary and secondary levels of education should also be exposed to sociology of sanitation. For primary level instruction, a set of the manners considered desirable in the context of (individual, social and environment) sanitation should be prepared along with their justification. For secondary level teaching, the details of success stories of the efforts of government and NGOs (for example, Sulabh International) should be prepared in Hindi, English and different vernaculars. The government of India and the state governments should be persuaded to take immediate steps for launching these projects for introducing the knowledge of the value of sanitation in the life of an individual and also in the life of a nation *vis-a-vis* the children and students (the future citizens of our country).

# 23

# Environmental Sanitation, Public Health and Social Deprivation

*G Ram*

## What does the Sociology of Sanitation deal with?

Sociology of Sanitation deals with the complex of social relations, actions and behaviour patterns that involve efficient disposal of human waste, dirt or any other disease-causing substances. Thus, sociological knowledge of sanitation has the following three aspects:

- It attempts to understand the social relations, social actions and behaviour patterns of people emerging out of their acts of sanitation.
- In broad sense, sanitation implies freeing from any kind of disease-causing substance; namely, human waste (excreta, urine, sweating, nails, etc.), animal excreta and carcasses, garbage, wreckage, dirt, spit, stagnant water, etc by their efficient disposal.
- The twin function of sanitation is hygenic living and health

When we talk of sanitation of a people it is necessary to know about these two aspects and, also, in relation to other fields of social life, as sub-systems of social system which is continuously changing. Thus, both the perspectives, cultural and structural, are complementary to each other for a holistic understanding of sanitation.

## The Cultural Perspective

As a cultural phenomenon, sanitation can be conceived at three interrelated levels of people's life in society; namely, personal, family/ household and community/ public.

- At personal level, an individual's sanitary habits and practices like regular and appropriate cleaning of bowels, proper urinating, bathing, washing of clothes, teeth-cleaning, paring of nails, etc., affect the state of his/ her living and health immediately and, as well, of those who come in contact with him/ her.
- At family level, the disposal practices of human and animal waste, garbage and drainage, and animal keeping practices which constitute the family culture of sanitation affect the living and health of the whole family and then affects other families and individuals in its vicinity, e.g., swine flu has frequently erupted from domestic or farm poultries.
- At community/public level, the sanitary practices comprise the disposal of human excreta, dirt, garbage, litters etc., drainage and sewerage, disposal of wreckage and stagnant water and restrained spitting at common places like roads, offices, markets, bus stands, railway stations, airports, common fields, fair grounds, cinema halls, educational institutions, etc.

These public practices comprise the environmental sanitation in community/society and also affect the living and health of all the families in its surroundings and the individuals who visit these places of common use.

The environmental sanitation is function of both the culture of sanitation prevailing at personal and family levels and the institutional arrangement of the community/society operative for sanitisation of the environment. Thus, the three levels are ultimately linked with each other in the general culture of health and sanitation in a society.

**The Structural Perspective**

As a sub-system, sanitation is closely related to economy, polity, law, education and religion as sub-systems of social system. One can see variation of efficiency in sanitation in terms of resources and classes, political leadership and goals, law-enforcement, educational levels and religious beliefs and rituals.

Sometimes, economic resources are available but because of beliefs and low or no education, an efficient way of sanitation is not accepted in a community.

In case of environmental sanitation, one generally observes poor law-implementation while it may be most effective in a town of tribal community like Aizawl in Mizoram where community writ about sanitation runs large across the tribal and non-tribal populations and nobody can make roads or public places dirty and the people have to use only public or private facilities of sanitation.

On the other hand, force of religious beliefs and ritual practices extended in public life make difference of sanitation practices between two slums in Silchar; namely, Kalibari Char and Rongpur. The former consists of poor Bengali migrants and the latter, of rural Hindu-Meitei Manipuris.

**Environmental Sanitation and the Public Health**

Environmental sanitation is a big problem in developing societies like India where the disposal system among majority of the people is not efficient/human-friendly and above all the culture of sanitation is lacking.

Rather, it is all expected from the government to carry out sanitation, which is insufficient.

The improper sanitation of environment affects public health through water, air and land in all public places. The source of the problem is both the poor culture of health and sanitation among the people and the inefficient and insufficient sanitation system in the public places of the urban centres.

**Social Deprivation as a Mechanism for Environmental Sanitation**

The inefficient disposal mechanisms used for sanitation have created a class of scavengers sustaining for centuries.

The scavengers have been stigmatised with manual sanitary works and sustained at various levels of sanitation, making the practice a part of culture.

However, it is observed that in recent times the multi-national companies have used modern and efficient sanitation systems where people from different castes and groups sporting in uniforms can be seen carrying out sanitation in malls and others.

**Conclusion**

Mechanisation of sanitation has helped in improving the lot of the deprived and alienated class of scavengers.

When improved methods are available and affordable, people adopt them gradually. It is observed at household level in the two cases of tribal groups, the *Mishing* in Golaghat district of Assam and the *Rongmei Naga* in Tamenglong district of Manipur who are moving from open defecation to *kachcha* to *pacca* latrines and bathrooms in their houses. The process accompanies the improvement in their houses and living, along with their improved economic conditions.

On the other hand, many of the *Nagas* and other tribals carry out menial scavenging in public places in Silchar town because that is the only means of survival for them.

Hence, a two-prong strategy needs to be used.

Both, improvement in economic conditions of scavengers, through education and other rehabilitation measures, and availability of affordable modern sanitary system to the people can help in eradicating the on-going deprivation of the vulnerable sections engaged in menial jobs for the society.

# 24

# Social Science and Public Health: An Anthropological Perspective

*Amarendra Mahapatra*

Issues of Sanitation are directly related to community and society since long, but it has been addressed by the social scientists only recently. Being social scientist we should work on working models to solve these sanitation related issues rather than working on other issues of the subject. In this paper, it is illustrated taking the example, how deep tube wells in rural and tribal areas are not used for drinking purpose and the other example of rural sanitation programme, under which household latrines were erected but not used by the community. In this regard, the role of social scientists to tackle such problems is of prime importance.

In this regard it is suggested that, the tool Advocacy method can be adopted by the social scientists to overcome these sanitation related issues. Social scientists can adopt any method to resolve these issues in a replicable model. This attempt can help the researchers and implementers to make corrections in the existing programmes, so that the community can accept the programme. Presently, the community is not identifying the programme, after the advocacy this can change.

## Background

Sanitation has always been a part and partial of the society since ages. Different norms and practices are attached to this issue of sanitation, which may vary from community to community/society in particular. The evidences can be traced back, right from civilisations like Mohenjo-Daro and Harappa period drain system excavation, even prior to that in many European civilisations, too. However, Social Science has given its perspectives only recently a couple of centuries back in literature. This implies as the society size increased and the waste disposal / safe water became a problem of common men, in other words, when the problem was a visible, than only we (Social Scientists) acted. However, there were references on different aspects of sanitation since long on water supply.

There is a lot to talk on the statistics like these many proportions of people have no access to safe drinking water / latrine etc. But are these figures going to overcome the problem. The answer is No. Hence Social Science should formulate a means to solve individual problem at the grass root level. In this direction we have enough background material to work upon for a practical solution. Government today is interested to look into this inter-phase in detail in a replicable model, on waste disposal (Solid and Liquid) or potable water or any other issues related to sanitation.

Here, I will take this opportunity to share an experience; you must be aware that the deep tube wells were set up in almost all the villages in India by now, for providing safe drinking water. Do you know, that 32 per cent of the population in Rural and Tribal areas do not use the tube well water for drinking purpose (Odisha/A.P. and WB), they prefer surface water. The reasons outlined were taste and smell of the water from the tube well. On the other hand, the experience in Rajasthan and Gujarat is well satisfactory in using the tube well water. The water of the tube well does not smell there, due to non-humid weather. At this juncture how to overcome this problem; we should come out with a working model for demonstration, which is viable and replicable.

Similarly, in the rural sanitation programme, household latrines are set up in rural areas by extending aid from the Block Funds to Households. But in a review it was estimated that the use of latrine was not satisfactory. The reasons pointed were habit or habit of going out for defecation/ water problem for flushing/foul smell etc.

In this case how to solve this problem? We should work out which Advocacy tool can be used and whom to target; in order to imbibe the habit of using the latrine in the community.

Here, the role of Social Science as a whole is of prime importance; but we lack in this action fields often. That is mainly due to lack of opportunity and initiative. This is purely my opinion. In this platform I would like to share an example of Safe Drinking water and Sanitation in Schools.

**Safe Drinking Water and Sanitation in Schools**

1. Water is intrinsically interconnected with the basic sanitation and was added to the catalogue at the 2002 World Summit on Sustainable Development in Johannesburg. It is targeted to halve the burden of the proportion of people without sustainable access to safe drinking water and basic sanitation by 2015. The provision of safe drinking water and basic sanitation is among the most critical challenges for achieving sustainable development over the next decade.
2. However, the provision of safe drinking water and basic sanitation contributes to sustainable improvements in peoples' live regarding their health and education, the preconditions for productive employment as well as for the eradication of extreme hunger and empowerment of women.
3. The impact of water supply and sanitation projects on the different aspects such as the health situation as well as the empowerment are not generally quantified.
4. Impact assessments are used to evaluate the programmes, but there are many methodological issues involved in making these assessments which mainly deal with problems about validity and reliability (whether observations of a particular impact will be seen similarly by different observers).

A favourable policy environment is essential to the success of projects that aim to improve hygiene, sanitation and water supply in schools. Political commitment to children's education and health creates an environment that is conducive to implementing, operating and maintaining such projects and that enables small-scale pilot projects to scale up effectively.

Advocacy and information sharing can be an important tool to build political commitment that can help national and local governments put priorities and policies in place as well as change political attitudes and mobilise activities for hygiene, sanitation and water in schools. Advocacy for school hygiene, sanitation, and water projects and programmes should illustrate the links among health, education, water and sanitation services, and outline the ways in which such projects can benefit students, school staff, families, communities and countries.

Experience with these projects and programs have shown that they can contribute significantly to development. Specifically, school hygiene, sanitation, and water supply projects have produced the following outcomes:

- Led to improved health, nutritional status and learning performance,
- Contributed to increased school enrolment and attendance, particularly for girls,
- Led to sustained improvements in hygiene and sanitation practices because behaviours and skills learned in schools can continue over a lifetime,
- Improved hygiene and sanitation practices in the community.

Below here certain steps are proposed, by adopting these desired results can be achieved.

**Building Political Commitment:** Advocacy in the context of hygiene, sanitation and water supply in schools is essential but challenging. When setting priorities for attention, both national and local governments tend to focus first on large projects in which many direct interests are at stake. They are less likely to devote attention to school hygiene, sanitation and water projects because most of these are small-scale interventions that focus on changing hygiene behaviour and require only low cost investments. However, the long term sustainability of such school projects depends on political commitment to their success.

Political commitment at both the national and the local level is built through an overall communication strategy that incorporates:

- Advocacy
- Social mobilisation
- Programme communication

Figure 1 illustrates the relationships among these three components within the wider continuum of communication processes.

Advocacy is an important tool for building political commitment and helping national and local governments to put priorities and policies in place. Advocacy is the action of presenting an argument in order to gain commitment from political and social leaders and educate a society about a particular issue. Advocacy involves selecting and organising information to create a convincing arguments and then delivering the argument through various interpersonal and media channels.

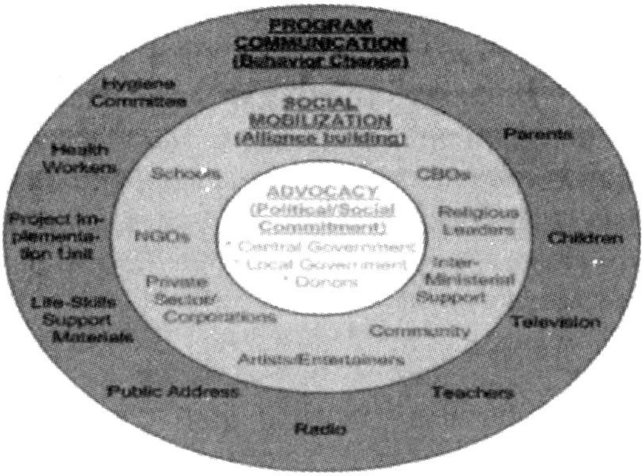


**Fig.1. Communication Continuum for Building Political Commitment.**

*Source*: McKee 1992.

**Advocacy has four dimensions**

- **Policy Dimension:** Changes in policy, attitudes, practices, programs and direction of resource allocation.
- **Civil Society Dimension:** Strengthening the capacity and power of civil society so that citizens can play effective roles in policymaking and decision-making.
- **Democratic Space Dimension:** Improving the accountability of those who lead and govern, by increasing the legitimacy of civil society participation in policymaking and decision-making.
- **Individual Gain Dimension:** Improving people's material gains in terms of quality of life, as well as expanding their awareness of themselves as citizens with rights and entitlements and the responsibility to act on them.

Social mobilisation is the process of bringing together allies from various sectors to raise awareness and demand for a particular development programme or policy change. The process mobilises partners at different levels in society to assist in the delivery of resources and services, to strengthen community participation for sustainability and self-reliance, and to bring about transparent and accountable decision-making.

Programme communication is the process of identifying, segmenting and targeting specific groups and audiences with particular strategies, messages, or training programmes. Communication is conveyed through various mass media and interpersonal channels, both traditional and non-traditional. Effective programme communication is a dialogue in which senders and receivers of information interact on an equal footing and the interchange of knowledge and experience leads to mutual discovery. During effective programme communication, planners, experts and field workers both listen to people's concerns, needs and suggestions and provide information about project possibilities.

**Identifying Stakeholders in the Advocacy Process:** As part of a larger process that also includes programme communication and social mobilisation, advocacy relies on identification of all stakeholders and defining the roles that they can play. The stakeholders in hygiene, sanitation and water supply projects for schools include those who use them, those who are indirectly affected by them, those who implement them, and those who pay for them.

**Schools, Teachers and Children:** As the key users, teachers and children are the primary stakeholders in the provision of hygiene, sanitation and water in schools. They are generally seen as the beneficiaries of advocacy efforts, but sometimes will also be the key decision makers when major decisions on practical implementation must be made.

**Parents, Family and Communities:** Families and communities are secondary stakeholders because they benefit indirectly from improved children's hygiene skills and hygienic school environment. A community is rarely a homogeneous stakeholder group, however; within any community there will be different groups of stakeholders (such as poor versus non-poor) with different perspectives on issues relating to hygiene, sanitation and water supply in schools.

**Local Government:** Local government officials may be keen to see hygienic conditions and water supply and sanitation facilities in schools to improve. On the other hand, they often have inadequate budgets to provide the services, and funding may well be reduced by corruption and other constraints. In some cases, officials from one government department may be able to influence those in another department, as well as being advocacy targets themselves.

**National Government:** National government officials, as policy makers, are often key advocacy targets, but some may also be influences or even allies on a particular issue. As with local government, some departments may be able to exert influence (or even power) over others; for example, the finance ministry may be able to affect the policy of another ministry through its influence over budget allocations.

**Civil Society:** NGOs and other civil society groups, as implementers of hygiene, sanitation and water supply projects in schools, may be partners in advocacy initiatives, or may be influences, providing examples of good practice and the working out of policy alternatives. International NGOs sometimes have a key opportunity to influence donors and other international organisations and can thus be strategic allies or influences. NGOs may themselves also be the targets of advocacy for better practice, or policy in their role as donors or as operational practitioners.

**The Private Sector:** The role of private water companies is increasing around the world, as the privatisation of water supply and sanitation services become more common. On issues of privatisation, they are likely to be advocacy targets or even adversaries; however, on other water supply-related issues. Other private sector organisations such as soap providers, domestic water companies, artisans and artisan associations, and consultants may be influences, allies, or targets in the advocacy process.

**International Donors and Multilateral Organisations:** International donors and multilateral agencies have an influential role to play in the development of hygiene education, water and sanitation policy. As key funders of national government programmes, they are in a position to impose criteria on national government development policy, including hygiene, sanitation and water supply in schools. They may, therefore, be both influences and advocacy targets themselves.

**Creating an Advocacy Strategy:** An effective advocacy strategy involves as many stakeholders as possible and lays the groundwork for advocacy through research into the needs and wishes of the community and the individuals within it. Table 1 below outlines the steps to follow in creating an advocacy strategy.

When developing an advocacy campaign, remember these key points:

- Link advocacy and communication posters, pamphlets and videos to a strategic communication plan.
- Only produce materials as part of a campaign. Use folk media in case of rural/tribal community.
- Pre-test messages, posters, pamphlets and pictures with a select group of target consumers.
- Develop a plan for measuring the impact of advocacy efforts.

**Table 1. Steps in Creating an Advocacy Strategy**

| No. | *Steps* | *Probes* |
|---|---|---|
| 1. | Identifying the issues: What do we want to change? | Limited attention given to impact of appropriate hygiene, sanitation, and water supply in schools |
| 2. | Finding out more thorough analysis: Analysing the issue; analysing the context and key stakeholders; understanding the time frame | Bottlenecks (political as well as practical) |
| 3. | Setting **SMART** objectives (SMART = Specific, Measurable, Achievable, Relevant, Time-Bound) | • Achieving **AMAR**<br>• Achieving (political) commitment for appropriate hygiene,<br>• Modifying sanitation needs,<br>• Attempting clean water supply in schools and<br>• Recording the process ( AMAR) |
| 4. | Identifying the target groups for advocacy activities: Whom do we want to influence? | Key players at different levels: schools, community, local government, national government including core ministries (education, health, water/sanitation authorities), civil society, private sector, international donors, and multi-lateral organisations. |
| 5. | Identifying allies: With whom can we work? | Positive stakeholder analyses |
| 6. | Defining the message | Consider the local culture and collabourate closely with local stakeholders. Take into consideration the policy dimension, civil society dimension, democratic space dimension, and individual gain dimension. |
| 7. | Choosing advocacy approaches and activities | Consider the local culture and collabourate closely with local stakeholders |
| 8. | Selecting tools | Consider the local culture and collabourate closely with local stakeholders. |
| 9. | Assessing the resources needed | |
| 10. | Planning for monitoring and evaluation | |
| 11. | Drawing up an action plan | |

**Using Advocacy Tools:** An effective advocacy process employs a variety of tools and methods to accomplish its goals, selecting those that are most appropriate to the culture and the situation. Using multiple tools increases the likelihood that the message will be heard and absorbed by the target audience. Advocacy methods include the following common tools:

- *Meetings*: Meetings are a key tool for gathering and conveying information, developing motivation and encouraging participation. Meetings are often used as part or the start of a lobbying strategy.
- *Lobbying*: Lobbying aims to influence the policy process by working closely with individuals in political and government offices.
- *Negotiation or Finding the Middle Ground:* This type of interaction helps two or more interest groups reach a common position from different sides of a debate. It may be carried out on a one-to-one basis, or through a meeting between several representatives of each side.
- *Project Visits:* Project visits encourage government or other stakeholders to support or select a specific type of project or approach by providing positive examples. Project visits can be very effective in convincing decision makers, and also have the advantage of providing opportunities for school staff and children to speak on their own behalf.
- *Reports:* A detailed and thorough report can be a basic tool of advocacy planning. However, information from a report is usually not directly usable in an advocacy campaign; it must be tailored to the audience for which it is intended.
- *Letters:* Letter writing is best used as a support for other tools, for example to raise an issue with the advocacy target prior to requesting a meeting. Because public figures receive many letters, an effective letter is based on research that ensures that it targets the right audience in the most appropriate way.
- *Leaflets and Posters*: Leaflets and posters are effective only if the target will read or notice them. They should be attractive and present a limited amount of text, showing what can be done about the issue or problem addressed.
- *Drama and Video*: Drama, folk media provides an opportunity to present facts and issues in an entertaining, culturally sensitive, and accessible way. In many societies, drama is a form of indigenous communication through which people can comfortably express their views. If the target audience is too large to reach with drama, video shows can be an appropriate alternative.

- *Mass Media:* Folk media, electronic media (television, radio) and print media play a significant part in advocacy, both by influencing policymakers directly and by changing public opinion on an issue.

Each method or tool has advantages and disadvantages in terms of its cost effectiveness and its potential to reach a large number of people. Table 2 below summarises in a simple way some of the pros and cons of various methods, while recognising that the value of most methods depends on the manner and context in which they are used.

**Table 2. Advantages and Disadvantages of Selected Advocacy Tools**

| | *Potential to Reach Poorest* | *Participatory Potential* | *Potential Audience* | *Cost Effectiveness* |
|---|---|---|---|---|
| Leaflets and fact sheets | + | + | ++ | + |
| Meetings | + | ++ | -- | - |
| Video | - | + | + | -- |
| Television | -- | -- | ++ | -- |
| Audio cassettes | + | - | + | - |
| Radio | ++ | + | +++ | ++ |
| Theatre/Drama Folk Media | ++ | ++ | ++ | ++ |
| Posters | + | - | + | - |
| E-mail/internet | -- | ++ | ++ | ++ |

*Source:* Burke, 1999.

Hope, this article and the present workshop forum provides a platform for the social scientists to think more in this light and act upon in future to deal these issues to come to a conclusion to tackle the problem in the society. Social research in this line, where Advocacy can help the planners and implementers to follow the steps advised by the social scientists in future.

# 25

# Sanitation

*Ram Updesh Singh*

Let me start by saying that since the mid-seventies, I have been a keen witness to the ever-expanding and laudable activities of the *sulabh* Organisation and its redoubtable Founder Dr Bindeshwar Pathak to whom the spirit of Gandhism has been a guiding star. With an inborn sense of realisation of the conditions under which the scavengers and other downtrodden sections of the society lived, Dr Pathak started transalating into action his sublime thoughts from a scratch and has succeeded in developing this organisation up to gaining international and universal recognition. I heartily admire and salute his spirited endeavours which have never been allowed to be overshadowed by any kind of egoist traits. He chose to follow the footsteps of a great man who in his life had come to a crossroad from which two roads emerged and who had taken the less travelled road, which made all the difference!

**Sulabh Sauchalayas**: The 'latrines made easy', or a 'pour flush latrine' with a slight variation, popularly called the *sulabh sauchalayas* are indeed a popular adjunct and an aide to hygienic development in most of the cities of India and abroad. It is also a befitting appliance for the semi-urban as well as the rural areas. A *sulabh* type of latrine, the precursor of the now gigantic *sulabh* movement, is a simple and cost-effective device which consists of an Indian type commode joined to a couple of underground receptacles which are used one by one and serve as a soakage pit also. Latrines apart, the *sulabh* movement has grown and gone side by side with the social upgrading of the families of a large number of scavengers in regard to their schooling, sanitation and status in society.

**Defecation**: 'Sanitation and hygiene' have 'cause and effect' relationship. V.S. Naipaul in his book, 'An Area of Darkness' repeatedly referred to the Indian women and men defecating in the open air generally and on the roadside flanks specially. After 65 years of independence, the phenomenon is still not quite out of sight to a motorist who drives in the wee hours of the morning or during the hours after dusk and switches on his headlights to encounter the bizarre scenes. The human excreta thus gets exposed for being trampled by a pedestrian besides throwing an obnoxious smell all around. On the other hand, the concept of ecological sanitation which aims at protecting eco-systems treats excreta as a valuable input if scientifically recycled for generation of power and production of organic manure. I am glad to say that *sulabh* has experimented in that direction with proven results.

**Sanitation**: Environmental sanitation calls for interventions aimed basically at improved management of excreta. Water is the most essential and basic ingredient for any effort towards development of hygiene and sanitation through improved toilet system. In a large number of villages of India, the supply of piped water continues to remain a distant dream. According to a source, 240 crores of people the world over live under highly unsanitary conditions and due to their unhygienic behaviours, they are exposed to the risk of falling prey to diarrhea and other infectious diseases. The share of the Indian population facing similar unsanitary situations is estimated to be about 60 per cent. Several schemes have been launched by the central and state governments for provision of water supply in the rural areas as also for the construction of latrines, but the achievements fall far short of the overwhelming requirements. There have also been praiseworthy efforts aimed at development of sanitation and hygiene by the civil society including some international organisations like WHO and *sulabh* International. But still there is a long way forward to be traversed.

**Waste Management**: Sanitation by way of disposal of excreta in the rural areas and collection, segregation and disposal of solid waste in the urban areas still continues to remain a formidable challenge, more so because the interventions of the governmental agencies have fallen far short of the required dimensions. So have the supplemental efforts of the civil society, despite laudable achievements of the *sulabh* Organisation. Soliciting social co-operation for meeting the challenges is essential. It is there that the concept of Sociology of Sanitation which forms the basic theme of this national workshop acquires utmost relevance.

**Social Mobilisation**: Social mobilisation is an essential pre-requisite for the success of any intervention for the development of environmental sanitation and hygiene in the urban as well as the rural areas. It is also essential that for identifying the needs, raising the awareness of and ascertaining the demands for sanitation and hygiene, all feasible social partners and allies must get together to face the emerging challenges and carry out well-defined tasks through planned and forceful advocacy. Otherwise, the efforts by way of the governmental and non-governmental interventions alone would not suffice without obtaining popular public participation.

**Way Forward**: Having been born and brought up in a very backward rural area of eastern UP, I have considered all aspects of sanitation and hygiene in the villages of India where over 70 per cent of the people live. The successive stages of dropping and disposal of human excreta are: (a) Open air defecation, (b) Pit-hole dry latrine, (c) Sulabh Sauchalaya, (d) Pour-Flush-latrine which uses small quantities of water poured from a bucket to flush away faeces and (e) State-of-the-Art latrine with septic tank and Sewage lines. From my childhood, I have heard of and promoted in my own way recourse to the age-old concept of a Pit-Latrine which entails making a small ditch on the earthy surface and covering it with the soil after defecation. Pit Latrine is, in fact, a latrine with a small pit for collection and decomposition of excreta. It costs little but delivers a lot. This would obviate the emission of foul smell and, in course of time, the excreta would melt into the earth, as it were, and at the same time add to the fertility of the soil. I feel that, as an interim measure till the *sulabh* Sauchalayas or the Pour-flush latrines or the other advanced models come in vogue, a campaign for the adoption of the age-old concept and practice of Pit-latrines could substantially supplement the other types of advanced interventions and thereby change the scenario of sanitation and hygiene at the grass-root level in rural India.

Making a speech, amidst the galaxy of intellectuals assembled here for this thematic workshop, has been to me a tall order. I am particularly thankful to the *sulabh* International Centre for Action Sociology and its 'role-model' Founder for giving me this unique opportunity to participate in this exceedingly meaningful workshop. I have no doubt that the outcome of this conference, i.e., 'Sanitation', would be included as a subject of study in the syllabi of under-graduate and post-graduate courses as well as a subject of thesis for a PhD degree.

Before I conclude, let me recall the inspiring lines of the American poet, Robert Frost: "The woods are lovely, dark and deep,/ But I have promises to keep,/And miles to go before I sleep,/ And miles to go before I sleep."

As we have a long way to go for developing the Sociology of Sanitation, I would with apologies to Frost, like to conclude by reciting my following lines:

Where the stakes run high and the stinks abound, Be not content only with a sermon on the mound; But join up to make the environment, safe and sound, And come to make the environment, safe and sound.

# 26

# Sanitation and Public Health Sanitation: An Essential Requirement for Public Health

*P.K. Sharma*

Providing environmentally-safe sanitation to millions of people is a significant challenge, especially in the world's second most populated country. The task is doubly difficult in a country where the introduction of new technologies can challenge people's traditions and beliefs (CUSS: 2010). The World Health Organisation finds inadequate sanitation to be a major cause of disease world-wide and improving sanitation as a tool to ensure a significant beneficial impact on health, both in households and across communities (TCS: 2011).

**Sanitation Means**: Professionals agree that "sanitation" as a whole is a "big idea" which covers—

- safe collection, storage, treatment and disposal/re-use/recycling of human excreta (faeces and urine);
- management/re-use/recycling of solid wastes (trash or rubbish);
- drainage and disposal/re-use/recycling of household wastewater (often referred to as sullage or grey water);
- drainage of storm water;
- treatment and disposal/re-use/recycling of sewage effluents;
- collection and management of industrial waste products; and
- management of hazardous wastes (including hospital wastes, and chemical/radioactive and other dangerous substances).

"Ecological" approach to sanitation which seeks to contain, treat and reuse excreta where possible–thus minimising contamination and making optimum use of resources. The key issue here is that each community, region or country needs to work out what is the most sensible and cost effective way of thinking about sanitation in the short and long term and then act accordingly.

**UNO States that**: Wherever humans gather, their waste also accumulates. Progress in sanitation and improved hygiene has greatly improved health, but many people still have no adequate means of disposing of their waste. This is a growing nuisance for heavily populated areas, carrying the risk of infectious disease, particularly to vulnerable groups such as the very young, the elderly and people suffering from diseases that lower their resistance. Poorly controlled waste also means daily exposure to an unpleasant environment. The buildup of fecal contamination in rivers and other water is not just a human risk: other species are affected, threatening the ecological balance of the environment.

The discharge of untreated wastewater and excreta into the environment affects human health by several routes:

- By polluting drinking water;
- By entry into the food chain, for example via fruits, vegetables, or fish and shellfish;
- By bathing, recreational and other contact with contaminated water;
- By providing breeding sites for flies and insects that spread diseases.

The urban growth in India is faster than the average for the country and far higher for urban areas over rural. The proportion of population residing in urban areas has increased from 27.8 per cent in 2001 to 31.80 per cent in 2011 and likely to reach 50 per cent by 2030. The number of towns has increased from 5,161 in 2001 to 7,935 in 2011. The rapid growth in urban areas has not been backed adequately with provisioning of basic sanitation infrastructure and thus leaving many Indian cities deficient in services as water supply, sewerage, storm water drainage, and solid waste management.

Sanitation is intrinsically linked to conditions and processes relating to public health and quality of environment, especially the systems that supply water and deals with human waste. The problem of sanitation gets further worsened in urban areas due to increasing congestion and density in cities resulting in poor environmental and health outcomes. As per 2011 census, the households having latrine facility within premises is 81.4 per cent which includes 72.6 per cent households having water closets and 7.1 per cent households having pit latrines and 1.70 per cent households having other latrines. Out of 72.6 per cent households, 32.70 per cent households are having water closets with piped sewer system, 38.20 per cent households are having water closets with pit latrines. The remaining 18.60 per cent household are both sharing public latrines (six per cent) and defecating in open (12.60 per cent).

To improve the sanitation situation in urban areas, in October 2008, the Government of India announced the National Urban Sanitation Policy (NUSP). The NUSP laid down the framework for addressing the challenges of city sanitation. The policy emphasises the need for spreading awareness about sanitation through an integrated city-wide approach, assigning institutional responsibilities and due regard for demand and supply considerations, with special focus on the women and urban poor.

All the states were requested to act with par with the NUSP to develop respective State Sanitation Strategies (SSS) and the cities for the preparation of City Sanitation Plans (CSPs) given that the sanitation is a state subject as per the constitutional provisions.

A study conducted by Asian Development Bank, 2009, Philiphines in which it was mentioned that;

**1. Successful Pro-poor Sanitation Programmes must be Scaled Up**

Assistance is still not reaching large numbers of the poorest of the poor. Successful models must be replicated and scaled up to serve those who cannot provide for their own needs under existing service delivery systems.

**2. Investments must be Customised and Targeted to Those most in Need**

With more than 450 million Indians living below the poverty line, only a few of the poor who have inadequate sanitation can be assisted right away. Due to limited resources, programmes should target groups, or locations lagging behind the furthest.

**3. Cost-effective Options must be Explored**

Appropriate lower-cost solutions offer a safe alternative to a wider range of the population. Higher-cost options can be explored when economic growth permits. Regardless of cost, all systems should address sanitation all the way "from toilet to river."

### 4. Proper Planning and Sequencing must be Applied

Investing in incremental improvements is an approach that one could consider if affordability of sanitation investment is an issue. Careful planning is required to ensure that investments do not become wasteful and redundant.

### 5. Community-based Solutions must be Adopted where Possible

An approach known as Community-Led Total Sanitation (CLTS) has been found to be effective in promoting change at the community level. Efforts must address socio-cultural attitudes toward sanitation and involve women as agents of change. Another innovation is the socialised community-fund raising, which has met great success among the rural poor.

### 6. Innovative Partnerships must be Forged to Stimulate Investments

The key is to stimulate investments from a wide range of sources as possible, including the private sector, non-government organisations (NGOs) and consumers themselves. This may require working with a wide range of partners through innovative public–private partnerships.

## Sanitation in India

India may be "on track" in achieving the MDG sanitation target-2008. MDG goals simply represent achievable levels if countries commit the resources and power to accomplish them. They do not necessarily represent acceptable levels of service.

This is especially true for India's sanitation situation. Despite recent progress, access to improved sanitation remains far lower in India compared to many other countries.

An estimated 55 per cent of all Indians, or close to 600 million people, still do not have access to any kind of toilet. Among those who make up this shocking total, Indians who live in urban slums and rural environments are affected the most.

In rural areas, the scale of the problem is particularly daunting, as 74 per cent of the rural population still defecates in the open. In these environments, cash income is very low and the idea of building a facility for defecation in or near the house may not seem natural. And where facilities exist, they are often inadequate. The sanitation landscape in India is still littered with 13 million unsanitary bucket latrines, which require scavengers to conduct house-to-house excreta collection. Over

700,000 Indians still make their living this way. The situation in urban areas is not as critical in terms of scale, but the sanitation problems in crowded environments are typically more serious and immediate. In these areas, the main challenge is to ensure safe environmental sanitation. Even in areas where households have toilets, the contents of bucket latrines and pits, even of sewers, are often emptied without regard for environmental and health considerations. Sewerage systems, if they are even available, commonly suffer from poor maintenance, which leads to overflows of raw sewage. Today, with more than 20 Indian cities with populations of more than one million people, including Indian megacities, such as Kolkata, Mumbai and New Delhi, antiquated sewerage systems simply cannot handle the increased load.

### Condition of Chhattisgarh

Implying growth rate of 23.81 per cent in 9 years in the capital city of Raipur, the expansion in urban population due to spatial extension and increased immigration is as high as 49 per cent. Urban population constitutes around 18.87 per cent of the total population in Chhattisgarh. There are 162 urban local bodies in CG.

### Chhattisgarh Urban Sanitation Strategy, 2010

Around 50 per cent of the urban population is poor. Most of these live in slums. Over 95 per cent of the slum-dwellers do not have a dedicated, individual toilet at home. The estimated number of urban dwellers practising open defecation is estimated to be 2.34 m. The number of toilets required on the basis of individual households being equipped with a dedicated toilet is estimated to be around 50 lacs. The major reasons for slum-dwellers not choosing to have a dedicated toilet in their homes, in the order of gravity, are as follows:

(i) Most slum-dwellers have a rustic mind and are traditionally accustomed to defecation in open. Some, in fact, complain of claustrophobia if required to use an enclosed toilet.

(ii) Building a dedicated toilet is considered extravagance. The person considers it financially prudent to build instead a living space and lease it for a stable monthly income.

(iii) There is no stringent punishment at present for open defecation. Many urban-poor families still consider it 'dirty' to have a toilet attached to their living space.

(iv) Flush toilets require more water, a common issue in localities of urban poor.

Sanitation-related Major Issues in Chhattisgarh Include the Following:

(i) Open defecation;

(ii) Unsafe open defecation (as upon railway tracks, or perched perilously upon the retention wall of a large pit or gutter);

(iii) Rustic mind-set, reluctant to migrate to in-house toilet use;

(iv) Reluctance to pay for pay-toilets, even on subsidised terms;

(v) Absence of concealed drainage;

(vi) Use of storm water drains for letting in domestic waste water;

; (vii) Absence of scientific solid waste management system;

(viii) Urinating and spitting upon walls and in public places;

(ix) High incidence of vector borne and water-borne diseases.

Sanitation problems can be solved with

| *Category* | *Domain* | *General Condition* |
|---|---|---|
| Dedicated toilets in homes and public buildings | Private / public | Fair to good. |
| Pay toilets- Community facilities | Public | Fair |
| Public toilets | Public | Poor to very poor |

Some other Problems are:

1. There is no enforcement mechanism for stopping defecation in public in the state at present.
2. City/town in the state has concealed sewerage system at present.
3. Sewer and storm water drains are common in most cities/ towns in the state.
4. No city/town in the state has a scientific system for solid waste management at present.
5. No city/town in the state has a system for harvesting waste water and treating it for re-use.
6. Further there is no provision for proper disposable of industrial waste.
7. The people should come out of the old belief like Sanitation is unaffordable, the poor have other basic requirements besides sanitation, it is costly to construct, etc.

**Totally Sanitised, Healthy and Livable Cities and Towns**

The vision for urban sanitation in India is the state goal, for urban sanitation includes:

(a) Causing awareness generation and behaviour change;

(b) Achieving open defecation free cities;

(c) Promoting integrated city-wide sanitation through:

(i) Reorienting sanitation and mainstreaming sanitation,

(ii) Sanitary and safe disposal: 100 per cent of human excreta and liquid wastes from all sanitation facilities including toilets,

(iii) Proper operation and maintenance of all sanitary installations.

(d) The Millennium Development Goals (MDGs) require that access to improved sanitation be extended:

- To at least half of the urban population by 2015;
- To 100 per cent of the urban population by 2025.

(e) The State Urban Sanitation Strategy will revolve around achieving, within towns and cities in the state, the goals contained in the National Policy.

The Government of India launched the Central Rural Sanitation Programme in 1986 with the objective of accelerating sanitation coverage in rural areas. It was restructured in 1999, exhibiting a paradigm shift in the approach, and the Total Sanitation Campaign (TSC) was introduced. Implemented by the Ministry of Rural Development, Government of India, the TSC aims to:

(a) Improve the general quality of life in rural areas;

(b) Accelerate sanitation coverage in rural areas through access to toilets to all by 2012;

(c) Motivate communities and *Panchayati Raj* Institutions through awareness creation and health education;

(d) Cover schools and *Anganwadis* in rural areas with sanitation facilities by March 2012, and promote hygiene education and sanitary habits among students;

(e) Encourage cost effective and appropriate technologies for ecologically safe and sustainable sanitation;

(f) Develop community managed environmental sanitation systems focusing on solid and liquid waste management.

**Need for Proper Sanitation**

Human excreta have been implicated in the transmission of many infectious diseases including cholera, typhoid, infectious hepatitis, polio, cryptosporidiosis and ascariasis. WHO (2004) estimates that about 1.8

million people die annually from diarrhoeal diseases where 90 per cent are children under five, mostly in developing countries.

Poor sanitation gives many infections the ideal opportunity to spread: plenty of waste and excreta for the flies to breed on, and unsafe water to drink, wash with or swim in. Among human parasitic diseases, schistosomiasis ranks second behind malaria in terms of socio-economic and public health importance in tropical and subtropical areas. Ascariasis is found worldwide. Infection occurs with greatest frequency in tropical and subtropical regions, and in any areas with inadequate sanitation. Ascariasis is one of the most common human parasitic infections. Up to 10 per cent of the population of the developing world is infected with intestinal worms– a large percentage of which is caused by Ascaris. Worldwide, severe Ascaris infections cause approximately 60,000 deaths per year, mainly in children.

Trachoma is the leading global cause of preventable blindness: trachoma is closely linked to poor sanitation and is one of the best examples of an infection readily preventable through basic hygiene. Six million people worldwide are permanently blind due to Trachoma. Trachoma is spread by a combination of:

- Poor sanitation, allowing the flies that spread the infection to breed;
- Poor hygiene associated with water scarcity and poor water quality;
- Lack of education and understanding of how easily the infection can spread in the home and between people.

Infectious agents are not the only health concerns associated with wastewater and excreta. Heavy metals, toxic organic and inorganic substances also can pose serious threats to human health and the environment—particularly when industrial wastes are added to the waste stream. For example, in some parts of China, irrigation for many years with wastewater heavily contaminated with industrial waste, is reported to have produced health damage, including enlargement of the liver, cancers and raised rates of congenital malformation rates, compared to areas where wastewater was not used for irrigation.

**Conclusion**

Sanitation system to provide the greatest health protection to the individual, the community and society at large must:

- Isolate the user from their own excreta;

- Prevent nuisance organisms (e.g. flies) from contacting the excreta and subsequently transmitting disease to humans; and
- Inactivate the pathogens before they enter the environment or prevent the excreta from entering the environment. It is important to understand that sanitation can act at different levels, protecting the household, the community and society. In the case of latrines, it is easy to see that this sanitation system acts at a household level. However, poor design or inappropriate location may lead to migration of waste matter and contamination of local water supplies putting the community at risk. In terms of waterborne sewage the containment may be effective for the individual and possibly also the community, but health effects and environmental damage may be seen far downstream of the original source, hence affecting society.

## References

India's Sanitation for All: How to Make it Happen Series, ADB, 2009, Philliphines.

WHO in cooperation with UNICEF and WSSCC.

Dueñas, Christina. 2005. *Water Champion: Joe Madiath - Championing 100 per cent Sanitation Coverage in Rural Communities in India*. November. www.adb.org/Water/Champions/madiath.asp Dueñas, Christina. 2009. *Country Water Action: India - Changing the Sanitation Landscape*. February. ww.adb.org/Water/Actions/IND/Sanitation-Landscape.asp

ADB. 2006. *Planning Urban Sanitation and Wastewater Management Improvements. Appendix 3: Some Global Case Studies*. May. www.adb.org/Water/tools/Planning-US-WSS.asp.

Tigno, Cezar. 2009. *Country Water Action: Bangladesh - Breaking a Dirty Old Habit*. January. www.adb.org/Water/Actions/Ban/Breaking-Dirty-Habit.asp

ADB. 2006. *Bringing Water Supply and Sanitation Services to Tribal Villages in Orissa the Gram Vikas Way*. April. www.adb.org/water/actions/IND/gram-vikas.asp.

V. Srinivas Chary, A. Narender, K. Rajeswara Rao. 2003. *Serving the Poor with Sanitation: The Sulabh Approach*. 3rd World Water Forum, Osaka, 19 March. PPCPP Session.

ADB. 2007. *Dignity, Disease, and Dollars: Asia's Urgent Sanitation Challenge*. www.adb.org/water/operations/sanitation/pdf/dignity-disease-dollars.pdf

Saxena N.C and A.K. Shivakumar-Social Policy, Planning, Monitoring and Evaluation (SPPME), UNICEF India-TCS, 2011.

Chhattisgarh Urban Sanitation Strategy, 2010-CG.Govt-2011.

Dignity, Disease and Dollars: Asia's urgent sanitation Challenges. Why Invest in Sanitation, ADB.

# 27

# Indian Garbage Garbed in Grand Theories

*Paras Nath Chudhary*

Living healthy and long: this has been one of the primal urges of man. Initially, all his efforts to fight teeming infections and diseases surrounding him had been to no avail. But man did not give up and kept struggling for a solution. Finally, the French invented the word and concept 'hygiene' and with it developed the idea of keeping oneself and the ambience clean. It bears special mention that this meant the beginning of organised systematic sanitary practices. The latter transformed the world. That is to say, man began living longer and healthier. Attainment of basic hygienic standards turned out to be one of the hallmarks of the advancement of a modern human society. In contrast, the lack or absence of it is acknowledged as being a mark of a failed society. Against this background, sanitation became a goal of deeper sociological enquiry.

It is a pity that India has yet to imbibe the idea of general hygiene and sanitation. However, our refusal to access even the most elementary civilisational gains has only reduced us to the status of a sick society in the literal sense of the term.

India has been ranked as a notoriously unclean society. The management of human faeces in particular has been abysmal. This can easily be put down to the lack of toilet facilities. All of us know, the public crapping is a common thing in this country. We betray the total ignorance of social hygiene. There has been a surfeit of studies conducted on this aspect of our society and all of them have yielded the conclusion that dirt management barely figures in Indian scheme of things so the country reeks of dirt. Nobel laureate V.S. Naipaul when visited India in the early 50s was appalled by the squalor he saw lying all around. He wrote a book 'an area of darkness' in which he says, Indians defecate everywhere and one sees human excreta on road-side, home side and in sum every side. He has described India as a defecating society. I wish, the book had been translated into Hindi. One can draw a whole list of international dignitaries who have equally barbecued incredible India's image by their caustic comments on its lack of sanitation.

Last year I was in Patna with a group of film makers from Europe. I was assisting them as a local consultant. It was a pleasure working with these wonderful Europeans and hearing them sing praise for our beautiful Bihar. But soon I was in for a shock when I had the unenviable task of answering their persistent question why Indians are adept at the preservation of dirt and loving it. They had become worn out throughout their stay inspecting stubborn, decayed and voluminous dirt all over the city. They were unhappy also because it was something that had compromised the experiences they wanted to take back home. One of them said, this simply meant Indians had a very low self-esteem. I kept mum as I had no answer.

I had an American student who lived in an upscale neighbourhood in south Delhi–not too far from the ring road. One day, she looked depressed and overcome with a deep hatred of this country. She had to daily negotiate a mass of human excreta lying on the road when going to her workplace. The dirt was forbidding and all over. That the dirt existed in the country's capital passed her comprehension. She called India the dirtiest country in the world.

Another student of mine from Manchester was riled by the sheer lack of basic civic sense on the part of the residents in the colony he lived in. It was difficult for him to understand why the residents themselves keep littering the park with foul smelling dirt where they and their ladies sit and gossip. He was flummoxed by such behaviour. I am sorry to say, hardly a day passed without my students sharing with me their stories on Indians' passionate attachment to dirt.

I had a mail from a young man from Stuttgart, Germany who recently visited India as a tourist. He spent about twenty days in Tamil Nadu and Kerala. He had nice experiences wherever he went. He met scores of interesting people especially in kerala. He was, however, shocked about the huge problem of waste that weighed down this country. He had not expected it to be so bad and he was appalled. According to this young German, India faces an enormous challenge in this regard.

At Nizamuddin in Delhi a girl was shot dead when she objected to a man urinating in front of her house. The man simply could not abide the girl's audacity to tell him off. Instead of making amends for the dirty act and indecent exposure he had indulged in, he went away but immediately came back with a gun to kill the girl who had asserted her right to cleanliness. The incident was instant copy for the media including the international portion of it.

One theory that is often advanced is that while Indians exhibit very high standards of personal hygiene, they are only a little wanting in public cleanliness. This is a theory that does not seem to stand scrutiny. There is a close relationship between the two and sanitation happens only when the two meet. The Euro-American belt is an example. This part of the world enjoys both public cleanliness and personal health. It is entirely thanks to their efficient and quick dirt management. Apart from very few civilisational diseases, most of the common diseases that seriously challenge our health are wholly absent there. The state is always willing to invest resources in keeping the environment clean. The west is antiseptically clean and it is said one can eat from a road without being exposed to any infection. Maintainance of this kind of cleanliness is no mean achievement considering the world's highest per capita waste output obtains there. The less said about us the better. There are millions of men and women still working as manual scavangers and their continuing to engage in this abominable profession is an annoying commentary on our sense of priority as a nation. No wonder there are hardly any countries in the world that could dare surpass us in dirt. It is the ubiquitous stinking dirt that prompted one of our union ministers recently to say India could easily annex noble laurels in being the dirtiest country on the planet.

There is another of repeated theory that puts forward poverty as the explanation for India's dirt. The theory has no legs to stand on in that there are a number of countries poorer than us that have much better sanitary conditions. To our embarrassment, some of these countries exist in our close neighbourhood. One can mention impoverished Burma and Bangladesh, for example. That Pakistan happens to be still cleaner only compounds our sense of humiliation.

There is yet another theory that on occasions gets deployed to defend India's dirt. This is the transcendental theory that argues Indians strive for an elevated spiritual cleanliness and do not give a fig about the mundane cleanliness. According to the theory, Indians consider this world as a relative truth and thus as an illusion. Their preoccupation with the absolute truth and a different kind of purity is barely appreciated creating incomprehension about them. However, the theory is dismissed outrightly as nonsense unlimited and a defence of the indefensible. A saying that bears recall in this context is-cleanliness is next to godliness.

All these theories are groundless and merely a smorgasbord of illogic, non-sequiters and hogwash. They dc not help us understand and fix the problem at all. But India is not bare of ingenuity and genius. Dr Bindeshwar pathak the founder of Sulabh International has shown it. When appalled by his country's squalor, he did not weave theories, nor did he withdraw into the academia's cocoons. Instead, he had a resolution to make a difference. The rest of the story is too well known to merit repetition. I would close by saying the good work he began on a modest scale has expanded over the years acquiring the status of a social revolution.

# 28

# Sociology of Sanitation

*Om Prakash Yadav*

To study the behavior of the society, a new subject was born widely known as Sociology. Sociology is defined as a science of society. In other words, one can say that whatever information we get about the functioning and behaviour of the society is termed as sociology. It has been present right from through the stone age to the present time.

Sociology of sanitation tells us how to keep ourselves clean. What are the basic standards of cleanliness? What were the standards of cleanliness in the past and what do they mean in the present time? To discuss all these aspects, this present seminar 'Sociology of Sanitation' has been organised.

In a broader sense we believe that sanitation is all about wearing clean cloth and living in a clean place. But question arises as to whether people wearing clean clothes and living in clean houses are really clean? But when we talk about a clean society and refer to a period from the stone age to present time, we come to the conclusion that earlier people were short of money and even the population of our country was not so alarming. Most of the people lived in villages. The clothes that they wore were not so fine, nor the houses they lived in were good. But the thoughts of the people were full of human values. There was peace of mind everywhere. Today, the world is full of luxurious items. Houses are good. And yet there is no peace of mind. Of course, people wear clean clothes and live in nice places, but they are living in strain.

With all the above aspects when we think of cleanliness we come across three points.

1. We should remain physically clean.
2. Our mind should be clean.
3. Our soul should be clean.

Firstly, when we talk about physical cleanliness, we mean all around cleanliness. This include our body, the place where we live and work, the clean environment, clean air, clean drinking water and the provision of a clean toilet.

Secondly, when we talk about clean mind, we mean clean and creative thoughts, so that no action from our side should harm anyone. There should be no place for jealousy and revenge in our mind.

When our body and mind are clean, our soul will naturally also be clean and healthy. This will motivate us for some creative work making us always happy.

So, in my view, we should always try to keep ourselves clean in all the ways, i.e., physically, psychologically and spirituality.

# 29

# Health Strategies for Information Technology Professionals

*R. Shankar*

Technology, Media and Telecommunications are three sectors that are combining to change the way people live and work and enabling products and services, that were previously unimaginable, changing the entire social fabric. Giving individuals control over where, how and why they consume information and entertainment and allowing people to communicate across geographic boundaries at the push of a button! The common thread that ties these sectors together is 'Information'. Mastering the powerful forces of technology, media and telecommunications takes more than information, it takes knowledge; seeing patterns in the noise and making sense out of chaos, viz., turning information into insight. In a world of limitless information the key to success is converting information into insight. Countries around the world will continue to make unparalleled investments in thought leadership and intellectual capital combining sophisticated analysis and thorough research with hands-on experience and practical insight. This will result in knowledge and expertise that can help the countries survive and thrive in the topsy-turvy world of technology, media and telecommunications, and hence the connecting thread 'Information'.

The single most important source of social change is technological innovation according to sociologists. Technological advancement spurs social change. Sociological changes take place due to the proliferation of technology in our society. Societies are changing constantly. Some of these changes are subtle and barely noticeable. Other changes are abrupt and blatant. Social changes can affect the norms, values, roles and institutions within a particular community. Some of the technological breakthroughs being made today will impact our culture, our relationships and our individual lives. In order to study these cultural and social changes we should understand the connection of the past to conditions today; examine the relationship between innovation and our living standard; explore how information technology has been a catalyst for change; assess how the job market has evolved and will continue to evolve; hypothesise on future trends of health hazards and suggest suitable strategies to keep our future Indian generations, i.e., young IT professionals' health is attempted in this paper.

With the introduction of computers in India in the 1960's, computers have proved remarkably effective at creating jobs. The logical question is, if the jobs in the service sector also are taken away one day by somebody unknown from a far off place, who will work for peanuts, then what? The answer is you, your creativity, your innovative instincts that nobody could replicate and no machine can match. So, the world would be ultimately conquered by those who would excel in creativity and others would just follow. Can we, the Indians, be the next generation of creative geniuses? Only time will tell.

The complex social and cultural matrix of change due to Information Technology is not properly known yet. At present, cyberspace as the emerging social space is perceived merely by technological metaphors and a market-driven development of the broadband Information Technology infrastructure.

We are in the electronic age where we wear all mankind as our skin. The heritage of the age-old philosophical dream of a universal language and a common understanding may become true. The Global Village does not take into consideration the severe social constraints which determine life in a village. This can be interpreted that the information society is becoming as culturally homogeneous as village lifestyle is.

Societies are basically conservative. They resist change. India is no exception. Any change in society is gradual. This change could be studied by taking a segment of the society and analysing the changes it went through due to the recent developments.

There may be a risk of serious physical injuries from working at our computer workstation.

Some studies have suggested that long periods of typing, improper workstation setup, incorrect work habits, or problems in our personal health may be linked to injuries. These injuries could include carpal tunnel syndrome, tendonitis, tenosynovitis, and other musculoskeletal disorders.

**Warning Signs**

The warning signs of these disorders can occur in the hands, wrists, arms, shoulders, neck, or back, and can include:

- Numbness, burning, or tingling soreness, aching, or tenderness pain, throbbing, or swelling, tightness or stiffness, weakness or coldness;
- Discomfort and fatigue, whether personal or work-related, not only cut into productivity, but left unattended, may get worse.

**Eyes-care**

*We spend the greater part of our life before the computer screens, unaware that it causes a condition known as CVS or Computer Vision Syndrome.*

CVS is characterised by eye strain associated with prolonged computer use.

**Eye-care Tips**

- Position the monitor 20 to 26 inches away the eyes,
- Take breaks between 20 to 60 minutes for about 2-4 minutes,
- Arrange light source to minimise glare and reflections on the screen,
- Blink frequently to moisture the eyes, and
- Use anti-glare spectacles.

**What are RSIs (Repetitive Stress Injuries)**

RSIs are not so much diseases as they are a response to excessive and repetitive demands placed on the body. The hundreds of known repetitive stress injuries, or RSIs, all have a similar cause: excessive wear and tear on the soft tissues of the body (tendons, nerves, circulatory system, etc.).

CTD-Cumulative Trauma Disorder

MSD-Musculo-skeletal Disorders

OOS-Occupational Overuse Syndrome

RMI-Repetitive Motion Injury

UEMSD-Upper Extremity Musculo-skeletal Disorder

WRULD-Work-Related Upper Limb Disorders.

Black Characters on a white background are usually the best. Avoid dark backgrounds.

**Typical Symptoms**

Typical injury symptoms include tightness, general soreness, dull ache, throbbing, sharp pain, numbness, tingling, burning, swelling and loss of strength in your upper extremities (hands, arms, shoulders, and neck). Some injury symptoms are not 'obviously' work related; Carpal Tunnel Syndrome (CTS) is an example of this, where hand numbness, pain, tingling frequently occurs at night while trying to sleep.

**RSI–Risk Factors**

*Repetition* - performing repeated motions in the same way with the same body part.

*Posture*-placing a joint towards its extreme end of movement in any direction away from its neutral, centered position.

*Force*-performing an activity with excessive muscular exertion/force.

*Static Exertion*-holding an object or a body position in a still, fixed manner.

*Contact Stress*-direct pressure on nerves or tendons due to resting the body part against a hard and possibly angled surface.

**Note:** Our bodies are designed to perform all of these activities, however, as they are done in combination, and for extended periods of time, risk of injury increases. This is true whether the activities are performed at work or play.

**Don't Let Food Do You In! Who are you ......?**

**The Stress Snacker:** You eat in response to how you feel—tired, sad, angry, happy, or upset. Your emotions—rather than your hunger—dictate your food choices.

**The Social Eater:** You look at food as a chance to bond with others, so your eating habits vary depending on where you are and who you're with.

**The Weekend Binger:** You're very disciplined during the week—eating right and exercising—but then you let yourself go on the weekends or whenever you have a few days off.

**The Nighttime Nosher:** You're so busy during the day that you eat almost nothing for breakfast or lunch. Then, at night, you're so hungry that you overeat or can't stop snacking.

**Stay in Shape: Don't let Desk Jobs Do You In**

It's easy to put on weight as we get older, especially when we have a sedentary lifestyle. Any exercise, even if it's done for just a few minutes each day, is better than none at all.

**Habits Are Made to be broken....but try these Strategies**

- Take exercise breaks instead of coffee breaks
- Get up a little earlier in the morning to fit in a 30 minute brisk walk
- Instead of using the elevator, use the stairs
- Get off the bus one or two stops early and walk the rest of the way
- Take a walk after dinner instead of watching television
- Drink lots of water every day.

**Exercise–Necessary to Keep You Fit!**

Make Physical activity a part of your life. Lack of physical activity is now clearly shown to be a risk factor for heart disease. Most of us have sedentary jobs. Work takes up a significant part of the day.

What can you do to increase your physical activity during the work day?

*You can*: Swim, cycle, jog, dance, walk, and

*Choose* : Activities that are fun, not exhausting.

**Do's and Don'ts**

**Do's**

- Go out for a short walk before breakfast or after dinner or both! Start with 5-10 minutes and work up to 30 minutes.
- Stand up while talking on the telephone.
- Walk down the hall to speak with someone rather than using the telephone.
- Take the stairs instead of the elevator. Or get off a few floors early and take the stairs the remainder of the way.
- Walk around your building for a break post-lunch.
- Space and limit your drinks (hard drinks...)

**Don't....**

- Over do it,
- Over eat,

- Slouch,
- Eat stale food,
- Over exert yourself,
- Don't eat out of frustration or a sense of being under stress,
- Don't skip your meals, and
- Stretching for health.

Performing simple stretches throughout the workday increases circulation and flexibility, improves posture and reduces tension and the chance of injury. Given in the 'handout' are some stretches specifically designed for individuals who spend time sitting while working at a desk, or on a computer. How they adapt and adjust to the new environment and make life as happy as possible and move forward in the adopted country.

## References

Aggarwal, Kuntal, (1991). Survival of Females in India. In Sociology of Health in India, edited by T.M. Dak, Rawat Fublications; Jaipur.

Baus, Amitabha et al., (1991). Sex Differentials in Nutritional Status and Child mortality: Some results from micro-level studies. In: *Health of the young and the female child*, edited by Ashok Shani; Indian Society for Health Administrators, Bangalore.

Chowdhry, A.I. et al., (1996). Differences in neonatal mortality by religious and socio-economic covariates in rural Bangladesh; the *Journal of Family Welfare*, Vol. 42, No. 2.

Das Guta, Monica, (1995). Fertility Decline in Punjab, India: Parallels with Historical Europe; *Population Studies*; Vol. 49, No. 3, London, England.

Deshpande, R.V., (1993). Determinants of Child mortality: A district level analysis for major Indian states; XVI Annul conference of the Indian Association for the Study of Population; Bhubaneswar, India.

George, Sabu et al. (1992). Female infanticide in rural South India; *Economic and Political Weekly*; Vol. 27, No. 22.

www.mmm.com

www.compaq.com

www.ahealthyme.com

www.cornell.edu

www.osha.gov

www.ergonomics.org

# 30

# Issues Related to Sanitation from the Perspective of Development

***S.K. Mishra*** and ***Prabhleen Kaur***

## Introduction

A society cannot progress unless its members progress and achieve refinement. The opportunity for progress and refinement should percolate down to the last member of society. Health plays a prominent role in achieving this goal. Thus, a vital component of a developed society is the health of its citizens. A healthy body harbours a healthy mind and there is an urgent need to create awareness regarding health and sanitation. Proper sanitation is needed to build a healthy society. Despite all progress and development today the modern world, especially India, suffers from poor sanitation. This lack of proper sanitation leads to ill health of members of the society.

It seems that lack of sanitation has emerged as one of the prominent stumbling blocks in the process of development of society in the 21st century. Keeping this in view as a serious challenge before us, the present paper makes an attempt to raise issues related to sanitation. These concerns have been raised by a number of social scientists time and again at different platforms.

## Problem of Sanitation in India

The absence of required sanitation in India has caused a loss of 6.5 per cent of the GDP per annum by the 20 per cent of the slum dwellers in India. Overall sanitation coverage in rural India is a dismal 34.8 per cent; for Scheduled castes and Scheduled tribes it is 23.7 per cent and 25 per cent respectively. The situation of sanitation is even worse in the tribal society of India. This is an indication of alarming situation regarding Public Health, Social Deprivation, and Environmental Sanitation and so on in India.

As a matter of fact, the situation of sanitation has not been so bad in India if analysed from a historical perspective. The archeological excavations in India have revealed the Harappan Model of urban sanitation. We also know the views of the father of the nation, Mahatma Gandhi on sanitation. In the modern period, the world witnessed another economical and most effective Sulabh International Model of Sanitation introduced by Mr Bindeshwar Pathak. But even then the coverage of sanitation is far less than what is required on the developmental scale. Till now, access to proper sanitation has remained the privilege of only a small section of the society in India.

### Important Data Related to Situation of Sanitation in India

As far as the access to improved sanitation is concerned, it is 54 per cent in urban areas, 21 per cent in rural areas and the total stands at 31 per cent in the year 2008 in India. The share of collected wastewater treated was 27 per cent in the year 2003. Also, the annual investment in water supply and sanitation stood at US $ 5 per capita.

### Institutions and Laws in this Sector

If we focus on the existence of various institutions and laws in this sector in India, the following picture is revealed:

- Water and Sanitation regulator – No;
- National Water and Sanitation co. – No;
- Sector Law – No;
- Decentralisation to municipalities – Partial; and
- Number of Service Providers:
  Urban – 3,255
  Rural – about 1,00,000

### National Urban Sanitation Policy

As regards the sanitation policy, 12 states in India were in the process of either elaborating or had completed the state sanitation policy. Around 120 cities in India were in the process of framing city sanitation plans in 2010. Also, 436 cities rated themselves in terms of their achievements and process concerning sanitation. The rating serves as the base line to measure improvements in the future and to prioritise action. The following data reveals the rating:

- About 40 per cent were in the Red category (in need of immediate remedial action);
- 50 per cent were in the Black category (needing considerable improvement);
- Only handful in Blue category (recovering); and
- Not a single one in the Green category.

**Investment**

The 11th Five Year Plan (2007-2012) foresees investments worth Rs. 127.025 crores for urban water supply and sanitation, including urban (stormwater) drainage.

**Review of Performance in the 11th Five Year Plan:**

The 11th Five Year Plan was successful in improving the situation of sanitation to a certain extent. Rural sanitation coverage in India in the beginning of the 11th Five Year Plan was at 39 per cent and by the end of the 11th Five Year Plan it was 71 per cent. The National Sample Survey Organisation (NSSO), 2010 data show that 65.2 per cent (Rural) and 11 per cent (Urban) areas have no sanitation facility in households. Also the Joint Monitoring Report of WHO/UNICEF, 2010 mentions that 638 million people defecate in open. According to the report, the sanitation coverage in rural areas in 2008 was – 21 per cent (improved), four per cent (shared), six per cent (unimproved) and rest 69 per cent in open.

Percentage of open defecation in Rural areas in South Asian countries (2008):

- India - 69 per cent
- Nepal - 60 per cent
- Pakistan - 40 per cent
- Afghanistan - 20 per cent
- Maldives - 4 per cent
- Bangladesh - 8 per cent
- Bhutan - 11 per cent
- Sri Lanka - 1 per cent

**NSSO (2008-09)**

The data collected by National Sample Survey Organisation (2008-2009) regarding the availability of latrine facilities has been mentioned below. As per the findings of the NSSO:

- 75 per cent Scheduled Tribes,
- 76 Scheduled Castes,
- 69 Other Backward Classes, and
- 43 Other communities; posses no latrine facility.

## Relevant Issues to be Raised

The present situation of sanitation in India calls for an immediate action. There is need to hold comprehensive dialogue with the academia, administrators and representatives of civil society. This will help frame issues for further researches.

The Department of Sociology, Janardan Rai Nagar Rajasthan Vidyapeeth (Deemed) University, Udaipur, Rajasthan has been involved in doing research in the field of sanitation. The Department has conducted empirical studies concerning the existence and condition of sanitation facilities in urban areas of Rajasthan. The study covered various cities of Rajasthan including Alwar, Bhilwara, Chittorgarh, Hanumangarh, Jodhpur, Kapasan, Pali, Pushkar, Shahpura, Tonk and Udaipur. The issue of sanitation is extremely essential and there is immense scope for research in this field.

## Conclusion

There is a need to conceptualise the perspectives of development from the sanitation point of view. There should be a future road-map to strengthen and enhance the methodology of interventions. Sanitation, especially with regard to the Tribal, Rural, Urban Divide; the conditions of the Scheduled Castes and the Scheduled Tribes in India as well as their ethnic practices need special attention. As far as the Public Health is concerned, specific Actions Programmes have to be developed. The role of the professionals and the civil society in this regard is important. The socially deprived sections of the society and their condition as regards sanitation, also needs to be looked at and improved through focussed interventions. Drawing attention to such vital issues, related to sanitation is a key to the development of society.

## References

Census of India, New Delhi: Government of India, 2001.

National Sample Survey Organisation, New Delhi: Government of India, 2008.

National Sample Survey Organisation, New Delhi: Government of India, 2010.

www.wikipedia.org

# 31

# Complete Cleanliness Campaign Project

*Anil Vaghela*

**Q. 1.** *Will you give information about Complete Cleanliness Campaign Project?*

**Ans.** The Complete Cleanliness Campaign Project is a special project awarded and operated by the Government of India. The main objectives of this campaign are making hundred per cent public conveniences available in rural area and ensure its permanent maintenance. It will stop open defecation and make village clean.

Through health related education, the purpose is to make cleanliness a habit and generate public awareness. The demands of public will be fulfilled.

Through individual toilets, people will be encouraged towards health and cleanliness. Shalas and Anganwadis will be made Cleanliness Campaign oriented. Planned actions are afoot for the proper disposal of liquid and solid wastes.

**Q. 2.** *What is the outline of Complete Cleanliness Campaign Project?*

**Ans.** Implementation of the project, under the supervision of secretary or commissioner, Rural Development and Sate Coordinator, CCDUTS is done by district level Village Development Agency. District Development Chairman is district development officer. Controller also functions.

**Q. 3** *Have the targets of complete cleanliness campaign progress bee fixed?*

**Ans.** This project is not target based. This project moves ahead through the creation of public awareness and demands emerging from that. Through different activities, decision is taken for the construction of toilets. Once toilet related fraternity is developed, it is properly utilised. It is cleaned daily. This toilet is not for any other interest.

**Q. 4** *What is Clean Gujarat project?*

**Ans.** It is a project of the Gujarat Government launched in 2007. In the beginning, the work was taken up for the construction of private toilets for APL people. Such families were given assistance of Rs. 750 each. It was enhanced to Rs. 1250 in 2009. Since then, there have also been arrangements for pollution management, liquid waste disposal and technical support.

**Q. 5.** *What is the difference between Complete Cleanliness Campaign Project and Gujarat Projects?*

**Ans.** Both the projects engage in the construction of toilets, disposal of liquid and solid wastes and conduct activities to create cleanliness related public awareness. Still there are some differences between the two. The Complete Cleanliness Campaign gives Rs. 3,200 each to the BPL families for construction of individual toilets as incentive. The BPL families of difficult and hilly regions are given Rs.3,700 each. On the other hand, under the clean project the amount is Rs. 1250 only.

**Q. 6.** *I belong to a BPL family. Can I get assistance for toilet construction? To whom should I approach?*

**Ans.** Under revised rules, you can get Rs. 3,200 for toilet construction. For difficult and hilly areas the amount is Rs. 3700. The beneficiary has to pay Rs. 300. It is necessary to contact the *sarpanch* of the concerned *panchayat* and the minister. The welfare committee of each village can also extend assistanee.

**Q. 7.** *I hail from the BPL family. I face stiff objection as there is no toilet in my house. How can I get it constructed?*

**Ans.** Under Clean Gujarat Project the APL family gets Rs. 1250 for toilet construction.

**Q. 8.** *After the construction of toilet, for which other purposes assistance will be available?*

**Ans.** Gujarat Government gives an incentive of Rs. 1,250 to APL families. After that under Clean Gujarat Project, monetary help is given for the following purposes:

1. Disposal of solid waste,
2. Disposal of Liquid waste,
3. Appointment of tehsil and village level mobiliser.
4. For monitoring the work.
5. For the education of villagers and cooperating youth.
6. For the motivational efforts of the village panchayat officials and effective leaders.
7. For cleanliness related public awareness trend.

**Q. 9.** *Is the amount given to the BPL or APL an incentive or for the construction of toilets?*

**Ans.** So that the people are motivated to construct toilet, the amount is given as an incentive.

**Q. 10.** *I am an urban APL. Shall I get assistance for the construction of toilet under Complete Cleanliness Campaign?*

**Ans.** This project is only for rural people. You can get assistance from the municipality and so contact them.

**Q. 11.** *Open defecation is free while one has to spend money for constructing toilet?*

**Ans.** It is dangerous to evacuate in open. It harms personal health and causes ecological harms. For health one can spend some money. Illness will affect professional activities. *Bacteria* is absorbed in the pit if the toilet is in the residence. Family remains healthy. Invalid old and ladies get the facility of privacy.

**Q. 12.** *Toilet construction takes more money than received as incentive. Can one get money from other sources?*

**Ans.** Over and above the governmental incentive, other agencies like dairy farms, milk producer units and banks also give money on cheap interests and subsidies for the construction of toilets.

**Q. 13.** *I am neither a BPL nor I have money to construct a toilet. What can I do?*

**Ans.** Depending on your convenience, you can dig a simple pit with plastic or cotton cover erected on all sides for privacy.

**Q. 14.** *Should I construct a pucca toilet?*

**Ans.** If you intend to avoid open defecation, it is necessary that one should have only a *pucca* toilet. Where there is no provision for toilet, after defecation, put some soil on the excreta so that the *bacteria* do not remain alive.

**Q. 15.** *In our village several milk groups have no toilet in their house. What is the way out?*

**Ans.** Make an APL/ BPL list of such residents and inform the *panchayat*. Rs. 1,250 to APL family and Rs. 3,200 to BPL family will be given. Similar action in respect of other groups can accelerate the pace of toilet construction.

**Q. 16.** *We are the ladies who cannot defecate in day-time and have to suppress the urge till it is dark in the evening. How to get rid of it?*

**Ans.** It is a reality in respect of women. Heads of the families should be told about it. Such affected ladies should unitedly raise their voice. Women groups should take up this responsibility. The ladies should take a solid step today itself so that no house remains without a toilet.

**Q. 17.** *What cooperation can be extended by the energetic youth to keep the village clean?*

**Ans.** Youth is the future of the country. They can give their contribution in the following ways:

1. After getting full guidance from the district Complete Cleanliness Campaign related development agencies of the villages, they can start their work.
2. After moving in all villages and listing the toilet-less houses, they can put pressure on the heads of such families.
3. Open defecators should be so humiliated that they are compelled to get toilet constructed.
4. Toilets in schools and *anganwadis* should remain clean and well maintained so that people could use.
5. There should be a programme for keeping public places *tardy*.
6. People should remain alert for complete cleanliness so that their village wins *Nirmal Gram Puraskar*.

**Q. 18.** *What contribution the sisters of lady groups can give in Complete Cleanliness Campaign Project?*

**Ans.** Ensure the construction of toilets in toilet-less houses. Lady groups should prove helpful. They should adopt protest measures including fast. Combined pressure on concerned family is necessary. The sale of toilet related raw materials like cement, sand and sanitation should be arranged.

**Q. 19.** *Since there is no water-tap in my house, what is wrong in going out for defecation?*

**Ans.** To defecate on river banks is prohibited. The river is mother, worshipped, giving water to the people. Water is the life source of birds, animals and human beings which is polluted through defecation and cause diseases like cholera, gastro and polio.

**Q. 20.** *How a person, working in an agricultural field can go to his house for defecation?*

**Ans.** There should be an emergency toilet in the field. If defecation is in open, soil should be put on the excretion.

**Q. 21.** *Sea beaches, where water level is higher, pit will be water logged. How to operate a toilet there?*

**Ans.** There are two options. Firstly, instead of digging a pit, on the ground, walls should be made in the shape of a *tunkey* for receiving excretion which may be emptied in due course.

The second option is to construct ecosan toilet in such expanses. It is specially designed. On the ground itself wall is made on which specially designed tube is kept. There are two pits in the bottom of the tube. In one waste and in other water collects. In the area of waste from time to time ash is put and after some time the converted manure should be taken out by removing the lid. This way, the problem of constructing toilet on sea-beaches is solved.

**Q. 22.** *I have no space for toilet in my house. What is the solution?*

**Ans.** Such families should approach the panchayat for land on which a public toilet complex could be constructed. Through public contribution, it is possible. Its maintenance should also be the combined responsibility. Both sexes should have separate toilets.

**Q. 23.** *I am infirm. Can I get a suitable toilet?*

**Ans.** For such users, specially designed toilets are available. In this, sloping space can be used. One can approach the panchayat or the development agency.

**Q. 24.** *What is the solution for my daughter having problem in the school due to the absence of toilet?*

**Ans.** There is provision of Rs. 35,000 under complete cleanliness campaign for schools. For this, it is necessary to contact the village panchayat or the district village development agency.

**Q. 25.** *What is the toilet facility in the co-education schools?*

**Ans.** There is the provision of separate toilets for both sexes under the complete cleanliness campaign.

**Q. 26.** *Urinals and toilets in my school are not clean. What should I do?*

**Ans.** In each primary school, from the education department an amount of Rs. 400 is spent on its maintenance covering acid, phenyl, brush, cotton and payment for cleaning staff. The principal and teachers should be informed.

**Q. 27.** *How can I inculcate the habit of cleanliness in my children?*

**Ans.** They should take bath daily and put on clean clothes.

1. Trim their nail ends.
2. Should use pot for drinking water.
3. After defecation, should clean their hands with soap.
4. Pencil, paper and other wastes should be thrown in the dus-bin.
5. Besides self, they should also suggest others to remain clean.

**Q. 28** *Will you tell us about child cleanliness adalats (courts)?*

**Ans.** The central government advisory stresses cleanliness in children. Children accept easily. Teachers are advised to conduct child *adalat*. They should apprise students of child mortality caused by drinking contaminated water. There should be minor punishment for causing dirt.

**Q. 29.** *As a teacher, what should I do to teach the quality of cleanliness to my students?*

**Ans.** These activities will impart the importance of cleanliness to the students.

1. If clean children are given preference, others will be motivated.
2. The winners of cleanliness related debate, essay writing, painting competition should be given proper incentives.

3. Cleanliness related quotes should be exhibited on walls.
4. There should be dramas, music etc programmes emphasising cleanliness.
5. Cleanliness related formula should be written on books and note-books.

**Q. 30.** *There are two anganwadis in my village and their government building has no toilet. Private houses have no toilets. What should be done for that?*

**Ans.** Either the tenants should change their accommodation or the house owner should be convinced to construct toilet.

**Q. 31.** *What should be done for the disposal of heaps of wastes at public places in my village?*

**Ans.** Under complete cleanliness campaign project, village panchayats are given aids for cleanliness. Panchayats can appoint cleaning staff who can collect wastes from individual householders. Self-help and youth groups should also carry out cleaning work. There should be such permanent arrangement.

**Q. 32.** *Can we get information about recycling of household wastes?*

**Ans.** Through some chemical treatment, wastes are recycled to produce compost cooking gas and generating electricity. It will lead to the disposal of wastes, cleanliness and income to the panchayat.

**Q. 33.** *Is any assistance available for recycling wastes?*

**Ans.** Complete cleanliness campaign gives some assistance for collecting wastes from individual houses. Under Clean Gujarat Project village panchayats get Rs. 9,000 for removal of wastes and their composting for solid waste management related different projects like MGNREGBRGETSC, 13th Finance Commission gives conversion assistance to panchayat, 'Dhan Sandesh'.

**Q. 34.** *How to go for safe disposal of waste?*

**Ans.** After collecting the wastes, they should be put on fire in a pit. One can earn some money by selling plastic wastes.

**Q. 35.** *How to dispose of growing polythene and plastic wastes in villages?*

**Ans.** There should be provision of dust-bins at public places for collecting wastes. People should be made aware of using these dust-bins. Collected wastes can be sold out for some earning.

**Q. 36.** *Is it proper to throw dirty used water of our houses in rivers?*

**Ans.** It is a harmful practice. It leads to the breeding of mosquitoes and other worms causing epidemics. They, who drink contaminated water of ponds, fall ill. There is always fear of water contamination.

**Q. 37.** *How to dispose of dirty water? Is there any assistance for that?*

**Ans.** The construction of drainage is the best solution. Later, this water can be purified and re-used. For this different projects like MNREGBRGFTSE, 13th Finance Commission extends assistance to panchayat.

**Q. 38.** *What is the treatment for the problems caused by flies and mosquitoes breeding on dirty water in the village?*

**Ans.** The village panchayat should level the ground. In the water-logging areas, collection pits should be dug out in which the dirty water will enter and the village will be disease free.

**Q. 39.** *What precautions are required at the places of public water taps and the animals water drinking points?*

**Ans.** At such places more water-logging is avoided. From time to time phenyl and gamosin should be used to stop mosquito breeding. There should be a permanent drainage for the flowing away of water.

**40.** *If the waste heaps are not harmful, why it should be removed?*

**Ans.** Wastes on roads or infront of houses, spoil the beauty of the village. Bad smell prevails. The village will be beautiful only after removing them. Land can be given on rent for cow-dung which will generate income. By constructing walls of 3-4″, wastes can be dumped there.

**Q. 41.** *Are some other uses of waste heaps?*

**Ans.** For animals dropping manure, worm compost, *gobar* gas, cooking gas and power generation can be utilised. Animal dung based manures increase the land fertility and increases agricultural produce. Kitchen will get cooking gas.

**Q. 42.** *Please give information about public toilet based bio-gas plant?*

**Ans.** In the area of good population public toilet related bio-gas plant can be constructed for compost and cooking gas. In the courtyard of the house, bio-gas plant is installed with which is connected toilets without the need of collection pit. Even dirty water is also handled. It gives bio-gas and compost. From Complete Cleanliness Campaign and some NGOs one can get assistance.

**Q. 43.** *What is Worm-compost?*

**Ans.** Animal dropping manure is used in worming-composting. Worms are mixed in *gobar*-manure to prepare fertiliser. Near residence, in open area worm-composting is possible for income. Animal husbandry people should carefully keep *gobar* for a longer period.

**Q. 44.** *Worm Composting is possible where?*

**Ans.** Anybody can do this work in the open area of his/her house.

**Q. 45.** *Under self-help group project, can separate groups of sisters working in villages do worm composting?*

Ans. These sisters will have to approach the tehsil or panchayat level officials of green project to procure full information. Through district support centre, technical and financial help can be procured. They also help in training the sisters. Assistance is also available for constructing sheds and purchasing worm and *gobar*-mixed fertilised. *Under Nirmal Gujarat Yojana* also sisters can get assistance to utilise their time and become self-dependent. Out of the income of the centre also they can get aids for different purposes.

**Q. 46.** *NRIs and some financially strong organisations of our village want to contribute to the cause of conveniences. Please guide?*

**Ans.** Such individuals and organisations have to meet the complete cleanliness campaign coordinator for getting financial AMU. They can give technical, financial and monetary support. Such bodies can also give loan for toilet construction.

**Q. 47.** *What should be done for adopting a village to make it a nirmal gram?*

**Ans.** Financial technical and manpower assistance are required for adopting a village as a *nirmal gram*.

Houses without toilets should be identified to know the reasons and the family heads should be persuaded to get toilet constructed. A ban has to be put on open defecation. Such people should be kept in continuous contact till toilets are built in their houses. Sisters of self-help groups should be made aware of worming compost. Villages have to be shown a new direction by keeping them clean by good use of cow-dung. Financial help will have to the given for digging *pucca* pits for collecting wastes. Schools and *anganwadis* will have to arrange different competitions, which will require funding assistancc.

**Q. 48.** *What are the yardsticks for giving nirmal gram puraskar?*

**Ans.** *Nirmal Gram Puraskar* is given for stopping open defecation and keeping clean villages to tehsils and district panchayats. These are the requirements:-

(a) Hundred per cent toilets and its utility is essential in the areas of village panchayat, tehsil panchayat and district panchayat.

(b) Toilets of all schools should remain clean. They should invariably be in use. There should be separate toilets for boys and girls.

(c) Open defecation should be totally banned.

(d) Open defecation should be punishable. The village army should pass a law for that purpose.

(e) In order to maintain cleanliness, there should be proper arrangements for liquid/solid wastes and drainage. The growing heaps of wastes and water-logging should not be permitted in the village.

(f) Source of water, proper platform and drainage for liquid disposal should essentially be ensured.

**Q. 49.** *What amounts are given to Nirmal Gram awarded villages?*

**Ans.** Depending on the basis of population as in 2001 census, the following awards are given to the winners of Nirmal Gram Purashkar:

| *Gram Panchayat* | *Rs.* |
|---|---|
| The village with the population of 1,000 | 50,000 |
| Village with 1,000-1999 population | 1,00,000 |
| Village with 2,000-4,999 Population | 2,00,000 |
| Village with 5,000-9,999 Population | 4,00,000 |
| Village with 10,000 and more | 5,00,000 |

| *Tehsil Panchayat* | *Rs.* |
|---|---|
| Tehsil Panchayat with a population of | |
| less than 50,000 | 10,00,000 |
| 50,001 and above | 20,00,000 |
| *District Panchayat* | |
| District Panchayat with a population of | |
| upto 10 lakh | 30,00,000 |
| More than ten lakh | 50,00,000 |

Along with the award money, *plaque* and certificates are also given.

**Q. 50.** *Where from I can get information about different projects like toilet in houses, schools, anganwadi, solid waste management, disposal of waste and worm-composting?*

**Ans.** For these information, one should contact following offices:-

1. Concerned village panchayat
2. Tehsil development officer and TSC department for tehsil panchayat
3. District controller, district village development agency and TSC department
4. Chairman, district development officer and district village development agency, etc.

If you are not satisfied with them, then you can contact state corrdinator, CCDUTSE Block-16, Dr. Jivraj Mehta Bhawan, Third Floor, Gandhi Nagar.

# 32

# Sociology of Sanitation: Issues and Concerns

*Manish Thakur*

It would be appropriate for any contemporary discussion of the larger societal context of sanitation to begin with a historical mapping of the twin notions of civic consciousness and public space. Historians of colonial India (Chakrabarty 1992; Kaviraj, 1997) have indicated the cultural incompatibility of the colonial and the 'native' notions of public health and hygiene leading to the latter's indifference to the related municipal injunctions and governmental expectations. They explain this disjunction in terms of the differing conceptualisations of the private and the public at the two ends of the spectrum. At times, they romanticise the prevalence of filth and garbage in the public sphere as the sign of the poor's refusal to submit to the demands of colonial modernity. Such refusal gets celebrated as acts of political defiance and also as testimony to the vibrancy of the political society in the country. In other words, they see continuity between the colonial and the post-colonial state and consider official discourses on public health, sanitation and hygiene as part of the complex apparatus of manufacturing citizens out of multitudinous communities.

Be that as it may, there has been no dearth of official discourses, plans and programmes concerning sanitation. Very often, these sanitation programmes are incentivised through subsidies and grants. Total sanitation campaigns have been underway in most of the states. Yet, they fail to achieve the desired effects. There are structural reasons for that which makes it imperative to bring in the economic status of households and habitations. In parts of Andhra Pradesh, toilets were used for storing grains as they happened to be the best parts of the habitation that the residents had. Besides, there is the impact of general corruption on issues of sanitation as they are perceived less important, and so less likely to raise public eyebrows. In many cases, toilets are just built on paper in active connivance with the state officials and municipal and school authorities, and do not attract much public scrutiny.

Likewise, issues of sanitation are intimately linked with our notions of human dignity. Construction workers across the country may erect huge buildings but their worksite would hardly have any toilet facilities. We pass on our responsibility to the contractors even in places like IIMs. Very few households allow domestic workers to avail of toilet facilities. In fact, some housing societies proscribe the use of such facilities for outsiders like maids, milk-*wallahs*, *newspaper-wallahs*. We have to fight the deep-seated notion of the differing human worth of different groups of people which get reflected in the facilities for sanitation that they may avail of or are provided with. In sociological jargon, we have to probe the implications of social stratification for an understanding of the complex sociology of sanitation. Sanitation is not merely a function of larger public culture.

And lastly, the sheer untranslatability of ritual cleanliness and purity into everyday practices of hygienic upkeep of public places poses great challenges. The conditions in pilgrim places such as Benaras and *dharmashalas* are cases in point. Interestingly, in the so-called secular places like universities and colleges, shopping complexes, one finds toilets under lock and key to discourage visitors from using them. At times, even in places where hundreds throng on a regular basis for work, authorities display great insensitivity in having arrangements for toilet facilities. Toilets in some of the village schools are exclusively meant for teachers while students are left to use open spaces in full public view.

## References

Chakrabarty, Dipesh. 1992. 'Of Garbage, Modernity and the Citizen's Gaze', *Economic and Political Weekly*, 27 (10-11), March-7-14.

Kaviraj, Sudipta. 1997. 'Filth and Public Sphere', *Public Culture*, 10 (1).

# 33

# Sociology of Sanitation: National Conference (Held on 28-29 January, 2013)

The National Conference on Sociology of Sanitation, organised by Sulabh International Centre for Action Sociology in collaboration with Sulabh International Social Service Organisation, was held on January 28 and 29, 2013 at Mavalankar Auditorium, New Delhi. The inaugural session had dignitaries like Hon'ble Mrs Meira Kumar, Speaker, Lok Sabha; Hon'ble Mr Jairam Ramesh, Minister of Rural Development, Government of India; Hon'ble Mr Bharatsinh Madhavsinh Solanki, Minister of State (Independent Charge), Department of Drinking Water and Sanitation, Government of India and Professor Yogendra Singh, Emeritus Professor, Jawaharlal Nehru University, New Delhi, as honoured guests and speakers. The function was attended by esteemed sociologists, social scientists and sanitation experts from all over the country, who were kind enough to contribute their scholarly papers for the occasion. The big auditorium was packed to the full with participating scholars, media and electronic personnel.

**Inaugural Function**

The function started at 11 am with the distinguished participants, sitting on the dais being garlanded, presented bouquets and shawls

by Dr Bindeshwar Pathak, Founder of the Sulabh Sanitation Movement, and his wife, Mrs Amola Pathak. They included Hon'ble Mrs Meira Kumar, Hon'ble Mr Jairam Ramesh, Hon'ble Mr Bharatsinh Madhavsinh Solanki, Professor Yogendra Singh and this was followed by singing of Sulabh Prayer by one and all present on the occasion. Thereafter to introduce the activities of Sulabh, videos prepared by *Voice of America* and a French Company were played, depicting the sanitation scenario in India. Showing realistic scenes of bucket or dry toilets being manually cleaned by scavenger women, the presentation accessed to Dr Bindeshwar Pathak talking about the gloomy scenario on the sanitation front. He personally intervened in the matter, innovating, inventing and developing a two-pit pour-flush compost toilet technology to replace bucket or dry toilets, which did not need cleansing by scavengers, who in their turn were being taken away from the inhuman and filthy job, educated and trained to earn their livelihood in a respectful manner through vocations like making eatables, beauty care, embroidery, stitching etc. They were thus brought into the mainstream of society, followed by social interaction with other communities in society leading to visiting temples, calling upon dignitaries like the Hon'ble President of India, Hon'ble President of the Congress Party, and Hon'ble Prime Minister (late Mr. Rajiv Gandhi), being invited to attend the General Assembly Session at the United Nations. These historical moments were shown in photographs displayed during the show.

Mr Arun Pathak, Chief Coordinator, Sulabh International Social Service Organisation, delivering his welcome address said, "It is significant that the hall where we are all sitting was named after Shri Mavalankar, the first Speaker of the Lok Sabha, in independent India, and today we have among us the first lady Speaker of the esteemed House. The Hon'ble Speaker and the esteemed Ministers have to deal with cut motions in the House, whereas Sulabh International is concerned with motion, as such (in some cases, loose one, as well)". Mr Pathak expressed gratefulness for the esteemed guests, scholars, scientists and media and electronic personnel to have spared their time and made it convenient to attend the conference that was going to introduce a new vista in the sphere of sociology as well as sanitation.

Mr Arun Pathak was followed by Mrs Usha Chaumar, Hony. President, Sulabh International Social Service Organisation (a liberated scavenger woman from Alwar, Rajasthan), who expressed her great pleasure specially to see Hon'ble Mr Jairam Ramesh at the function, who, she said, talked so freely that she used to enjoy his company. Always referring to Dr Pathak as Founder Sir, she said, when he went to Alwar and met her and her companions, he asked them to give up the work they were doing, on being told that they were scavengers cleaning human excreta from bucket toilets and carrying it on their heads in a vessel to throw it away at a place outside the habitation. He further said he would make them take up respectful jobs after proper training. No one among them was ready to be convinced. When some of them ventured to take a chance, what happened was an unbelievable

transformation. They now sit and dine with people belonging to higher classes, attend functions like marriage and birthdays at their residence, visit temples and offer worship there. Led by Founder Sir they have called upon VIPs like Hon'ble President of India, Hon'ble Ministers, visited UNO in New York and gone to Paris and Africa and attended high-level meetings.

Mrs Chaumar was followed by Mrs Mannu Ghosh, a widow from Vrindavan who expressed her gratitude for the help from Sulabh of Rs 1000 every month being given to the widows, besides ambulances and medical care there.

**Journey in Sanitation**

Dr Bindeshwar Pathak after welcoming the esteemed guests, including sociologists from all over the country, the rehabilitated scavenger women from Rajasthan, Bihar and New Delhi and the widows from Vrindavan, began telling his own story as to how he started his journey in the field of sociology and sanitation. Dr Pathak said: "I took up sociology as a subject in B.A. Part-I in Patna University and later as a subject in the Honours Class. I wanted to be a lecturer in the subject; however, after passing my Secondary School Examination, I became a school teacher. In the year 1968, by sheer coincidence, I joined the Bihar Gandhi Centenary Celebration Committee as a social worker. The General Secretary of the Committee asked me to engage myself fully to fulfill the dreams of Mahatma Gandhi – his unfinished agenda to restore the human rights and dignity of 'Untouchable' scavengers. This, he said, would be the best tribute from the committee to the Mahatma.

I told him my story when, as a boy, I, out of curiosity, touched an 'Untouchable' Dom lady who used to come to deliver utensils made of bamboo at my house and after whose departure, my grandmother used to sprinkle water to purify the place. My grandmother seeing me having touched the lady forced me to take cow-dung and cow urine with Ganga water to purify me. I added, I belong to Brahmin caste, and further, I am not an engineer to find out an alternative to the toilets needing manual cleaning. The General Secretary looked at me seriously and said, 'I don't know your caste or whether you are an engineer or not, I see light in you having seen your dedication and commitment'."

Dr Pathak further said, "My background of Sociology prodded me to build a rapport with the community for which I had to work. I went to Bettiah, Champaran in Bihar, to live with the scavengers, the place, where incidentally, Mahatma Gandhi started his *Satyagraha* movement. My father and father-in-law had turned hostile seeing me going to work for scavengers. One afternoon, while going with some friends to the town, I saw a boy in a red shirt being attacked by a bull. People rushed to help him, in the meanwhile someone shouted from the back of the crowd that the boy belonged to the 'Untouchable' colony. On this everybody left him in an injured state. We took him to the local hospital but he died on the way. That day I took the solemn vow, forgetting my family, my caste, to work to fulfill Mahatma Gandhi's dream to rescue the 'Untouchables' from the shackles of slavery that are 5000 years old. Once again, the background of Sociology came to my help indicating the need for some tools to test the hypothesis one is going to work upon. The tool, here, would be a technology that could find an alternative to bucket or dry toilet which needed manual scavenging. One such technology available was the sewerage system, which was costly to construct and maintain and hence existed in very few towns. I went through literature on the subject including the book, Excreta Disposal for Rural Areas and Small Communities by Edmund A. Wagner and J.N. Lanoix. Thereafter I innovated, invented and developed two-pit pour-flush Sulabh toilet, where one pit is used at a time; when it is filled up the flow is diverted to the other pit. After two years the residue in the first pit gets converted into bio-fertiliser which can be taken out by the householder himself. Sulabh alone has converted 1.3 million bucket toilets into Sulabh Shauchalayas and lakhs of scavengers have been freed from their inhuman profession of manually cleaning and carrying human excreta". The Sulabh Founder said, "To rehabilitate the scavengers, I took help of one of the tools of Mahatma Gandhi – the tool of non-violence. I didn't tear or burn the books of Vedas or Manusmriti. I persuaded the upper caste people and Pandits of temples to accept the scavengers as members of the society. I took them to Jagannath temple where after initial resistance the Pandits were convinced after discussion to let the erstwhile scavenger ladies perform *Pooja* in the temple. After the Nathdwara visit the scavengers were given audience by the Hon'ble President of India, Mr R. Venkataraman and the Hon'ble Prime Minister late Mr Rajiv Gandhi. They were taken to Jagannath temple, Alwar. The head priest Pandit Devendra Kumar Sharma is here today amongst us. He will be awarded a cheque of Rs. five lakh by Sulabh in this function. There after they were taken to Varanasi where they worshipped Lord Shiva. The Pandits from Varanasi are also present here among us. They will take oath at this function today to eliminate untouchability from our society. The erstwhile scavengers have attended the UN General Assembly session and visited the Statue of Liberty in New York. They visited France to attend the Summit at Le Havre and Marseilles as well as Phoenix Ashram of Mahatma Gandhi in South Africa. The tool for this transformation has been education and training in vocations like making eatables, beauty care, stitching and embroidery in a Sulabh institute called Nai Disha in Rajasthan. They are sitting here among us in blue saris. Similarly, rehabilitated scavenger ladies from Arrah (Bihar) as well as New Delhi will be given blue saris at lunch today. Their children get free education, school dress and books and stationery in the Sulabh Public School in New Delhi".

Dr Pathak said he termed the present National Conference as one on Sociology of Sanitation as he was convinced that sanitation should

be included as a discipline in sociology as core problem areas embodying sanitation like social deprivation, hygiene, ecology, poverty, etc., require sociological intervention. Dr Pathak was followed by Prof Yogendra Singh, Emeritus Professor, Jawaharlal Nehru University, New Delhi, who is a renowned sociologist. He said, sociology emerged as a subject much later after history, philosophy and political science. Social awareness, individuals' relationship with one another and their participation as a community–all these are vital factors in sociological studies. Sanitation, hygiene, education are the sociological inter-locking factors. It is a well-known truism that sociology is practically nonexistent in dictatorial regimes. It has been a remarkable step taken by Dr Bindeshwar

Pathak to organise this National Conference where various aspects of sociology like sanitation, public health, gender equality and social discrimination will be explored in the coming discussions.

Hon'ble Mr Bharatsinh Madhavsinh Solanki, Minister of State (independent charge), Department of Drinking Water and Sanitation, speaking on the occasion named sanitation and drinking water as the basic needs of society. We have to gear up and streamline our efforts at the national scale to make provision for their availability for all, we will seek the active participation and cooperation of all, specially the nongovernmental organisations in these endeavours, he added. Hon'ble Mr Jairam Ramesh, Union Minister for Rural Development started his address with drawing attention of the audience to the sanitational situation in the country with provision for sanitary toilets still to be made on a large scale, specially in the villages, where even now, about 25 lakh scavengers are engaged in cleaning toilets. The government has taken a pioneering step by constituting Mahila Swayam Sahayata Samooh. The effort is to provide what has been termed as Aajeevika to sponsor self-help activities arranging bank loans for the purpose. 25,000 such

Samooh have been constituted targeting to reach 75,000 in a year. The Department of Drinking Water and Sanitation has initiated Nirmal Bharat Abhiyan. So far 2,500 Panchayats have become Nirmal, whereas their

total number is 2.5 lakh. It has been planned to reach all of them in ten years' time. There is a bill before Parliament to make prohibitory provisions against manual scavenging stricter, since the existing Act preventing the practice has not been effective. The Minister said, "I shall request the Hon'ble Speaker to use her good offices to get the proposed bill through to be enacted soon. Only one state so far has been able to totally prevent defecation in the open, that is Sikkim. Kerala is expected to be the second such state, to be followed, hopefully by Maharashtra. Efforts are to be concentrated on states like Bihar, U.P., Madhya Pradesh, which are big states to be taken care of. The issue of sanitation is too important and big to be left as a governmental mission. NGOs are to be associated on a large scale in the drive for cleanliness; Sulabh's work in the field has been really pioneering".

Hon'ble Speaker, Lok Sabha Mrs Meira Kumar, addressing the audience recalled her long association with Sulabh where she is always remembered. She said, "The organisation has been doing great work in the field of sanitation and social reform. The sewerage system was introduced in Calcutta in 1870. Out of 7,933 towns only 160 have sewerage treatment plants. The problem of the 'untouchables' in our

society is an old one. We do not have slavery as America had; slaves were liberated at some point of time or the other, not so with our 'untouchables'. The problem is mainly our mental attitude, our minds are dirty. We are so much concerned about cleanliness that touching a scavenger or even his shadow will pollute us. I went to Japan. Houses as well as streets are quite clean there. There are no scavengers there. Housewives clean their houses and the portion outside in front of their house. We get to the Dalits at the time of elections; when we tell them they are vital components of our society. Their votes make or mar a candidate. Our Sansad has their significant contribution. But seeing their general condition in our society, I thought it will not change, at least not during my life time. But it has now started changing, thanks to Sulabh".

Pandit Devendra Kumar Sharma, head priest of the Jagannath temple, Alwar, was awarded a cheque of Rs 5 lakh on behalf of Sulabh by Hon'ble Mr Jairam Ramesh, Union Minister. He also administered oath to the Pandits of Varanasi, led by Dr B.N. Chaturvedi not to discriminate against anyone on the basis of untouchability and caste and readily worship deities in temples with the 'Untouchables' as well as share meals at functions with them.

Mr S.P. Singh, Chairman, Sulabh International Social Service Organisation, proposed vote of thanks. The inaugural session concluded with singing of the National Anthem by one and all present there.

**Technical Sessions**

After lunch, the First Technical Session on Sociology of Sanitation was held under the Chairmanship of Prof Hetukar Jha (Retired),

Department of Sociology, Patna University. It may be pointed out that the scholarly papers and articles received for the National Conference were compiled and published in book form in two volumes. They were released by the Hon'ble Speaker and the Hon'ble Ministers. During the First Technical Session the learned sociologists included Mr Manish Thakur, Dr S.K. Mishra and Ms Prabhleen Kaur, Dr Mohammad Akram, Dr Sadan Jha and Prof Shakuntala C. Shettar.

Mr Manish Thakur from the Indian Institute of Management, Kolkata, pleaded for a historical mapping of the twin notions of civil consciousness and public space. Historians of colonial India indicated the cultural incompatibility of the colonial and native notions of public health and hygiene. In parts of Andhra Pradesh, toilets were used for storing grains. Construction workers may erect huge buildings but hardly they have any toilet facilities. Very few households allow domestic workers to avail of toilet facilities.

Dr S.K. Mishra and Mrs Prabhleen Kaur delineated the issues related to sanitation from the perspective of development. A vital component of a developed society is the health of its citizens. Overall coverage in rural India is a dismal 34.8 per cent; for Scheduled Castes and Scheduled

Tribes it is 23.7 per cent and 25 per cent respectively. Sanitational situation was not so bad during the Harappan period where model of urban sanitation was discovered. It is also to be noted that there are no water and sanitation regulator and there are no sector laws either. Percentage of open defecation in rural areas is 69 per cent, the highest in South Asia.

Dr Mohammad Akram, Associate Professor of Sociology, AMU, Aligarh, held that poor sanitation is something that not only affects the health of the people, but also the economic and social development of the nation. It is the joint responsibility of individual, community and state. A study conducted by a unit of WHO estimated that India loses Rs 240 billion annually due to lack of proper sanitation. Fifty-five per cent of our population has no access to toilets and sanitation in India is yet to become an integral part of development paradigm, although the sanitation coverage has increased significantly from 21 per cent in 2001 to more than 65 per cent.

Prof Shakuntala C. Shettar, Department of Sociology, Karnataka University, Dharwad held that sociology of sanitation is already a sub-branch of medical sociology that emerged in the USA during 1940s. The relations between the two are extremely intimate. The gender issues in sanitation relate to the women who are responsible for water and hygiene of family, specially of children. Securing good sanitation facilities has direct bearing not only on women's health but also on their access to education and employment.

Prof Sadan Jha was of the view that the discourse on sanitation has primarily been west centric. In the non-west differentiation along caste and gender lines shape the cosmology of sanitation and hygiene. Mahatma Gandhi, on the other hand, included in his *swaraj* both *swa* as well as the collective.

The Second Technical Session on 'Environmental Sanitation' was held under the Chairmanship of Mr Pankaj Jain, IAS, Secretary, Ministry of Drinking Water and Sanitation. Dr R. Shankar, Co-Chairman and Professor of Sociology, Bharathidasan University, Tiruchirapalli, held that in research methodology qualitative research involves an in-depth understanding of human behaviour. The measures often used in the study of healthcare are quality-adjusted life years and the related disability-adjusted life years. Health is closely related to nutrition as well as spread of education. Many factors make up the balance of nature. Human body, after all, is nature's creation. All lives depend on water, air and minerals.

Dr V. Chandrasekhar and Dr Karuppiah, Department of Sociology, University of Madras, Chennai, described unregulated industrialisation and urbanisation disaster. In India, 47 children out of 1,000 die after birth, 80 per cent die of diseases caused by water, sanitation and environmental pollution. Population explosion places higher demands on natural resources. Development planning in India gives high priority to economic criteria and fails to incorporate the environmentalist's concern; soft cultural and hard cultural factors are to be cautiously modulated for any significant change.

Dr Sharmila Chhotaray, Assistant Professor of Sociology, Tripura University, indicated lack of adequate knowledge and scarcity of water as primary reasons for insanitary conditions in tribal populated villages of West Tripura District. Dr Hema Gandotra, Department of Sociology, University of Jammu, estimated that only 31 per cent of India's population is using improved sanitation facilities as of 2008. The Ganga river in India has a stunning 1.1 million litres of raw sewage being disposed into it every minute, when a community gets displaced as in the state of JandK, there is discussion usually on their socio-economic conditions and hardly any on the issue of sanitation and water or environment.

Dr Saroj Ranjan Mania, Research and Analysis Consultant, Bhubaneswar, revealed that there is great disparity amongst various states. 10 per cent rural households in Madhya Pradesh use toilet as compared to over 80 per cent in Kerala or 60 per cent in Assam. In

Odisha, one-fourth of the total population belongs to ST category. Due to poverty they lack sanitation awareness. Defecation in the open is a common practice.

Dr Anil Vaghela from Samaldas Arts College, Sociology Department, M.K. Bhavnagar University, Bhavnagar, Gujarat, laid out a detailed syllabus of Sociology of Sanitation, suggesting five units as follows: 1. Introduction of the Subject, 2. Research method like survey, questionnaire and interview, 3. Theory and approach – community theory, personal theory and government approach, 4. Relation with other sectors, 5. Relation with and differences with other social sciences like Psychology, History, Philosophy.

Mr Paras Nath Chaudhary, (formerly associated with the University of Heidenberg), held that India has yet to imbibe the idea of general hygiene. While we may exhibit, some people say, high standards of personal hygiene, we are only a little cautious for public cleanliness.

Mr Ram Updesh Singh, IAS (Retired), quoted V.S. Naipaul from his book, 'An Area of Darkness' referring to the scene of Indian men and women defecating in the open. Social mobilisation is an essential prerequisite for sanitational development. Sulabh initiative in the matter has really been laudable.

Prof V.P. Singh, Head, Centre for Globalisation and Development Industries, University of Allahabad, and Mr Ashish Saxena, Associate Professor, Department of Sociology, University of Allahabad, cautioned against global warming and degradation of environment, pollution of rivers like Ganga, the negligence adopted towards the cleaners, specially at massive locations like the age old Kumbha Mela, who are the lowest paid while they work round the clock. The Day 1 concluded with a lively and realistic drama played in the evening – 'Dreams of Mahatma Gandhi – from Serfdom to Freedom' depicting the erstwhile lamentable plight of scavengers and their redemption through the efforts of Sulabh International educating and training them and their children.

**Second Day of the Conference**

Started with a visit by the esteemed participants to the Sulabh Campus in the morning. They went round the Sulabh International Museum of Toilets, different models of Sulabh two-pit pour-flush

toilet displayed at the campus as well as the biogas plant and the effluent treatment system. The gas generated is used to light mantle lamp and cooking food in the kitchen. They saw flask full of effluent treated through Sulabh technology rendering it odourless and pathogen-free. There were also shown dry lumps of human excreta which after a period of two years turned into hard balls free of odour and pathogens.

The Day 2 of the National Conference had two Technical Sessions. The third session on Public Health was held under the Chairmanship of Prof Ishwar Modi, President, Indian Sociological Society. Dr Amarendra Mahapatra, Assistant Director, Regional Medical Research Centre, Bhubaneswar, held sanitation to have always been a part and parcel of the society for ages. He also made surprising revelations that 32 per cent of the population in rural and tribal areas do not use the tube well water for drinking purpose and that in rural areas, the use of latrine was not satisfactory because of the habit of going out for defecation or foul smell or water problem for flushing, building political commitment, advocacy, lobbying and folk media are necessary for this cause.

Prof Pramod Kumar Sharma, Head of Sociology, Department, Pandit Ravi Shankar University, Raipur, Chhattisgarh, named provision of environmentally safe sanitation to millions of people as a significant challenge. Urban growth in India is faster than rural one. Proportion of population residing in urban areas has increased from 27.8 per cent in 2001 to 31.80 per cent in 2011. Successful pro-poor sanitation programmes must be scaled up, investments must be customised and targeted to those most in need. There ought to be an enforcement mechanism for stopping defecation in public.

Mr Kamal Nath Jha (Save the Children) indicated the provision of functional toilets in only 20 per cent of schools according to a recent survey. These are to be prioritised in any sanitation programme.

Prof Madhu Nagla, Department of Sociology, M.D. University, Rohtak, considered ideas about dirt and hygiene to vary from culture to culture and from century to century. Simply providing public services in the field of sanitation does not in itself guarantee improvement in health status.

**MDG Target**

Prof Shaukath Azim from Karnataka University, Dharwad, held the poor and marginalised groups to be the worst sufferers in respect of health and hygiene. According to WHO and UNICEF's Joint Monitoring Programme for Water Supply and Sanitation, 17 states such as Kerala, Haryana, Meghalaya, Himachal Pradesh, Punjab and most of the Union Territories have reached the MDG target; Assam and Andhra Pradesh will achieve it in next 10 years; Karnataka and Maharashtra in the next 25 years and Madhya Pradesh and Odisha only in the next century. Scavengers are being used in Karnataka to clean human excreta. In case of BPL families, most of the sanctioned toilets were found only on official records.

Dr Richard Pais, Professor of Sociology (Retired), Mangalore, Karnataka University, talked of India's fast urbanised growth. Referring to Mangalore, he said around 1940s, wet latrines became common. The scavengers were absorbed in the Corporation. The Corporation employed around 400 people to clean streets.

The Fourth Session on Day Two, was held on Social Deprivation under the Chairmanship of Prof M.N. Karna, Emeritus Professor of Sociology, North-Eastern Hill University, Shillong. According to the Co-Chairman of the session, Dr Jitendra Prasad, Professor and Head of Department of Sociology, M.D. University, Rohtak, Haryana, it is paradoxical that people who provided a particular service to the society were labelled as 'Untouchables'. It is a pleasant surprise to learn that the great freedom fighter, Shaheed Bhagat Singh had said, if religion means blind faith by mixing rituals and philosophy, then it should be blown away. About 7-8 thousand *Mehtars* work to keep Mahakumbh Mela clean. The law passed in 1993 outlawing the practice of manual scavenging has not been effective. This aspect was also stressed by Dr Akhilesh Ranjan stating that, the community involved in maintaining hygiene holds lower position in society.

Dr Radheshyam Tripathi, Professor of Sociology, Tilak College, Katni, Madhya Pradesh, saw light on the horizon with people of the deprived classes coming up in greater numbers in services, their children joining schools and colleges. This is leading to elimination of labour market exclusion, service exclusion and exclusion from social relations.

Dr Vishav Raksha, Associate Professor, Department of Sociology, University of Jammu, highlighted the social deprivation scavengers faced

with low rate of literacy among SC and ST females at 41.9 per cent and 47.8 per cent respectively. These are hereditary negativities. There is, however, a redeeming factor in recent political awakening that has taken place.

The Fifth Session was on the way forward and road map ahead. The Valedictory Session was held under the Chairmanship of Dr Bindeshwar Pathak. Mr Pankaj Jain, Secretary, Department of Drinking Water and Sanitation addressing the valedictory session said, the Sulabh technology relating to the disposal of excreta had been found satisfactory even by scientists who had examined it. The only caution they advised was the construction of Sulabh toilets be away from water bodies underground to safeguard against any bacterial pollution. The remarkable thing about Sulabh technology toilets was that they did not cause any environmental pollution. Considering the fact that 600 million people in the country go for open defecation, they have to be provided with proper sanitation facilities and Sulabh and such other NGOs have a great role to play.

Mr Jain said, a part of the sanitation problem in India was due to the reluctance of people to pay for the use of toilets. Generally, people would go for defecation in the open and would not like to pay for use of toilets for this purpose. In view of this, the government had made it mandatory for filling stations in the country to have provision of toilets for the convenience of people travelling long distance in their cars. Sulabh has succeeded in motivating people to pay for the use of its toilets. "How could the government motivate people to pay for such facilities is a question still defying us". Mr Jain commended and praised Sulabh, again, for its success in this regard.

Dr Pathak summarising the discussions said that an India Declaration has been prepared and agreed upon with specific recommendations to prioritise the issue of sanitation in the broad discipline of sociology. Dr Pathak expressed his gratitude and thankfulness for the great success of the National Conference by virtue of active participation of eminent dignitaries like the Hon'ble Speaker, Lok Sabha, Hon'ble Ministers of Government of India and eminent scholars of sociology.

# 34

# Sanitation: An Essential Requirement for Public Health

*P.K. Sharma*

Providing environmentally-safe sanitation to millions of people is a significant challenge, especially in the world's second most populated country. The task is doubly difficult in a country where the introduction of new technologies can challenge people's traditions and beliefs. (CUSS 2010). The World Health Organisation finds inadequate sanitation to be a major cause of disease world-wide and improving sanitation as a tool to ensure a significant beneficial impact on health, both in households and across communities. (TCS 2011)

**Sanitation Means**: Professionals agree that "sanitation" as a whole is a "big idea" which covers

- safe collection, storage, treatment and disposal/re-use/recycling of human excreta (faeces and urine);
- management/re-use/recycling of solid wastes (trash or rubbish);
- drainage and disposal/re-use/recycling of household wastewater (often referred to as sullage or grey water);
- drainage of storm water ;
- treatment and disposal/re-use/recycling of sewage effluents;
- collection and management of industrial waste products; and
- management of hazardous wastes (including hospital wastes, and chemical/radioactive and other dangerous substances).

"Ecological" approach to sanitation which seeks to contain, treat and reuse excreta where possible – thus minimising contamination and making optimum use of resources. The key issue here is that each community, region or country needs to work out what is the most sensible and cost effective way of thinking about sanitation in the short and long term and then act accordingly.

**UNO States that**: Wherever humans gather, their waste also accumulates. Progress in sanitation and improved hygiene has greatly improved health, but many people still have no adequate means of disposing of their waste. This is

a growing nuisance for heavily populated areas, carrying the risk of infectious disease, particularly to vulnerable groups such as the very young, the elderly and people suffering from diseases that lower their resistance. Poorly controlled waste also means daily exposure to an unpleasant environment. The buildup of fecal contamination in rivers and other waters is not just a human risk: other species are affected, threatening the ecological balance of the environment.

The discharge of untreated wastewater and excreta into the environment affects human health by several routes:

- By polluting drinking water;
- Entry into the food chain, for example via fruits, vegetables or fish and shellfish;
- Bathing, recreational and other contact with contaminated waters;
- By providing breeding sites for flies and insects that spread diseases;

The urban growth in India is faster than the average for the country and far higher for urban areas over rural. The proportion of population residing in urban areas has increased from 27.8 per cent in 2001 to 31.80 per cent in 2011 and likely to reach 50 per cent by 2030. The number of towns has increased from 5,161 in 2001 to 7,935 in 2011. The rapid growth in urban areas has not been backed adequately with provisioning of basic sanitation infrastructure and thus leaving many Indian cities deficient in services as water supply, sewerage, storm water drainage, and solid waste management.

Sanitation is intrinsically linked to conditions and processes relating to public health and quality of environment, especially the systems that supply water and deals with human waste. The problem of sanitation gets further worsened in urban areas due to increasing congestion and density in cities resulting in poor environmental and health outcomes. As per 2011 Census, the households having latrine facility within premises is 81.4 per cent which includes 72.6 per cent households having water closets and 7.1 per cent households having pit latrines and 1.70 per cent households having other latrines. Out of 72.6 per cent households, 32.70 per cent households are having water closets with piped sewer system, 38.20 per cent households are having water closets with pit latrines. The remaining 18.60 per cent household are both sharing public latrines (6 per cent) and defecating in open (12.60 per cent)

To improve the sanitation situation in urban areas, in October 2008, the Government of India announced the "National Urban Sanitation Policy" (NUSP). The NUSP laid down the framework for addressing the challenges of city sanitation. The policy emphasises the need for spreading awareness about sanitation through an integrated city-wide approach, assigning institutional responsibilities and due regard for demand and supply considerations, with special focus on the women and urban poor.

All the states were requested to act with par with the NUSP to develop respective State Sanitation Strategies (SSS) and the cities for the preparation of City Sanitation Plans (CSPs) given that the sanitation is a State subject as per the Constitutional provisions.

A study Conducted by Asian development Banks,2009,Philiphines in which it was mentioned that;-

**1. Successful pro-poor sanitation programs must be scaled up:** Assistance is still not reaching large numbers of the poorest of the poor. Successful models must be replicated and scaled up to serve those who cannot provide for their own needs under existing service delivery systems.

**2. Investments must be customised and targeted to those most in need:** With more than 450 million Indians living below the poverty line, only a few of the poor who have inadequate sanitation can be assisted right away. Due to limited resources, programs should target groups or locations lagging behind the furthest.

**3. Cost-effective options must be explored:** Appropriate lower-cost solutions offer a safe alternative to a wider range of the population. Higher-cost options can be explored when economic growth permits. Regardless of cost, all systems should address sanitation all the way "from toilet to river."

**4. Proper planning and sequencing must be applied:** Investing in incremental improvements is an approach that one could consider if affordability of sanitation investment is an issue. Careful planning is required to ensure that investments do not become wasteful and redundant.

**5. Community-based solutions must be adopted where possible:** An approach known as Community-Led Total Sanitation (CLTS) has been found to be effective in promoting change at the community level. Efforts must address socio-cultural attitudes toward sanitation and involve women as agents of change. Another innovation is the socialised community-fund raising, which has met great success among the rural poor.

**6. Innovative partnerships must be forged to stimulate investments:** The key is to stimulate investments from as wide a range of sources as possible, including the private sector, nongovernment organisations (NGOs), and consumers themselves. This may require working with a wide range of partners through innovative public–private partnerships.

**Sanitation in India**

India may be "on track" in achieving the MDG sanitation target-2008 MDG goals simply represent achievable levels if countries commit the resources and power to accomplish them. They do not necessarily represent acceptable levels of service.

This is especially true for India's sanitation situation. Despite recent progress, access to improved sanitation remains far lower in India compared to many other countries .

An estimated 55 per cent of all Indians, or close to 600 million people, still do not have access to any kind of toilet. Among those who make up this shocking total, Indians who live in urban slums and rural environments are affected the most.

In rural areas, the scale of the problem is particularly daunting, as 74 per cent of the rural population still defecates in the open. In these environments, cash income is very low and the idea of building a facility for defecation in or near the house may not seem natural. And where facilities exist, they are often inadequate. The sanitation landscape in India is still littered with 13 million unsanitary bucket latrines, which require scavengers to conduct house-to-house excreta collection. Over 700,000 Indians still make their living this way. The situation in urban areas is not as critical in terms of scale, but the sanitation problems in crowded environments are typically more serious and immediate. In these areas, the main challenge is to ensure safe environmental sanitation. Even in areas where households have toilets, the contents of bucket-latrines and pits, even of sewers, are often emptied without regard for environmental and health considerations. Sewerage systems, if they are even available, commonly suffer from poor maintenance, which leads to overflows of raw sewage. Today, with more than 20 Indian cities with populations of more than 1 million people, including Indian megacities, such as Kolkata, Mumbai, and New Delhi, antiquated sewerage systems simply cannot handle the increased load.

### Condition of Chhattisgarh

Implying growth rate of 23.81 per cent in 9 years. In the capital city of Raipur, the expansion in urban population due to spatial extension and increased immigration is as high as 49 per cent. Urban population constitutes around 18.87 per cent of the total population in Chhattisgarh. There are 162 urban local bodies in CG.

### Chhattisgarh Urban Sanitation Strategy, 2010

Around 50 per cent of the urban population is poor. Most of these live in slums. Over 95 per cent of the slum-dwellers do not have a dedicated, individual toilet at home.The estimated number of urban dwellers practicing open defecation is estimated to be 2.34 m. The number of toilets required on the basis of individual households being

Equipped with a dedicated toilet is estimated to be around 50 lacs. The major reasons for slum-dwellers not choosing to have a dedicated toilet in their homes, in the order of gravity, are as follows:

(i) Most slum-dwellers have a rustic mind and are traditionally accustomed to defecation in open. Some, in fact complain of claustrophobia if required to use an enclosed toilet.

(ii) Building a dedicated toilet is considered extravagance. The person considers it financially prudent to build instead a living space and lease it for a stable monthly income.

(iii) There is no stringent punishment at present for open defecation. Many urban-poor families still consider it 'dirty' to have a toilet attached to their living space.

(iv) Flush toilets require more water, a common issue in localities of urban poor.

Sanitation-related major issues in Chhattisgarh include the following:

(i) Open defecation

(ii) Unsafe open defecation (as upon railway tracks, or perched perilously upon the retention wall of a large pit or gutter).

(iii) Rustic mind-set, reluctant to migrate to in-house toilet use.

(iv) Reluctance to pay for pay-toilets, even on subsidised terms.

(v) Absence of concealed drainage.

(vi) Use of storm water drains for letting in domestic waste water.

(vii) Absence of scientific solid waste management system.

(viii) Urinating and spitting upon walls and in public places.

(ix) High incidence of vector borne and water-borne diseases.

| *Category* | *Domain* | *General Condition* |
|---|---|---|
| Dedicated toilets in homes and public buildings | Private / public | Fair to good. |
| Pay toilets- Community facilities | Public | Fair |
| Public toilets | Public | Poor to Very poor |

Some other Problems are:

1. There is no enforcement mechanism for stopping defecation in public in the State at present.
2. City/town in the State has concealed sewerage system at present.
3. Sewer and storm water drains are common in most cities/ towns in the State.
4. No city/town in the State has a scientific system for solid waste management at present.
5. No city/town in the State has a system for harvesting waste water and treating it for re-use.
6. Further there is no provision for proper disposable of Industrial waste.
7. The people should come out of the old belief like:- Sanitation is unaffordable, poor's have other basic requirements beside sanitation, it is costly to construct, etc.

Totally sanitised, healthy and livable cities and towns.

The vision for urban sanitation in India is the state goal for Urban sanitation includes:

(a) Causing awareness generation and behaviour change.

(b) Achieving open defecation free cities.

(c) Promoting integrated city-wide sanitation through:

(i) Reorienting sanitation and mainstreaming sanitation.

(ii) Sanitary and safe disposal: 100 per cent of human excreta and liquid wastes from all sanitation facilities including toilets.

(iii) Proper operation and maintenance of all sanitary installations.

(iv) The Millennium Development Goals (MDGs) require that access to improved sanitation be extended –

- To at least half of the urban population by 2015.
- To 100 per cent of the urban population by 2025.

(iv) The State Urban Sanitation Strategy will revolve around achieving within towns and cities in the State the goals contained in the National Policy.

The Government of India launched the Central Rural Sanitation Programme in 1986 with the objective of accelerating sanitation coverage in rural areas.It was restructured in 1999, exhibiting a paradigm shift in the approach,and the Total Sanitation Campaign (TSC) was introduced. Implemented by the Ministry of Rural Development, Government of India, the TSC aims to:

(a) Improve the general quality of life in rural areas;

(b) Accelerate sanitation coverage in rural areas through access to toilets to all by 2012;

(c) Motivate communities and *Panchayati Raj*3 Institutions through awareness creation and health education;

(d) Cover schools and *Anganwadis* in rural areas with sanitation facilities by March 2012, and promote hygiene education and sanitary habits among students;

(e) Encourage cost effective and appropriate technologies for ecologically safe and sustainable sanitation;

(f) Develop community managed environmental sanitation systems focusing on solid and liquid waste management

**Need for Proper Sanitation**

Human excreta have been implicated in the transmission of many infectious diseases including cholera,typhoid, infectious hepatitis, polio, cryptosporidiosis, and ascariasis. WHO (2004) estimates that about 1.8 million people die annually from diarrhoeal diseases where 90 per cent are children under five, mostly in developing countries.

Poor sanitation gives many infections the ideal opportunity to spread: plenty of waste and excreta for the flies to breed on, and unsafe water to drink, wash with or swim in. Among human parasitic diseases, schistosomiasis ranks second behind malaria in terms of socio-economic and public health importance in tropical and subtropical areas. Ascariasis is found worldwide. Infection occurs with greatest frequency in tropical and subtropical regions,and in any areas with inadequate sanitation. Ascariasis is one of the most common human parasitic infections. Up to 10 per cent of the population of the developing world is infected with intestinal worms – a large percentage of which is caused by Ascaris. Worldwide, severe Ascaris infections cause approximately 60,000 deaths per year, mainly in children

Trachoma is the leading global cause of preventable blindness: trachoma is closely linked to poor sanitation and is one of the best examples of an infection readily preventable through basic hygiene.Six million people worldwide are permanently blind due to Trachoma. Trachoma is spread by a combination of:

- poor sanitation, allowing the flies that spread the infection to breed;
- poor hygiene associated with water scarcity and poor water quality;
- lack of education and understanding of how easily the infection can spread in the home and between people.

Infectious agents are not the only health concerns associated with wastewater and excreta. Heavy metals, toxic organic and inorganic substances also can pose serious threats to human health and the environment - particularly when industrial wastes are added to the waste stream. For example, in some parts of China, irrigation for many years with wastewater heavily contaminated with industrial waste, is reported to have produced health damage, including enlargement of the liver, cancers and raised rates of congenital malformation rates, compared to areas where wastewater was not used for irrigation.

**Conclusion**: Sanitation system to provide the greatest health protection to the individual, the community, and society at large it must:

- Isolate the user from their own excreta;
- Prevent nuisance organisms (e.g. flies) from contacting the excreta and subsequently transmitting disease to humans; and
- Inactivate the pathogens before they enter the environment or prevent the excreta from entering the environment. It is important to understand that sanitation can act at different levels, protecting

the household, the community and 'society'. In the case of latrines it is easy to see that this sanitation system acts at a household level. However, poor design or inappropriate location may lead to migration of waste matter and contamination of local water supplies putting the community at risk. In terms of waterborne sewage the containment may be effective for the individual and possibly also the community, but health effects and environmental damage may be seen far downstream of the original source, hence affecting 'society'

## References

1. India's Sanitation for All: How to Make it Happen Series,ADB,2009 Philliphines
2. WHO in cooperation with UNICEF and WSSCC.
3. Dueñas, Christina. 2005. *Water Champion: Joe Madiath - Championing 100 per cent Sanitation Coverage in Rural Communities in India.* November. www.adb.org/Water/Champions/madiath.asp
4. Dueñas, Christina. 2009. *Country Water Action: India - Changing the Sanitation Landscape*. February. ww.adb.org/Water/Actions/IND/ Sanitation-Landscape.asp
5. ADB. 2006. *Planning Urban Sanitation & Wastewater Management Improvements. Appendix 3: Some Global Case Studies*.May. www.adb.org/Water/tools/Planning-US-WSS.asp.
6. Tigno, Cezar. 2009. *Country Water Action: Bangladesh - Breaking a Dirty Old Habit*. January. www.adb.org/Water/Actions/Ban/Breaking-Dirty-Habit.asp
7. ADB. 2006. *Bringing Water Supply and Sanitation Services to Tribal Villages in Orissa the Gram Vikas Way*. April. www.adb.org/water/ actions/IND/gram-vikas.asp.
8. V. Srinivas Chary, A. Narender, K. Rajeswara Rao. 2003. *Serving the Poor with Sanitation: The Sulabh Approach*. 3rd World Water Forum, Osaka, 19 March. PPCPP Session
9. ADB. 2007. *Dignity, Disease, and Dollars: Asia's Urgent Sanitation Challenge*. www.adb.org/water/operations/sanitation/pdf/dignity-disease-dollars.pdf
10. Saxena N.C and A.K. Shivakumar-Social Policy, Planning,Monitoring and Evaluation (SPPME),UNICEF India-TCS,2011.
11. Chhattisgarh Urban Sanitation Strategy, 2010-CGGovt-2011.
12. Dignity, Disease and Dollars: Asia's urgent sanitation Challenges. Why Invest in Sanitation, ADB.

# National Conference Recommendations

India Declaration
Made on
29th January, 2013
at
National Conference
on
Sociology of Sanitation: Environmental Sanitation,
Public Health and Social Deprivation
Under the aegis of
Sulabh International Centre for Action Sociology
In Close collaboration with
Sulabh International Social Service Organisation
Mavalankar Auditorium, Rafi Marg, New Delhi

In the two days National Conference on Sociology of Sanitation: Environmental Sanitation, Public Health and Social Deprivation, organized by Sulabh International Social Service Organisation, held on 28th and 29th January 2013, Sociologists coming from various parts of the country agreed to the call of Dr. Bindeshwar Pathak that there is an urgent need of beginning a new sub-discipline of sociology, called 'Sociology of Sanitation'. It was strongly felt and argued in the conference that existing sub-disciplines of sociology do not adequately capture and address the varied aspects, nuances and social complexities related to sanitation. More than hundred papers were presented and delegates agreed to the following recommendations.

1. Sociology of Sanitation should be introduced as a new sub-discipline of sociology at national as well as global level.
2. The new sub-discipline will engage with sanitation at the theoretical, empirical and action level.

3. The primary objective of Sociology of Sanitation is to achieve total elimination of open defecation and empowerment of the disadvantaged communities. At the pragmatic level, Sulabh model and technologies are recommended to achieve ecological sanitation in affordable and efficient manner.
4. The Sulabh experience suggests that Sociology of Sanitation can generate employment opportunities and hence it is compatible to the UGC norms of 'employment generation potentiality' for introducing a new discipline/course.
5. It is also recommended that appropriate curriculum, literature and plan of action should be developed to achieve the above goals. Appropriate working groups should be formed under the leadership of Dr. Bindeshwar Pathak for each of the tasks.
6. A tentative syllabus is also proposed which should include the following:
    - Definition, nature, scope and subject matter of Sociology of Sanitation
    - Relation of Sociology of Sanitation with other sub-disciplines of sociology and other social sciences and humanities
    - Theoretical perspectives
    - Important concepts
    - Important thinkers
    - Methodology
    - Problems, issues and challenges
    - Dimensions of sanitation
    - Policies, planning and executing agencies
    - Advocacy for community interventions
    - Sulabh Shauchalaya: A tool of social change
    - Sustainable Technology: Sulabh Tools
    - Injustice, deprivation and strategies for empowerment
    - Practical field and project work
7. It is also recommended that Indian Sociological Society should be requested to begin a new research committee on Sociology of Sanitation and must promote research and teaching on sanitation at every possible level.

8. UGC should be approached to include Sociology of Sanitation as a recommended course in Sociology at UG, PG and Research levels in a graded manner.
9. ICSSR should be approached to give priority to sanitation studies while promoting research at academic and disciplinary levels.
10. All Departments of Sociology at universities, colleges and other educational institution including schools should be informed about this declaration.
11. Scholars should be encouraged to write comprehensive text and reference books on Sociology of Sanitation.
12. A journal on Sociology of Sanitation should be started.
13. Seminars and conferences should be organized in different parts of the country and world for promoting and popularizing Sociology of Sanitation.
14. E literature in the form of proceedings, papers, blogs and websites should be promoted.
15. Rich literature in the form of encyclopedia and dictionaries on sanitation be prepared and made available to all the concerned.
16. Association for Promotion of Sociology of Sanitation should be formed as a Forum to promote Sociology of Sanitation.

See more at: http://www.sociologyofsanitation.com/national-conference-recommendations/#sthash.3z3oWCQy.dpuf

# Session/Speakers

**January 28,2013 : Day One**

**Technical Session One: Sociology of Sanitation (2:00 p.m. to 03:30 p.m.)**

**Chairperson**

Prof. Hetukar Jha,
Department of Sociology (Retd.),
Patna (Bihar)

**Co-Chairperson**

Prof. A. Karuppiah,
Department of Sociology,
University of Madras, Tamil Nadu

**Speakers**

1. Sociology of Sanitation: Issues and Concerns – Manish Thakur
2. Issues Related to Sanitation from the Perspective of Development – Dr. S K Mishra/Ms. Prabhleen Kaur
3. Sanitation, Health and Development Defecit in India – Dr. Mohammad Akram
4. Right to Sanitation and Dignity of Women - Dr. Anil K.S. Jha
5. Aspirational Sphere of Sanitized Social: Knowledge and Experiences in the Discourses on Sanitation – Dr. Sadan Jha
6. Sociology of Sanitation: Incorporating Gender Issues in Sanitation – Prof. Shakuntala C Shettar

**Technical Session Two: Environmental Sanitation (03:30 p.m. to 05:00 p.m.)**

**Chairperson**

Hon'ble Shri Pankaj Jain, IAS,
Secretary,
Ministry of Drinking and Water Sanitation

**Co-Chairperson**

Hon'ble Dr. R. Shankar,
Prof. & Head,
Department of Sociology,
Tiruchirappalli

**Speakers**

1. Environment, Sanitation and Health – Prof. A Karuppiah and Dr. V Chandrasekaar
2. Displacement and Environment – Dr. Hema Gandotra
3. Situation of Sanitation with Reference to Odisha – Dr. Saroj Ranjan Mania
4. Challenges for the Total Sanitation Campaign in North East India – Dr. Sharmila Chottray
5. Sampoorna Swakshta Abhiyaan – Dr. Anil Vaghela
6. Sanitation – Paras Nath Chaudhry
7. Sociology of Sanitation – Ram Updesh Singh, IAS (Retd.)
8. Sanitation and Sustainable Water Conservation in Ganga River Basin – Prof. V. P. Singh
9. Movement Towards the Green Pilgrimage: Mapping Environmental Sanitation Issues in Kumbh Mela at Prayag – Dr. Ashish Saxena

**January 29, 2013 : Day Two**

**Technical session Three: Public Health (11:00 a.m. to 12:30 noon)**

**Chairperson**

Professor Ishwar Modi,
President, Indian Sociological Society,
Member Executive Committee,
President, Research Committee on Sociology of Leisure & Delegate to the Assembly of Councils, International Sociological Association.
Director, India International Institute of Social Sciences Jaipur, Rajasthan

**Co-Chairperson**

Professor Rajesh Mishra,
Head, Dept. of Sociology,
Lucknow University
Secretary Indian Sociological Society
Lucknow (UP)

**Speakers**

1. Public Health Services in Combatting Infant and Maternal Mortality in Rural India – Prof. Noor Mohammad
2. Social Science and Public Health – Dr. Amrendra Mahapatra
3. Sanitation and Public Health Sanitation – Prof. Pramod Kumar Sharma
4. Vidayalaya Balmanch as a Mechanism to Improve Sanitation and Hygiene in Schools – Kamal Nath Jha
5. Social Costruction of Hygiene Abstract – Prof. Madhu Nagla
6. An Analysis of Sanitation Deprivation in Karnataka – Dr. Shaukath Azim
7. Qualitative Research Methodology and It's Application in Health Research – Dr. Shankar Pillai
8. 'Sanitation in Mangalore: A Case-study'- Richard Pais

**Technical Session Four: Social Deprivation**
**(12:30 noon to 02:00 p.m.)**

**Chairperson**

Prof. M.N. Karna,
Emeritus Professor of Sociology,
North-Eastern Hill University, Shillong Camp – Patna

**Co-Chairperson**

Professor Jitendra Prasad,
Professor & Head Department of Sociology,
M. D. University Rohtak, Haryan

**Speakers**

1. Sanitation and Social Status – Dr. Akhhilesh Ranjan
2. Social Deprivation – Dr. Radhey Shyam Tripathi
3. Scourge of Untouchability and Social Deprivation of Scavengers – Dr. Jitendra Prasad and Dr. Satish Kundu

4. Social Deprivation and Scavengers – Dr. Vishav Raksha

**Session Five: Way forward and Road map ahead (3:00 p.m. to 04:00 p.m.)**

**Chairperson**

Professor K.L. Sharma,
Vice Chancellor,
Jaipur National University Jaipur, Rajasthan

**Co-Chairperson**

Professor Nil Ratan,
A. N. Sinha Institute of Social Studies Patna (Bihar)

**Valedictory Session (4.00 p.m. to 5.30 p.m.)**

**Chairperson**

Dr. Bindeshwar Pathak

**Co-Chairperson**

Prof. Shyam Lal,
Ex-Vice Chancellor,
Patna, University

Hon'ble Shri Pankaj Jain, IAS,
Seceretary,
Ministry of Drinking Water and Sanitation,
Govt. of India,
will deliver the Valedictory

- See more at: http://www.sociologyofsanitation.com/honble-guests/sessionspeakers/#sthash.hwoHGjzR.dpuf

# Index